# 325 NEW HOME PLANS

## FOR 2003

# Smart Designs for Today's Neighborhoods

HOME PLANNERS

Published by Home Planners, LLC
Wholly owned by Hanley-Wood, LLC
3275 West Ina Road, Suite 110
Tucson, Arizona 85741

Distribution Center:
29333 Lorie Lane
Wixom, Michigan 48393

President—Jayne Fenton
Vice President, Group Publisher—Eric Karaffa
Vice President, Group Content—Jennifer Pearce
Executive Editor—Linda B. Bellamy
Editorial Director—Arlen Feldwick-Jones
Managing Editor—Vicki Frank
Project Editor—Laura Hurst Brown
Plans Editor—Ashleigh Stone
Graphic Designer—Jay C. Walsh
Production Artist—Peter Zullo
Senior Production Manager—Sara Lisa
Production Manager—Brenda McClary

Front cover:
Plan Plan HPT840096
Design by Home Design Services, Inc.
Photograph by Russell Kingman
See page 70

Back cover:
Plan HPT840264
Design by Frank Betz Associates, Inc.
Photographs by Happy Terrabone
See page 189

Introduction (page 4):
Plan HPT840285 by Looney Ricks Kiss Architects, Inc.
Photograph ©Jeffrey Jacobs/Architectural Photography, Inc.
See page 206

Book design by Jay C. Walsh

First Printing, July 2002

10 9 8 7 6 5 4 3 2 1

Printed in the United States of America

Library of Congress Control Number: 2002100813

ISBN 1-931131-03-1 Softcover

# CONTENTS

This home, as shown in the photograph, may differ from the actual blueprints.
For more detailed information, please check the floor plans on page 206 carefully.

# Welcome

Here's a collection of cutting-edge designs, from 850 to 6,500 square feet, that step into the space age with plenty of style. Courtyards and porches are just the beginning of these 21st-Century houses. Featuring the top plans from our best designers—and a few fresh faces too—this compendium of tomorrow houses boasts ready-for-the-future interiors.

Sections are arranged by exterior style for easy browsing. Beginning on the facing page, *summer houses & cottages* features way-past-cool seaside bungalows. *Rustic getaways & retreats* includes fabulous new Craftsman-style homes. With *farmhouses & ranches,* we present the latest look in Americana (it's a little rugged). Bold yet gently familiar, these homes build in the wide-open spaces or an Arcadian suburb.

Ready for a new notion of home? Check out *urban designs & townhomes*—new plans by bang-up-to-date designers. *Colonials & history houses* has an into-the-future look that's still gently familiar. *English & provençal manors* lends new twists to Old World style. Finally, *mediterranean & spanish styles* features a climate-friendly palette of California Monterrey and Basque elements that suit today's homeowners—in any region.

When you're ready to order, visit our user-friendly instructions on putting together a blueprint package—with helpful tips, a price schedule and many extras. Many of our house plans can be ordered with deck and landscape sets too. Check pages 245 through 253, or call toll-free 1-800-521-6797.

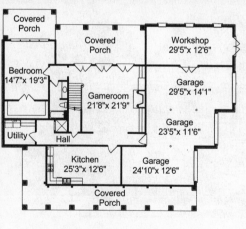

Covered Porch

Bedroom 14'7"x 19'3"

Utility

Covered Porch

Gameroom 21'8"x 21'9"

Hall

Workshop 29'5"x 12'6"

Garage 29'5"x 14'1"

Garage 23'5"x 11'6"

Kitchen 25'3"x 12'6"

Garage 24'10"x 12'6"

Covered Porch

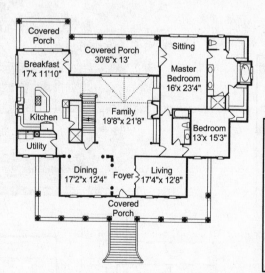

Covered Porch

Breakfast 17'x 11'10"

Kitchen

Utility

Covered Porch 30'6"x 13'

Family 19'8"x 21'8"

Sitting

Master Bedroom 16'x 23'4"

Bedroom 13'x 15'3"

Dining 17'2"x 12'4"

Foyer

Living 17'4"x 12'8"

Covered Porch

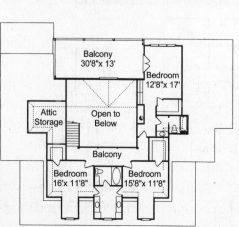

Balcony 30'8"x 13'

Bedroom 12'8"x 17'

Attic Storage

Open to Below

Balcony

Bedroom 16'x 11'8"

Bedroom 15'8"x 11'8"

## Plan HPT840001

**Price Code:** C4
**Bedrooms:** 5 **Bathrooms:** 4
**First Floor:** 3,143 sq. ft.
**Second Floor:** 901 sq. ft.
**Total:** 4,044 sq. ft.
**Finished Basement:** 1,818 sq. ft.
**Width:** 80'-3" **Depth:** 66'-0"

This stunning seaside home expresses the regional flavor of the Carolina coast. A wrapping covered front porch welcomes you into the main level. Inside, formal living and dining rooms flank the foyer. A fireplace and built-ins are featured in the family room, which views the rear covered porch. The gourmet island kitchen offers pantry storage and a breakfast nook. The main-level master bedroom provides a sitting area, private bath and two walk-in closets. A second bedroom is also located on this level, while three additional bedrooms and attic storage reside upstairs. The basement level provides a spacious garage, second kitchen, game room, guest bedroom, second utility room and a workshop.

## Plan HPT840003

**Price Code:** C4
**Bedrooms:** 3 **Bathrooms:** 3½
**First Floor:** 2,146 sq. ft.
**Second Floor:** 952 sq. ft.
**Total:** 3,098 sq. ft.
**Lower-Level Entry:** 187 sq. ft.
**Width:** 52'-0" **Depth:** 65'-4"

An inviting wraparound porch and plenty of other outdoor spaces extend the living area of this cottage. French doors and built-in cabinets adorn the great room. A private hall leads to the first-floor master suite. The upper level boasts a catwalk that overlooks the great room and the foyer. A secluded master wing enjoys a bumped-out window, a stunning tray ceiling and two walk-in closets.

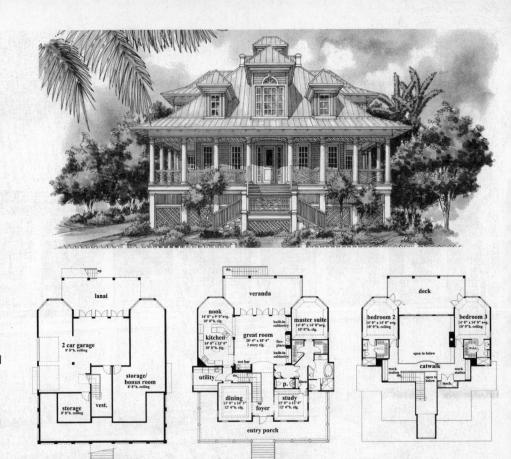

*summer homes & cottages*

## Plan HPT840002

**Price Code:** C4
**Bedrooms:** 4 **Bathrooms:** 4
**First Floor:** 3,294 sq. ft.
**Second Floor:** 1,202 sq. ft.
**Total:** 4,496 sq. ft.
**Finished Basement:** 1,366 sq. ft.
**Width:** 63'-0" **Depth:** 82'-0"

Suited for a golf resort or lakeview site, this two-story home includes room for plenty of guests. French doors open from the front porch to the foyer, dining room and a family bedroom. French doors also lead from the hearth-warmed living room to the rear porch. The island kitchen features a breakfast area, pantry and butler's pantry near the dining room.

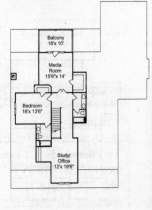

History-rich details lovingly rethink tradition throughout this waterfront plan to form a new notion of home and create comfort. The strength of the design lies in its simplicity, with an open interior and plenty of breezy outdoor spaces. Walls of energy-efficient glass filter sunlight to the heart of the home and allow generous views of the landscape. A gallery provides guest amenities, such as a powder room. A servery area with its own walk-in pantry links a well-equipped kitchen to the formal dining room. French doors lead from the master suite and morning area to an extensive outdoor space that includes a covered porch. Upstairs, a wraparound loft leads to an open library.

Three-Car Garage

**Plan HPT840004**

**Price Code:** C4

**Bedrooms:** 3  **Bathrooms:** 3½

**First Floor:** 2,331 sq. ft.

**Second Floor:** 988 sq. ft.

**Total:** 3,319 sq. ft.

**Width:** 53'-10"  **Depth:** 71'-10"

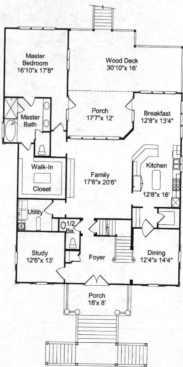

Master Bedroom 16'10"x 17'8"

Wood Deck 30'10"x 16'

Master Bath

Porch 17'7"x 12'

Breakfast 12'8"x 13'4"

Walk-In Closet

Family 17'6"x 20'6"

Kitchen 12'8"x 16'

Utility

Study 12'6"x 13'

1/2 Ba.

Foyer

Dining 12'4"x 14'4"

Porch 18'x 8'

Balcony 17'10"x 10'

Playroom 13'10"x 15'

Bath

Bedroom 12'2"x 11'4"

Bedroom 13'2"x 11'4"

Library/Office 11'8"x 12'

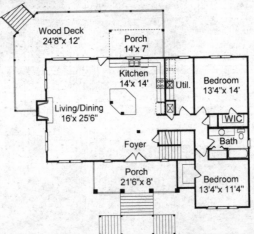

A split staircase adds flair to this coastal home where a fireplace brings warmth on chilly evenings. The foyer opens to the expansive living/dining area and island kitchen. A multitude of windows fills the interior with sunlight and ocean breezes. The wraparound rear deck finds access near the kitchen. The second-floor master suite offers a private balcony and a luxurious bath with a garden tub.

## Plan HPT840005

**Price Code:** A4
**Bedrooms:** 3 **Bathrooms:** 2
**First Floor:** 1,552 sq. ft.
**Second Floor:** 653 sq. ft.
**Total:** 2,205 sq. ft.
**Width:** 60'-0" **Depth:** 50'-0"

## Plan HPT840006

**Price Code:** C1
**Bedrooms:** 3 **Bathrooms:** 3
**Square Footage:** 2,413
**Width:** 66'-4" **Depth:** 62'-10"

An impressive hipped roof and unique turret-style roofs top the two front bedrooms of this extraordinary coastal home. An arched window in an eyebrow dormer crowns the double-door front entrance. A remarkable foyer creates quite a first impression and leads to the generous great room via a distinctive gallery with columns and a tray ceiling. The great room, master bedroom and master bath also boast tray ceilings. ©2000 Donald A. Gardner, Inc.

Multiple gables, a center dormer with an arched clerestory window, and a striking front staircase create visual excitement for this three-bedroom coastal home. Vaulted ceilings in the foyer and great room highlight a dramatic second-floor balcony that connects the two upstairs bedrooms, each with its own bath and private porch. The great room is generously proportioned with built-ins on either side of the fireplace. ©2000 Donald A. Gardner, Inc.

### Plan HPT840007

**Price Code:** C1
**Bedrooms:** 3 **Bathrooms:** 3½
**First Floor:** 1,620 sq. ft.
**Second Floor:** 770 sq. ft.
**Total:** 2,390 sq. ft.
**Width:** 49'-0" **Depth:** 58'-8"

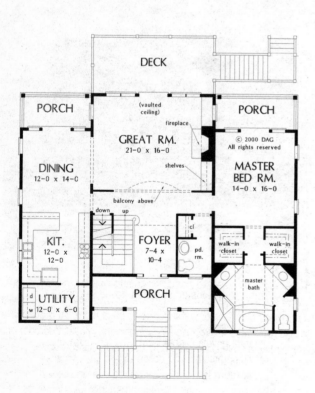

DECK

PORCH

(vaulted ceiling)

fireplace

PORCH

GREAT RM.
21-0 x 16-0

© 2000 DAG
All rights reserved

shelves

MASTER
BED RM.
14-0 x 16-0

DINING
12-0 x 14-0

balcony above

down    up

KIT.
12-0 x 12-0

FOYER
7-4 x 10-4

cl

pd. rm.

walk-in closet

walk-in closet

UTILITY
12-0 x 6-0

PORCH

master bath

d
w

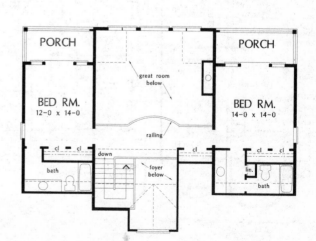

PORCH

PORCH

great room below

BED RM.
12-0 x 14-0

BED RM.
14-0 x 14-0

railing

cl    cl

down

cl

cl    cl

bath

foyer below

lin.

bath

## Plan HPT840009

**Price Code:** C1
**Bedrooms:** 3 **Bathrooms:** 2
**First Floor:** 1,623 sq. ft.
**Second Floor:** 978 sq. ft.
**Total:** 2,601 sq. ft.
**Width:** 48'-0" **Depth:** 57'-0"

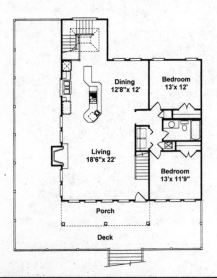

Offering a large wraparound porch, this fine two-story pier home is full of amenities. The living room has a warming fireplace and plenty of windows to enjoy the view. The galley kitchen features unique angles, with a large island/peninsula separating this room from the dining area. Two bedrooms share a bath and easy access to the laundry facilities. Upstairs, a lavish master suite is complete with a private covered porch.

## Plan HPT840008

**Price Code:** A3
**Bedrooms:** 4 **Bathrooms:** 2
**First Floor:** 1,122 sq. ft.
**Second Floor:** 528 sq. ft.
**Total:** 1,650 sq. ft.
**Width:** 34'-0" **Depth:** 52'-5"

Photo by Chris A. Little of Atlanta
This home, as shown in the photograph, may differ from the actual blueprints. For more detailed information, please check the floor plans carefully.

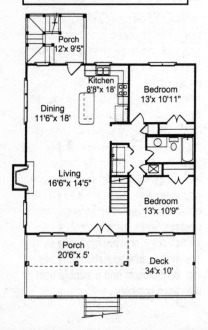

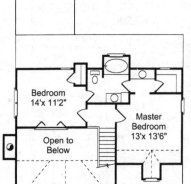

This lovely seaside vacation home is perfect for seasonal family getaways or for the family that lives coastal year-round. The spacious front deck is great for private sunbathing or outdoor barbecues, providing breathtaking ocean views. The two-story living room is warmed by a fireplace on breezy beach nights, while the island kitchen overlooks the open dining area nearby.

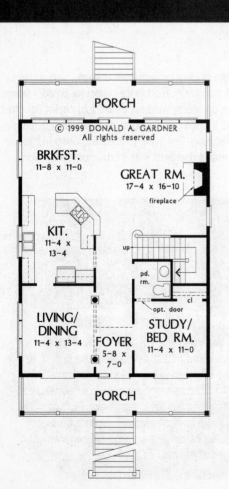

PORCH

BRKFST.
11-8 x 11-0

GREAT RM.
17-4 x 16-10

fireplace

KIT.
11-4 x
13-4

up

pd.
rm.

opt. door

cl

LIVING/
DINING
11-4 x 13-4

FOYER
5-8 x
7-0

STUDY/
BED RM.
11-4 x 11-0

PORCH

PORCH

MASTER
BED RM.
13-8 x 17-0

BED RM.
12-8 x 11-8

cl

bath

lin.

walk-in
closet

cl

railing

down

lin.

UTIL.

d   w

master
bath

lin.

foyer
below

BED RM.
11-4 x 11-0

cl

PORCH

## Plan HPT840010

**Price Code:** C1
**Bedrooms:** 4  **Bathrooms:** 2½
**First Floor:** 1,170 sq. ft.
**Second Floor:** 1,058 sq. ft.
**Total:** 2,228 sq. ft.
**Width:** 30'-0"  **Depth:** 51'-0"

An elevated pier foundation, narrow width, and front and rear porches make this home perfect for waterfront lots, while its squared-off design makes it easy to afford. The great room, kitchen and breakfast area are all open for a casual and spacious feeling. Numerous windows enhance the area's volume. Flexible rooms located at the front of the home include a formal living or dining room and a study or bedroom with an optional entry to the powder room. Upstairs, every bedroom (plus the master bath) enjoys porch access. The master suite features a tray ceiling, dual closets and a sizable bath with linen cabinets.

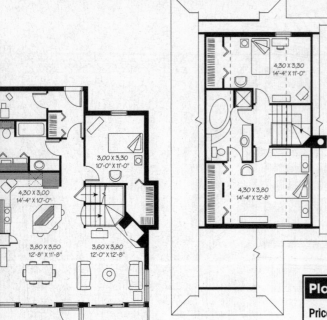

This vacation home enjoys a screened porch and an elevated living area. Truly a free-flowing plan, the dining room, living room and kitchen share a common space, with no walls separating them. A family bedroom and full bath complete the first level. Upstairs, two additional bedrooms—with ample closet space—share a lavish bath, which includes a whirlpool tub and separate shower. This home is designed with a basement foundation.

**Plan HPT840011**

**Price Code:** A2
**Bedrooms:** 3 **Bathrooms:** 2
**First Floor:** 895 sq. ft.
**Second Floor:** 576 sq. ft.
**Total:** 1,471 sq. ft.
**Width:** 26'-0" **Depth:** 36'-0"

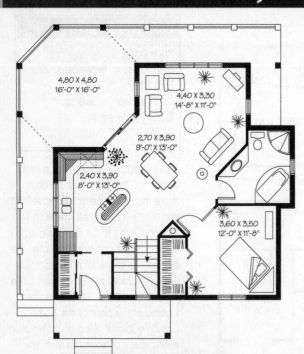

This charming home is ideal for waterfront property, with a wrap-around porch and a corner gazebo that's perfect for outdoor living. The vestibule offers an energy- and space-efficient pocket door that opens to the island kitchen and dining room where sliding glass doors open to the gazebo. The living room offers views in three directions. This home is designed with a basement foundation.

**Plan HPT840012**

**Price Code:** A1
**Bedrooms:** 1 **Bathrooms:** 1
**Square Footage:** 840
**Width:** 33'-0" **Depth:** 31'-0"

## Plan HPT840013

**Price Code:** A3
**Bedrooms:** 3  **Bathrooms:** 2
**First Floor:** 1,212 sq. ft.
**Second Floor:** 620 sq. ft.
**Total:** 1,832 sq. ft.
**Width:** 38'-0"  **Depth:** 40'-0"

This comfortable vacation design provides two levels of relaxing family space. The main level offers a spacious wrapping front porch and an abundance of windows, filling interior spaces with the summer sunshine. A two-sided fireplace warms the living room/dining room combination and a master bedroom that features a roomy walk-in closet. Nearby, the hall bath offers a relaxing whirlpool tub. The kitchen is open and features an island snack bar and pantry storage. A cozy sun room accesses the wrapping deck. Upstairs, two additional bedrooms feature ample closet space and share a second-floor bath. This home is designed with a basement foundation.

3,60 X 3,90
12'-0" X 13'-0"

4,90 X 3,60
16'-4" X 12'-0"

4,50 X 4,40
15'-0" X 14'-8"

4,10 X 3,40
13'-8" X 11'-4"

3,60 X 4,80
12'-0" X 16'-0"

4,10 X 4,40
13'-8" X 14'-8"

3,30 X 4,80
11'-0" X 16'-0"

MASTER BED RM.
15-0 x 17-0

PORCH

walk-in closet

walk-in closet

lin.

master bath

fireplace

GREAT RM.
20-0 x 16-4

seat

KITCHEN
13-0 x 13-4

DINING
15-4 x 12-8

down

w d

UTIL.

cl

walk-in closet

FOYER
6-4 x 9-6

bath

lin.

cl

BED RM.
11-4 x 12-0

PORCH

BED RM.
11-4 x 13-0

PORCH

## Plan HPT840015

**Price Code:** A4
**Bedrooms:** 3 **Bathrooms:** 2
**Square Footage:** 1,970
**Width:** 34'-8" **Depth:** 83'-0"

This slim design with triple gables, front and back porches and a quartet of bay windows is an optimal home for waterfront properties. The great room, dining room and kitchen are open to one another for a spacious, casual atmosphere. Numerous windows and volume ceilings enhance spaciousness throughout the home. ©2000 Donald A. Gardner, Inc.

*summer homes & cottages*

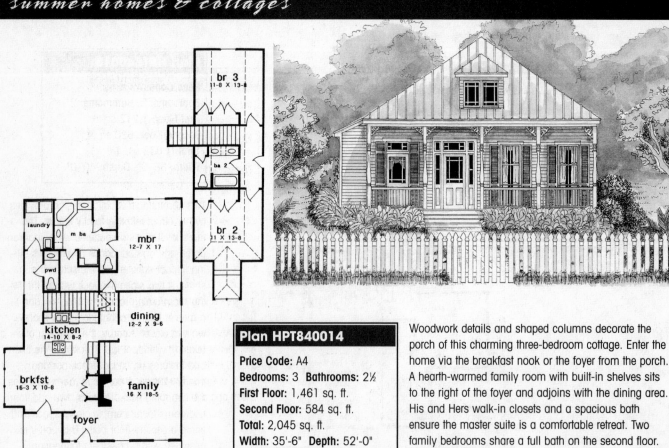

br 3
11-8 X 13-8

ba 2

br 2
11 X 13-8

laundry

m ba

mbr
12-7 X 17

pwd

dining
12-2 X 9-6

kitchen
14-10 X 8-2

brkfst
16-3 X 10-8

family
16 X 18-5

foyer

porch

## Plan HPT840014

**Price Code:** A4
**Bedrooms:** 3 **Bathrooms:** 2½
**First Floor:** 1,461 sq. ft.
**Second Floor:** 584 sq. ft.
**Total:** 2,045 sq. ft.
**Width:** 35'-6" **Depth:** 52'-0"

Woodwork details and shaped columns decorate the porch of this charming three-bedroom cottage. Enter the home via the breakfast nook or the foyer from the porch. A hearth-warmed family room with built-in shelves sits to the right of the foyer and adjoins with the dining area. His and Hers walk-in closets and a spacious bath ensure the master suite is a comfortable retreat. Two family bedrooms share a full bath on the second floor.

*summer homes & cottages* **15**

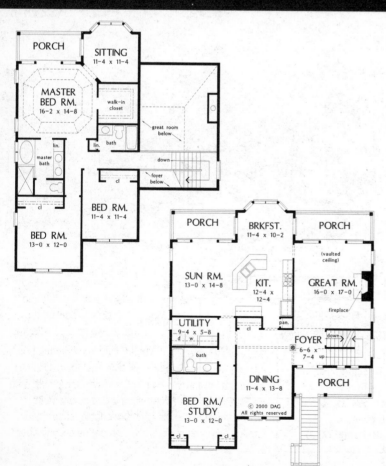

PORCH

SITTING
11-4 x 11-4

MASTER
BED RM.
16-2 x 14-8

walk-in
closet

great room
below

lin.

lin. bath

master
bath

down

cl

foyer
below

BED RM.
11-4 x 11-4

cl

BED RM.
13-0 x 12-0

PORCH

BRKFST.
11-4 x 10-2

PORCH

(vaulted
ceiling)

SUN RM.
13-0 x 14-8

KIT.
12-4 x
12-4

GREAT RM.
16-0 x 17-0

fireplace

UTILITY
9-4 x 5-8

d    w

bath

cl

pan.

FOYER
6-6 x
7-4 up

down

BED RM./
STUDY
13-0 x 12-0

DINING
11-4 x 13-8

© 2000 DAG
All rights reserved

PORCH

cl    cl

## Plan HPT840016

**Price Code:** C2
**Bedrooms:** 4 **Bathrooms:** 3
**First Floor:** 1,500 sq. ft.
**Second Floor:** 1,112 sq. ft.
**Total:** 2,612 sq. ft.
**Width:** 42'-0" **Depth:** 49'-6"

Porches front and back, a multitude of windows and a narrow facade make this elevated pier foundation perfect for a beach property or any waterfront lot. The main living areas are positioned at the rear of the home for the best views of the water. The great room features a vaulted ceiling, a fireplace and back-porch access. The open kitchen shares space with a bayed breakfast area and lovely sun room. The first floor includes a bedroom/ study and a full bath, while the master suite and two more family bedrooms can be found upstairs. The master suite boasts a private porch and a sitting room with a bay window.

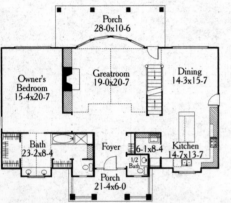

**Second Floor Plan**

Bedroom 14-2x10-2
Bath
Open To Below
Balcony
Bedroom 13-6x10-2
Bath
Study 10-7x8-7

**First Floor Plan**

Porch 28-0x10-6
Owner's Bedroom 15-4x20-7
Greatroom 19-0x20-7
Dining 14-3x15-7
Bath 23-2x8-4
Foyer
6-1x8-4
1/2 Bath
Kitchen 14-7x13-7
Porch 21-4x6-0

## Plan HPT840017

**Price Code:** C1
**Bedrooms:** 3 **Bathrooms:** 3½
**First Floor:** 1,760 sq. ft.
**Second Floor:** 853 sq. ft.
**Total:** 2,613 sq. ft.
**Width:** 56'-0" **Depth:** 46'-6"

Rustic details shape the exterior of this unique country cottage. A covered front porch opens to a foyer that leads directly to the great room, warmed by a country fireplace. A curved wall of windows invites nature indoors and overlooks the rear porch. The island kitchen is open to the formal dining room, also great for casual occasions. Upstairs, a balcony overlooks the two-story great room. Please specify basement, crawlspace or slab foundation when ordering.

*summer homes & cottages*

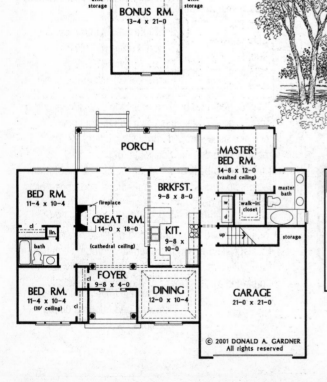

BONUS RM. 13-4 x 21-0
attic storage
attic storage
down

PORCH
BED RM. 11-4 x 10-4
fireplace
GREAT RM. 14-0 x 18-0 (cathedral ceiling)
BRKFST. 9-8 x 8-0
KIT. 9-8 x 10-0
MASTER BED RM. 14-8 x 12-0 (vaulted ceiling)
master bath
w d walk-in closet
up
storage
bath
cl lin.
FOYER 9-8 x 4-0
DINING 12-0 x 10-4
GARAGE 21-0 x 21-0
BED RM. 11-4 x 10-4 (10' ceiling)
cl

## Plan HPT840326

**Price Code:** A3
**Bedrooms:** 3 **Bathrooms:** 2
**Square Footage:** 1,377
**Bonus Room:** 322 sq. ft.
**Width:** 57'-8" **Depth:** 44'-0"

This delightful summer cottage design offers a simple layout, favorable to any family. The foyer is flanked by a dining room and two family bedrooms that share a hall bath. The great room is enhanced by a cathedral ceiling and a warming fireplace. A vaulted ceiling is offered in the master suite, which includes a walk-in closet and private bath. ©2001 Donald A. Gardner, Inc.

© 1998   Donald A Gardner, Inc.

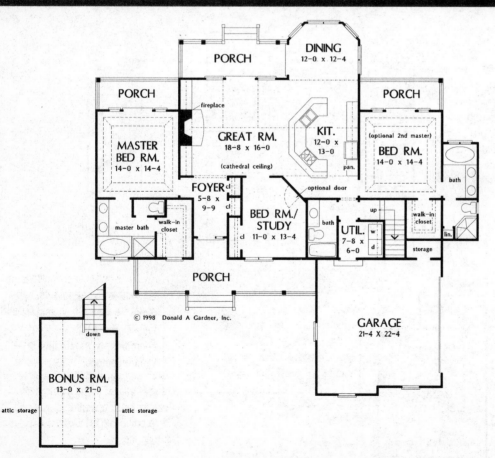

PORCH

DINING
12-0 x 12-4

PORCH

PORCH

PORCH

fireplace

MASTER
BED RM.
14-0 x 14-4

GREAT RM.
18-8 x 16-0

KIT.
12-0 x
13-0

(optional 2nd master)

BED RM.
14-0 x 14-4

bath

(cathedral ceiling)

pan.

master bath

walk-in
closet

FOYER
5-8 x
9-9

cl

cl
cl

optional door

BED RM./
STUDY
cl   11-0 x 13-4

bath

up

UTIL.
7-8 x
6-0

w
d

walk-in
closet

bath

lin.

storage

PORCH

© 1998   Donald A Gardner, Inc.

GARAGE
21-4 X 22-4

down

BONUS RM.
13-0 x 21-0

attic storage          attic storage

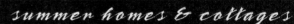

## Plan HPT840018

**Price Code:** A4
**Bedrooms:** 3 **Bathrooms:** 3
**Square Footage:** 1,792
**Bonus Room:** 338 sq. ft.
**Width:** 66'-4" **Depth:** 62'-4"

Cedar shakes and siding blend with the Craftsman details of a custom design in this stunning home. An open common area separates two suites, including an optional master suite that would be great for guests or a room- mate. Note the fireplace and direct porch access in the great room. Watch the glow of the fire from the kitchen's five-sided island. Enjoy the light-filled dining area for formal and informal dining occasions.

## Plan HPT840019

**Price Code:** C4
**Bedrooms:** 4  **Bathrooms:** 3½
**First Floor:** 1,980 sq. ft.
**Second Floor:** 1,492 sq. ft.
**Total:** 3,472 sq. ft.
**Width:** 74'-6"  **Depth:** 82'-3"

Here's a cozy 1920s bungalow with Arts and Crafts details that flourish inside and out. The facade combines the shingles favored by Craftsman bungalows with the textural interest of brick and stone. The optional porte cochere provides covered access to the family room as well as an invitation to entertain outdoors. This home is designed with a walkout basement foundation.

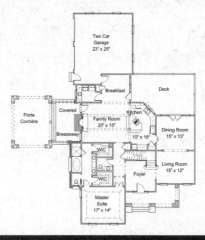

The vaulted ceiling in the great room and tray ceiling in the dining room add richness to this charming, elegant design. The arch in the master bedroom's tray ceiling tops a triple window, and note the shower seat in the master bath. The great room, with a fireplace and built-ins, features rear-deck access. ©2000 Donald A. Gardner, Inc.

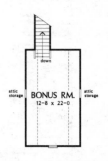

## Plan HPT840020

**Price Code:** A4
**Bedrooms:** 3  **Bathrooms:** 2
**Square Footage:** 1,593
**Bonus Room:** 332 sq. ft.
**Width:** 50'-0"  **Depth:** 54'-0"

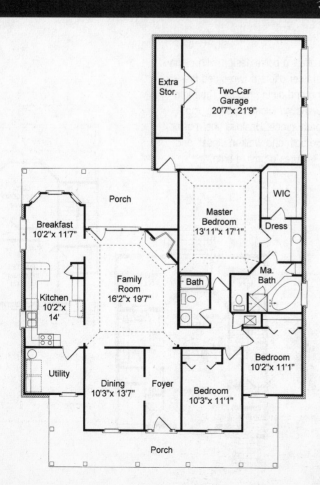

**Plan HPT840021**

**Price Code:** A3
**Bedrooms:** 3 **Bathrooms:** 2
**Square Footage:** 1,847
**Width:** 49'-6" **Depth:** 72'-5"

This rustic cottage design is perfect for any countryside or seaside setting. A wrapping covered front porch and dormer windows enhance the exterior. Inside, the foyer is flanked on either side by a family bedroom and a formal dining room. Straight ahead, the family room boasts a corner fireplace and access to the rear porch. The master bedroom is luxurious with a private bath, dressing room and walk-in closet. The two family bedrooms share a hall bath. The kitchen faces a bayed breakfast nook. A utility room and two-car garage with extra storage space complete this one-story design.

## Plan HPT840022

**Price Code:** A2
**Bedrooms:** 3 **Bathrooms:** 2
**First Floor:** 836 sq. ft.
**Second Floor:** 481 sq. ft.
**Total:** 1,317 sq. ft.
**Width:** 38'-2" **Depth:** 34'-0"

This sweet lakeside cottage is sure to please with its quaint charm and convenient floor plan. A covered porch greets family and friends and offers a place to sit and enjoy the summer breezes. Inside, the living room—with its warming fireplace—flows nicely into the kitchen/dining area. A snack bar and plenty of counter space are just some of the features found here.

*summer homes & cottages*

## Plan HPT840023

**Price Code:** A2
**Bedrooms:** 2 **Bathrooms:** 2½
**First Floor:** 756 sq. ft.
**Second Floor:** 580 sq. ft.
**Total:** 1,336 sq. ft.
**Width:** 32'-0" **Depth:** 36'-9"

This sweet Tudor cottage offers a petite design with plenty of family appeal. The first floor offers a two-sided fireplace that warms the living and dining rooms. The main level is completed by a U-shaped kitchen, powder room, laundry and plenty of porch space. Upstairs, the master bedroom features a private bath and walk-in closet, and the guest bedroom also features a private bath.

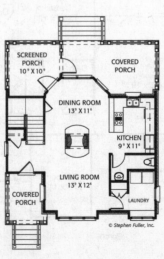

© Stephen Fuller, Inc.

## Plan HPT840024

**Price Code:** A2
**Bedrooms:** 2 **Bathrooms:** 2½
**First Floor:** 617 sq. ft.
**Second Floor:** 474 sq. ft.
**Total:** 1,091 sq. ft.
**Width:** 32'-0" **Depth:** 31'-0"

This charming cottage design is perfect for a vacation by the lake or in the country. European details and a bayed living-room window enhance the exterior. A petite covered front porch welcomes you inside where a two-sided fireplace warms the living and dining rooms. The kitchen is compact yet efficient and accesses a rear grilling porch. A powder room is located nearby. Upstairs, two family bedrooms feature ample closet space—and each bedroom features its own private bath.

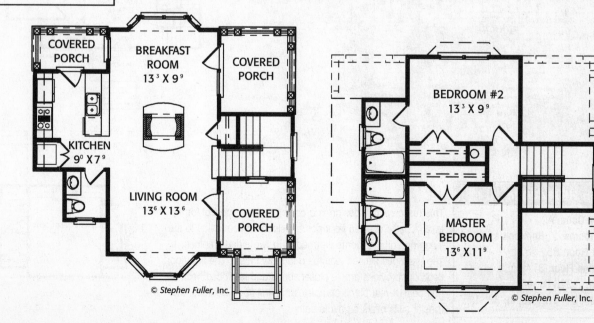

COVERED PORCH

BREAKFAST ROOM
13³ X 9⁹

COVERED PORCH

KITCHEN
9⁰ X 7⁹

LIVING ROOM
13⁶ X 13⁶

COVERED PORCH

© Stephen Fuller, Inc.

BEDROOM #2
13³ X 9⁹

MASTER BEDROOM
13⁶ X 11⁹

© Stephen Fuller, Inc.

## Plan HPT840025

**Price Code:** A4
**Bedrooms:** 3 **Bathrooms:** 3
**First Floor:** 872 sq. ft.
**Second Floor:** 734 sq. ft.
**Total:** 1,606 sq. ft.
**Width:** 40'-0" **Depth:** 29'-6"

Siding, shingles and a stone chimney give rustic charm to this cozy cottage. The large living room, with a wood-burning fireplace, built-in shelves and a wall of windows, opens to the covered side porch. The first-floor bedroom adjoins a full bath; the tranquil master bedroom and another family bedroom reside upstairs along with two full baths.

*summer homes & cottages*

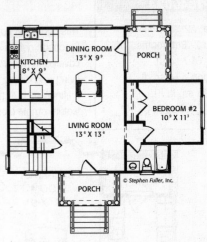

## Plan HPT840026

**Price Code:** A2
**Bedrooms:** 2 **Bathrooms:** 2
**First Floor:** 852 sq. ft.
**Second Floor:** 374 sq. ft.
**Total:** 1,226 sq. ft.
**Width:** 37'-10" **Depth:** 33'-4"

This rustic cottage design is a cozy getaway—perfect for the lake. A petite covered front porch welcomes you inside to the living and dining rooms warmed by a two-sided fireplace. The U-shaped kitchen features a laundry closet. The first-floor bedroom provides ample closet space and is placed near the hall bath. A rear porch completes the first floor. Upstairs, the master suite offers a private bath.

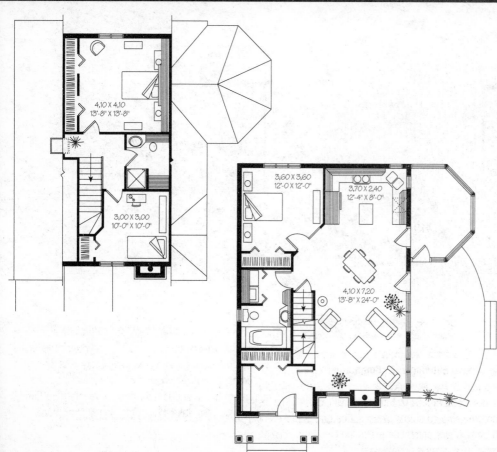

## Plan HPT840027

**Price Code:** A2
**Bedrooms:** 3  **Bathrooms:** 2
**First Floor:** 918 sq. ft.
**Second Floor:** 532 sq. ft.
**Total:** 1,450 sq. ft.
**Width:** 26'-4"  **Depth:** 37'-0"

Nature enthusiasts are right at home in this engaging two-story home with expansive views and a delightful sun room. The enclosed vestibule opens to the spacious living/dining room where sunlight abounds. The adjoining U-shaped island kitchen has access to the angular sun room for casual yet visually stimulating dining. The utility room is tucked away behind the stairs with the full bath. One bedroom is found on the first floor while two additional bedrooms share a full bath on the second floor. This home is designed with a basement foundation.

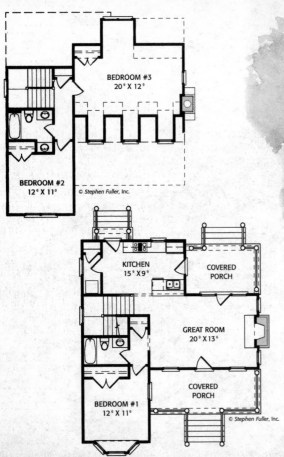

© Stephen Fuller, Inc.

BEDROOM #3
20⁹ X 12⁹

BEDROOM #2
12⁶ X 11⁰

© Stephen Fuller, Inc.

KITCHEN
15⁹ X 9⁹

COVERED PORCH

GREAT ROOM
20⁹ X 13⁶

COVERED PORCH

BEDROOM #1
12⁶ X 11⁶

© Stephen Fuller, Inc.

## Plan HPT840029

**Price Code:** A3
**Bedrooms:** 3  **Bathrooms:** 2
**First Floor:** 862 sq. ft.
**Second Floor:** 654 sq. ft.
**Total:** 1,516 sq. ft.
**Width:** 34'-0"  **Depth:** 39'-6"

The rustic simplicity of this country design is perfect for just about any setting. A covered front porch welcomes you inside to a spacious great room warmed by a fireplace. The compact kitchen features direct access to the rear covered porch. The first-floor bedroom is enhanced by a bayed window and is located next to a hall bath. Upstairs, two additional bedrooms share the second floor with a hall bath.

*summer homes & cottages*

KITCHEN
13⁹ X 9⁹

DINING ROOM
13³ X 10⁰

PORCH

MASTER BEDROOM
12⁹ X 11³

LIVING ROOM
13³ X 14³

BEDROOM #2
12⁹ X 11³

PORCH

© Stephen Fuller, Inc.

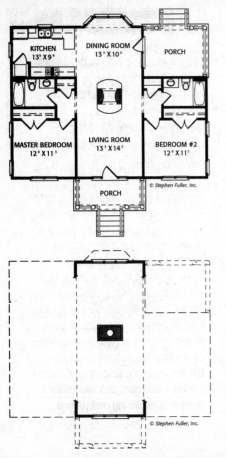

© Stephen Fuller, Inc.

© Stephen Fuller, Inc.

## Plan HPT840028

**Price Code:** A2
**Bedrooms:** 2  **Bathrooms:** 2
**Square Footage:** 1,070
**Width:** 40'-0"  **Depth:** 36'-6"

This quaint one-story design offers a simple vacation-style floor plan. A petite front porch welcomes you inside, where a two-sided fireplace warms the living room and dining room area. The kitchen easily serves the bay-windowed dining room and rear porch for outdoor meals. Two family bedrooms and two full baths complete the floor plan.

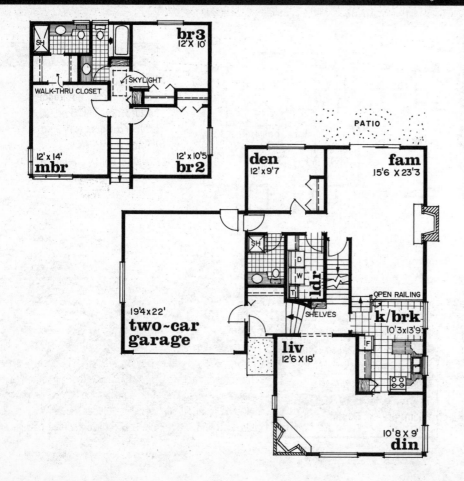

br3
12' X 10'

SH

SKYLIGHT

WALK-THRU CLOSET

12' x 14'
mbr

12' x 10'5
br2

PATIO

den
12'x9'7

fam
15'6 X 23'3

ldr

SH

D
W
T

OPEN RAILING

SHELVES

19'4x22'
two-car
garage

k/brk
10'3x13'9

F

liv
12'6 x 18

10'8 X 9'
din

## Plan HPT840030

**Price Code:** C1
**Bedrooms:** 3  **Bathrooms:** 3
**Main Level:** 1,283 sq. ft.
**Second Level:** 688 sq. ft.
**Total:** 1,971 sq. ft.
**Width:** 48'-0"  **Depth:** 47'-8"

A massive stone chimney stack combines with vertical wood siding on the exterior of this home to evoke a rustic feel. The interior opens through an offset entry to the formal living and dining areas, warmed by a corner fireplace. The sunken family room has a fireplace as well and accesses the rear yard through sliding glass doors. The kitchen and breakfast room sit between the two living spaces. A cozy den is tucked in a corner behind the service area with a full bath and laundry. Bedrooms on the second level include a master bedroom and two family bedrooms encircling a skylit hall.

## Plan HPT840032

**Price Code:** C1
**Bedrooms:** 3  **Bathrooms:** 3½
**First Floor:** 1,708 sq. ft.
**Second Floor:** 1,049 sq. ft.
**Total:** 2,757 sq. ft.
**Bonus Room:** 208 sq. ft.
**Suite:** 478 sq. ft.
**Width:** 84'-0"  **Depth:** 76'-7"

If your tastes run to cottage design, this could be the home of your dreams. The island kitchen overlooks both dining and great rooms and offers counter eating space. The master suite remains on the first floor, while the second floor features two bedrooms and two baths, plus a large bonus area. A full suite over the garage accommodates guests or live-in relatives.

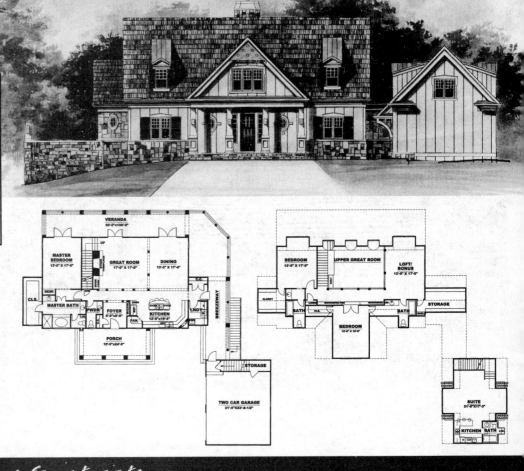

*rustic getaways & retreats*

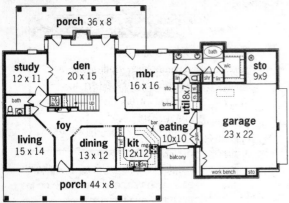

## Plan HPT840031

**Price Code:** C2
**Bedrooms:** 4  **Bathrooms:** 3½
**First Floor:** 1,925 sq. ft.
**Second Floor:** 1,173 sq. ft.
**Total:** 3,098 sq. ft.
**Width:** 78'-0"  **Depth:** 52'-0"

This rustic countryside design offers a simple floor plan and charming exterior details. A covered front porch welcomes you inside to a foyer flanked on either side by formal living and dining rooms. The rear offers a den warmed by a fireplace, a study and a master suite. A garage and back porch complete the first-floor plan. Please specify crawlspace or slab foundation when ordering.

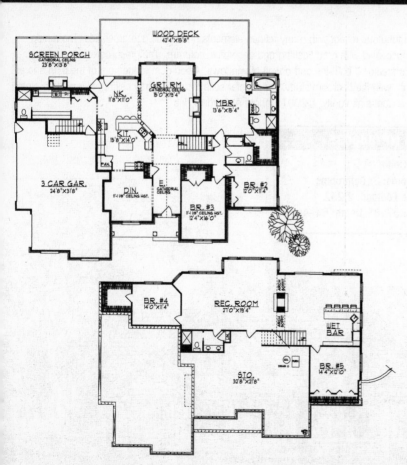

## Plan HPT840033

**Price Code:** A4
**Bedrooms:** 5  **Bathrooms:** 3½
**Square Footage:** 2,370 sq. ft.
**Finished Basement:** 1,469 sq. ft.
**Width:** 75'-4"  **Depth:** 54'-0"

This rustic ranch with Craftsman details will appeal to any family. Inside, a family bedroom and formal dining room flank the entry. The island kitchen connects to a nook. The great room is enhanced by a fireplace and built-ins. The rear screened porch is also warmed by a cozy fireplace. The master bedroom features a private bath and walk-in closet, while two additional bedrooms share a hall bath. The optional basement level offers room to grow with plans for two additional bedrooms, a recreation room, wet bar and plenty of storage.

## Plan HPT840034

**Price Code:** C4
**Bedrooms:** 4  **Bathrooms:** 3½
**Main Level:** 2,464 sq. ft.
**Lower Level:** 1,887 sq. ft.
**Total:** 4,351 sq. ft.
**Width:** 59'-0"  **Depth:** 81'-0"

Here is a gorgeous hillside design that offers an unassuming front perspective. Inside, the dining room, island kitchen, nook and great room enjoy an open plan. The master suite finds privacy to the right with a luxurious bath. The staircase near the kitchen leads to the lower level where three additional bedrooms are found. The game room offers a built-in media center with a wet bar and wine cellar close at hand.

Here's a fabulous retreat with many refined elements and space-age amenities. The dining room is accented with a tray ceiling and decorative columns. The great room has a vaulted ceiling, a fireplace, built-ins and a wall of windows. A bedroom to the front of the plan shares a full bath with the bedroom/study. The master suite includes a tray ceiling, two walk-in closets and a dual-sink vanity. ©2001 Donald A. Gardner, Inc.

## Plan HPT840035

**Price Code:** C1
**Bedrooms:** 3  **Bathrooms:** 2
**Square Footage:** 2,252
**Width:** 57'-8"  **Depth:** 64'-4"

© 2001 Donald A. Gardner, Inc.

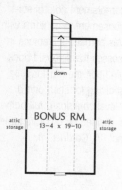

BONUS RM.
13-4 x 19-10

attic storage    attic storage

down

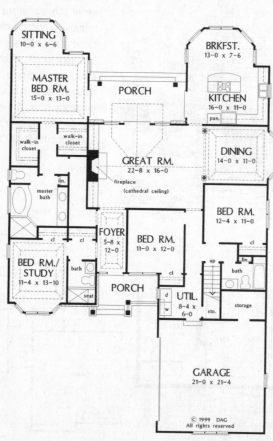

SITTING
10-0 x 6-6

MASTER
BED RM.
15-0 x 13-0

PORCH

BRKFST.
13-0 x 7-6

KITCHEN
16-0 x 11-0

pan.

walk-in closet    walk-in closet

lin.

master bath

DINING
14-0 x 11-0

GREAT RM.
22-8 x 16-0
fireplace
(cathedral ceiling)

cl    cl

BED RM./
STUDY
11-4 x 13-10

bath

seat

FOYER
5-8 x 12-0

BED RM.
11-0 x 12-0

PORCH

UTIL.
8-4 x 6-0

d
w

cl

sto.

up

lin.

bath

storage

BED RM.
12-4 x 11-0

cl

GARAGE
21-0 x 21-4

© 1999 DAG
All rights reserved

## Plan HPT840036

**Price Code:** C1
**Bedrooms:** 4 **Bathrooms:** 3
**Square Footage:** 2,290
**Bonus Room:** 355 sq. ft.
**Width:** 53'-0" **Depth:** 77'-10"

An appealing mixture of exterior building materials combines with decorative wood brackets in the gables to create undeniable Craftsman style for this four-bedroom home. Special ceiling treatments create volume and add interest throughout the home: tray ceilings in the foyer, dining room, bedroom/study and master bedroom, and a stunning cathedral ceiling in the great room. The great room is further enhanced by a rear clerestory dormer window and back-porch access. Bay windows expand several key rooms: the dining room, breakfast area, bedroom/study and the master bedroom's sitting area.
©1999 Donald A. Gardner, Inc.

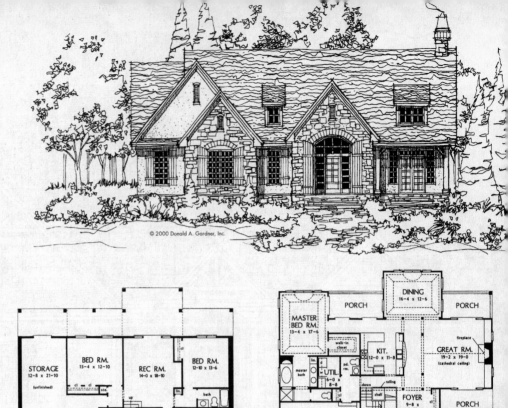

© 2000 Donald A. Gardner, Inc.

## Plan HPT840037

**Price Code:** A4
**Bedrooms:** 3 **Bathrooms:** 2½
**Main Level:** 1,694 sq. ft.
**Lower Level:** 971 sq. ft.
**Total:** 2,665 sq. ft.
**Width:** 60'-6" **Depth:** 61'-2"

An arched and gabled entry and Craftsman details create an appealing facade for this hillside home. The great room with a cathedral ceiling is flanked by front and back porches, while two back porches similarly border the dining room with a tray ceiling and an arch-top picture window. The spacious master suite features a tray ceiling and an arch-top picture window. ©2000 Donald A. Gardner, Inc.

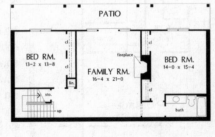

This hillside home features stone, stucco and cedar shake shingles to complement natural surroundings and a walkout basement to conform with sloping lots. Built-in shelves border the fireplace in the great room, which accesses the splendid back porch. Located on the main floor, the master suite enjoys a walk-in closet, shelving for linen and a generous bath. The lower level contains a full bath and two family bedrooms, divided by a comfortable family room. ©2000 Donald A. Gardner, Inc.

## Plan HPT840038

**Price Code:** A4
**Bedrooms:** 3 **Bathrooms:** 2½
**Main Level:** 1,769 sq. ft.
**Lower Level:** 1,135 sq. ft.
**Total:** 2,904 sq. ft.
**Width:** 65'-4" **Depth:** 59'-4"

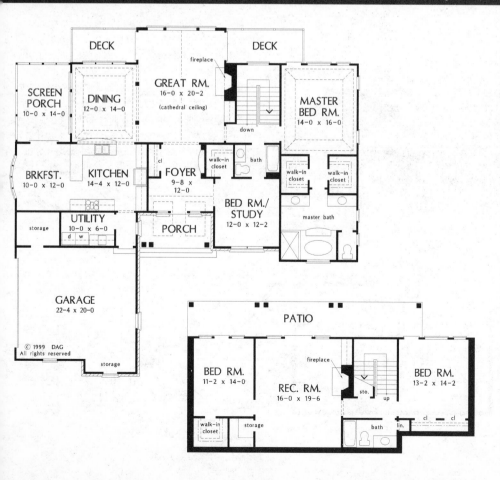

DECK

DECK

SCREEN PORCH
10-0 x 14-0

DINING
12-0 x 14-0

GREAT RM.
16-0 x 20-2
(cathedral ceiling)

fireplace

down

MASTER BED RM.
14-0 x 16-0

BRKFST.
10-0 x 12-0

KITCHEN
14-4 x 12-0

FOYER
9-8 x 12-0

cl

walk-in closet

bath

walk-in closet

walk-in closet

storage

UTILITY
10-0 x 6-0

d   w

PORCH

BED RM./ STUDY
12-0 x 12-2

master bath

GARAGE
22-4 x 20-0

storage

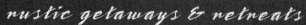

PATIO

BED RM.
11-2 x 14-0

fireplace

REC. RM.
16-0 x 19-6

sto.

up

BED RM.
13-2 x 14-2

walk-in closet

storage

bath

lin.

cl      cl

---

## Plan HPT840039

**Price Code:** C2
**Bedrooms:** 4  **Bathrooms:** 3
**Main Level:** 1,901 sq. ft.
**Lower Level:** 1,075 sq. ft.
**Total:** 2,976 sq. ft.
**Width:** 64'-0"  **Depth:** 62'-4"

The vaulted foyer of this home receives light from two clerestory dormer windows and includes a niche for displaying collectibles. The generous great room enjoys a dramatic cathedral ceiling, a rear wall of windows, access to two rear decks, a fireplace and built-in bookshelves. A recreation room is located on the lower level. Two bedrooms can be found on the main floor, while two more flank the rec room downstairs. The master suite boasts an elegant tray ceiling, His and Hers walk-in closets and a luxurious bath with dual vanities, a garden tub and separate shower.

## Plan HPT840041

**Price Code:** C2
**Bedrooms:** 4 **Bathrooms:** 3½
**Main Level:** 1,662 sq. ft.
**Upper Level:** 585 sq. ft.
**Lower Level:** 706 sq. ft.
**Total:** 2,953 sq. ft.
**Bonus Room:** 575 sq. ft.
**Width:** 81'-4" **Depth:** 68'-8"

A stunning center dormer with an arched window embellishes the exterior of this Craftsman-style home. An arched window allows light into the foyer. A generous back porch extends the great room, which features an impressive cathedral ceiling and a fireplace. The master suite includes a tray ceiling and enjoys back-porch access. Two more bedrooms are located upstairs, while a fourth is in the lower level along with a family room.
©1999 Donald A. Gardner, Inc.

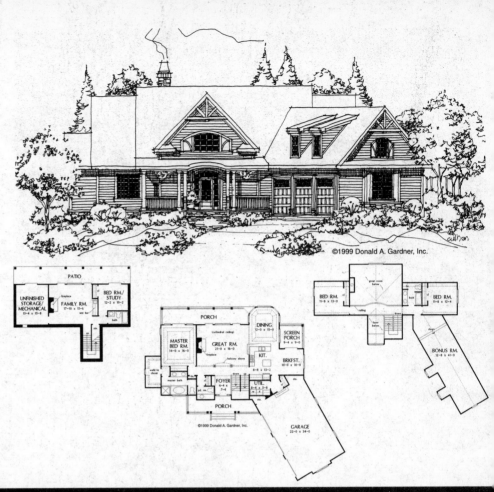

©1999 Donald A. Gardner, Inc.

## Plan HPT840040

**Price Code:** C3
**Bedrooms:** 4 **Bathrooms:** 4
**First Floor:** 2,477 sq. ft.
**Second Floor:** 742 sq. ft.
**Total:** 3,219 sq. ft.
**Bonus Room:** 419 sq. ft.
**Width:** 100'-0" **Depth:** 66'-2"

A prominent center gable with an arched window accents the facade of this custom Craftsman home. The vaulted great room boasts a rear wall of windows and a fireplace bordered by built-in cabinets. A second-floor loft overlooks the great room for added drama. The master suite is completely secluded and enjoys a cathedral ceiling and a luxurious bath. The home includes three additional bedrooms and baths as well as a vaulted loft/study and bonus room. ©1999 Donald A. Gardner, Inc.

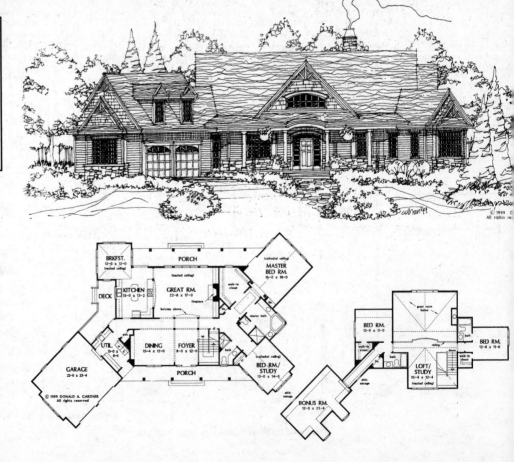

© 1998 Donald A Gardner, Inc.

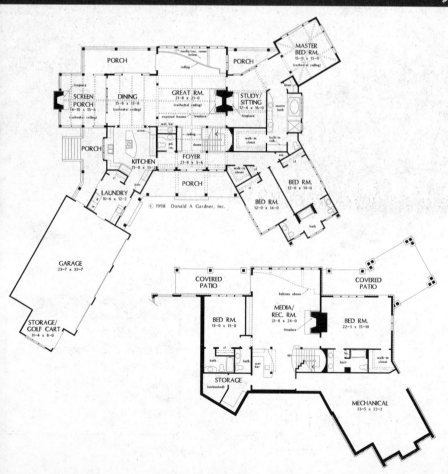

© 1998 Donald A Gardner, Inc.

## Plan HPT840042

**Price Code:** L2
**Bedrooms:** 5   **Bathrooms:** 4½
**Main Level:** 3,040
**Lower Level:** 1,736 sq. ft.
**Total:** 4,776 sq. ft.
**Width:** 106'-5"   **Depth:** 104'-2"

Looking a bit like a mountain resort, this fine Craftsman home is sure to be the envy of your neighborhood. Inside, a spacious great room welcomes you with a cozy fireplace directly ahead. A lavish master suite begins with a sitting room complete with a fireplace, and continues to a private porch, large walk-in closet and sumptuous private bath. Two family bedrooms share a bath and have a wing to themselves. The efficient kitchen sits adjacent to a large, sunny dining area and offers access to a screened porch with yet another fireplace! The lower level features a huge media room with a fourth fireplace.

## Plan HPT840044

**Price Code:** C3
**Bedrooms:** 4 **Bathrooms:** 3
**Main Level:** 2,122 sq. ft.
**Lower Level:** 1,290 sq. ft.
**Total:** 3,412 sq. ft.
**Width:** 83'-0" **Depth:** 74'-4"

A Craftsman combination of cedar shake shingles and wood siding lends warmth and style to this custom-designed home. A stunning cathedral ceiling spans the open great room and spacious center-island kitchen. A deep tray ceiling heightens the formal dining room, while the breakfast room is enhanced by a vaulted ceiling. Two rear decks and a screened porch enhance the living space. ©1999 Donald A. Gardner, Inc.

The interior of this home boasts high ceilings, a wealth of windows and an open arrangement of rooms. A covered portico leads into a roomy foyer, which is flanked by an office/study, accessible through French doors. Just beyond the foyer, a huge vaulted family room highlights columns decorating the entrance and positioned throughout the room. The island kitchen leads to the beautiful dining room.

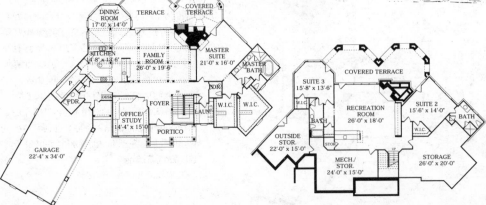

## Plan HPT840043

**Price Code:** L2
**Bedrooms:** 3 **Bathrooms:** 3½ +½
**Main Level:** 2,932 sq. ft.
**Lower Level:** 1,556 sq. ft.
**Total:** 4,488 sq. ft.
**Width:** 114'-0" **Depth:** 82'-11"

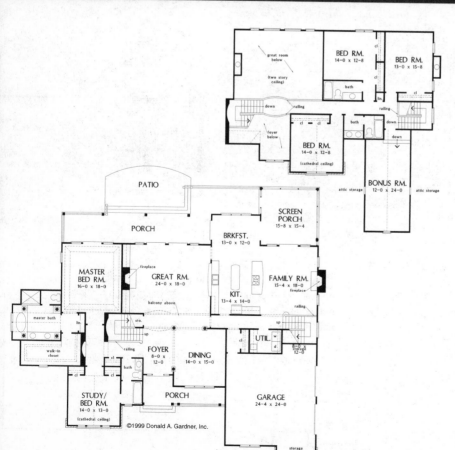

**great room below** (two story ceiling)

BED RM.
14-0 x 12-8

BED RM.
13-0 x 15-8

down / railing / foyer below / railing

BED RM.
14-0 x 12-8
(cathedral ceiling)

bath

down

BONUS RM.
12-0 x 24-0

attic storage / attic storage

PATIO

PORCH

BRKFST.
13-0 x 12-0

SCREEN PORCH
15-8 x 15-4

MASTER BED RM.
16-0 x 18-0

fireplace

GREAT RM.
24-0 x 18-0

KIT.
13-4 x 14-0

FAMILY RM.
15-4 x 18-0
fireplace

master bath

balcony above

railing

walk-in closet

railing / up / sto.

FOYER
8-0 x 12-0

DINING
14-0 x 15-0

UTIL.

w / d

8-0 x storage 12-0

up

STUDY/ BED RM.
14-0 x 13-0
(cathedral ceiling)

PORCH

GARAGE
24-4 x 24-0

storage

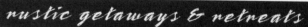

## Plan HPT840045

**Price Code:** C4
**Bedrooms:** 5 **Bathrooms:** 4
**First Floor:** 2,908 sq. ft.
**Second Floor:** 1,021 sq. ft.
**Total:** 3,929 sq. ft.
**Bonus Room:** 328 sq. ft.
**Width:** 85'-4" **Depth:** 70'-4"

Siding and stone embellish the exterior of this five-bedroom traditional estate for an exciting, yet stately appearance. A two-story foyer creates an impressive entry. An equally impressive two-story great room features a fireplace, built-ins and back-porch access. The first-floor master suite enjoys an elegant tray ceiling, back-porch access and a lavish bath with all the amenities including an enormous walk-in closet. Down the hall, a second first-floor bedroom easily converts to a study. The island kitchen easily serves the dining and breakfast rooms.

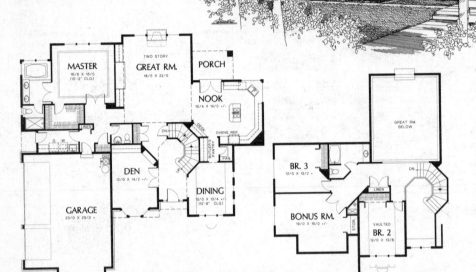

## Plan HPT840046

**Price Code:** C2
**Bedrooms:** 3 **Bathrooms:** 2½
**First Floor:** 2,141 sq. ft.
**Second Floor:** 662 sq. ft.
**Total:** 2,803 sq. ft.
**Bonus Room:** 287 sq. ft.
**Width:** 65'-0" **Depth:** 63'-0"

MASTER
16/8 X 15/0
(10'-3" CLG.)

TWO STORY
GREAT RM.
18/0 X 22/0

PORCH

NOOK
10/4 X 14/0 +/-

OVENS REF

BUTLER'S PANTRY

DESK

DN.

DEN
12/0 X 14/2 +/-

DINING
12/0 X 13/4 +/-
(12'-8" CLG.)

GARAGE
23/0 X 29/0 +

D. W.

GREAT RM.
BELOW

BR. 3
12/0 X 12/2 +/-

LINEN

DN.

BONUS RM.
19/0 X 15/0 +/-

STOR.

VAULTED
BR. 2
12/0 X 13/6

Grand Palladian windows make this brick/stone facade amazingly bright inside and out. The foyer extends to a winding staircase upstairs and leads to the den through French doors downstairs. The dining room has an amazing ceiling and plenty of natural sunlight. A breakfast nook shares the same space as the island kitchen—corner windows allow light to flood in. The master suite is located on the second floor for privacy.

## Plan HPT840047

**Price Code:** C2
**Bedrooms:** 4 **Bathrooms:** 3
**Square Footage:** 2,720
**Width:** 67'-4" **Depth:** 74'-8"

©2000 Donald A. Gardner, Inc.

MASTER
BED RM.
15-8 X 16-8

BRKFST.
11-0 x 10-2
(11' ceiling)

PORCH

wet bar

BED RM.
12-0 x 13-0

walk-in closet

walk-in closet

KITCHEN

pan.

lin.

walk-in closet

master bath

13-0 x 13-4

fireplace

GREAT RM.
18-8 x 20-8
(13' ceiling)

shelves

lin.

bath

BED RM.
13-0 x 12-0

cl

STORAGE
8-8 x 6-6

UTIL.

d   w

lin.

pantry

cl

DINING
12-0 x 14-0

sto.

FOYER
6-0 x
11-0

cl

BED RM./
STUDY
12-0 x 13-0

seat

bath

cl

GARAGE
22-4 x 24-8

PORCH

PORCH

storage

This lavish design boasts luxury and practicality. Enter through the foyer into the open great room, which overlooks a rear porch. An island kitchen sits opposite of a breakfast room and features a walk-in pantry. Three bedrooms, including a master suite, are available to the family. A fourth bedroom can be made into a study. ©2000 Donald A. Gardner, Inc.

**DINING**
12-0 x 15-0

**PORCH**

**MASTER BED RM.**
14-0 x 18-0

**PORCH**

fireplace

**KITCHEN**
12-0 x 15-0

**GREAT RM.**
22-0 x 18-8

(cathedral ceiling)

walk-in closet

walk-in closet

**BRKFST.**
9-8 x 10-0

railing

down

**UTIL.**
5-8 x 6-8

pantry

storage

pd. rm.

cl **FOYER**
6-8 x 10-0

master bath

seat

**GARAGE**
21-8 x 23-4

**PORCH**

storage

©1999 Donald A. Gardner, Inc.

**PATIO**

wet bar

fireplace

**BED RM.**
11-6 x 13-4

cl

cl

lin.

**REC. RM.**
19-8 x 18-8

**BED RM.**
13-6 x 11-0

cl

bath

bath

up

sto.

### Plan HPT840048

**Price Code:** C2
**Bedrooms:** 3  **Bathrooms:** 3½
**Main Level:** 1,725 sq. ft.
**Lower Level:** 1,090 sq. ft.
**Total:** 2,815 sq. ft.
**Width:** 59'-0"  **Depth:** 59'-4"

Arched windows and arches adorn the covered front porch and complement the gable peaks on the facade of this stylish Craftsman home. Designed for sloping lots, this home positions its common living areas and master suite on the main level, while a generous recreation room and two family bedrooms reside on the lower level. An exciting cathedral ceiling expands the foyer and great room, while the dining room and master bedroom and bath enjoy elegant tray ceilings. The island kitchen opens to the great room, dining room and breakfast area.

## Plan HPT840049

**Price Code:** C3
**Bedrooms:** 3  **Bathrooms:** 3
**First Floor:** 2,215 sq. ft.
**Second Floor:** 708 sq. ft.
**Total:** 2,923 sq. ft.
**Bonus Room:** 420 sq. ft.
**Width:** 76'-4"  **Depth:** 69'-10"

This rustic farmhouse design features a variety of today's most up-to-date amenities. A country front porch welcomes you inside through a set of double doors. The foyer is flanked by the formal dining room and the study. The grand room boasts a fireplace flanked by built-ins—decorative art niches are found here and in the dining room. Please specify basement or crawlspace foundation when ordering.

## Plan HPT840050

**Price Code:** C2
**Bedrooms:** 3  **Bathrooms:** 2½
**Square Footage:** 2,329
**Width:** 72'-6"  **Depth:** 73'-4"

This rustic mountain farmhouse features all the favorite amenities for today's family. A front covered porch welcomes you inside to a foyer flanked on either side by a dining room and study. The great room is enhanced by a fireplace, built-ins and two sets of double doors to the rear. The master suite is luxurious with two walk-in closets and a private bath. The kitchen offers a pantry and casual nook.

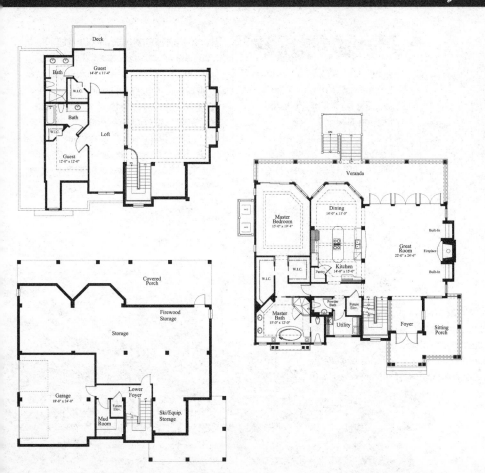

Deck

Bath

Guest
14'-0" x 11'-4"

W.I.C.

Bath

W.I.C.

Loft

Guest
12'-0" x 12'-0"

Covered
Porch

Firewood
Storage

Storage

Garage
18'-6" x 24'-0"

Lower
Foyer

Future
Elev.

Mud
Room

Ski/Equip.
Storage

DN

Veranda

Master
Bedroom
15'-0" x 19'-4"

Dining
14'-0" x 11'-0"

Great
Room
22'-0" x 24'-6"

Built-In

Fireplace

Built-In

W.I.C.

W.I.C.

Pantry

Kitchen
14'-0" x 15'-0"

Master
Bath
15'-0" x 12'-0"

Powder
Bath

Future
Elev.

Utility

Foyer

Sitting
Porch

## Plan HPT840051

**Price Code:** C3
**Bedrooms:** 3  **Bathrooms:** 3½
**First Floor:** 2,096 sq. ft.
**Second Floor:** 892 sq. ft.
**Total:** 2,988 sq. ft.
**Finished Basement:** 1,948 sq. ft.
**Width:** 56'-0"  **Depth:** 54'-0"

Siding and shingles give this home a Craftsman look while columns and gables suggest a more traditional style. The foyer opens to a short flight of stairs that leads to the great room, which features a lovely coffered ceiling, a fireplace, built-ins and French doors to the rear veranda. To the left, the open island kitchen enjoys a pass-through to the great room and easy service to the dining bay. The secluded master suite has two walk-in closets, a luxurious bath and veranda access.

## Plan HPT840052

**Price Code:** C4
**Bedrooms:** 3 **Bathrooms:** 3½
**First Floor:** 2,138 sq. ft.
**Second Floor:** 944 sq. ft.
**Total:** 3,082 sq. ft.
**Bonus Room:** 427 sq. ft.
**Width:** 77'-2" **Depth:** 64'-0"

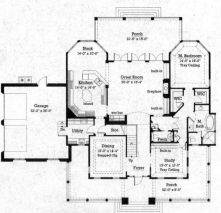

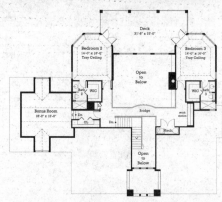

Rustic details highlight this luxury farmhouse design. A wraparound porch welcomes you inside to a foyer flanked on either side by a study with built-ins and a formal dining room easily served from the kitchen. The two-story great room features a country fireplace flanked by built-ins and access to the rear porch. Please specify basement or crawlspace foundation when ordering.

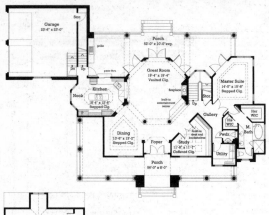

## Plan HPT840053

**Price Code:** C3
**Bedrooms:** 3 **Bathrooms:** 3½
**First Floor:** 1,874 sq. ft.
**Second Floor:** 901 sq. ft.
**Total:** 2,775 sq. ft.
**Bonus Room:** 424 sq. ft.
**Width:** 90'-6" **Depth:** 61'-0"

This modern farmhouse blends well into a mountain or seaside setting. The wrapping front porch welcomes you inside to a foyer flanked by a dining room and study. The octagonal great room features a fireplace and three sets of double doors to the rear porch. The gourmet kitchen serves a bayed nook. The master suite offers two walk-in closets. Please specify basement or crawlspace foundation when ordering.

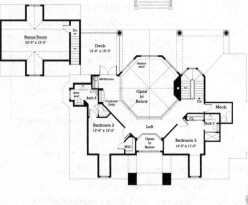

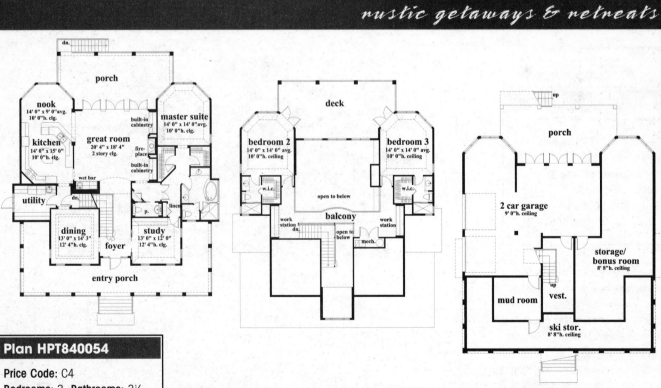

porch

nook
14' 0" x 9' 0" avg.
10' 0" h. clg.

kitchen
14' 0" x 15' 0"
10' 0" h. clg.

great room
20' 4" x 18' 4"
2 story clg.

built-in cabinetry

master suite
14' 0" x 14' 0" avg.
10' 0" h. clg.

fireplace

built-in cabinetry

wet bar

utility

dn.

p.

linen

dining
13' 0" x 14' 3"
12' 4" h. clg.

foyer

study
13' 0" x 12' 0"
12' 4" h. clg.

entry porch

deck

bedroom 2
14' 0" x 14' 0" avg.
10' 0" h. ceiling

bedroom 3
14' 0" x 14' 0" avg.
10' 0" h. ceiling

w.i.c.

w.i.c.

open to below

balcony

work station

dn.

open to below

work station

mech.

up

porch

2 car garage
9' 0" h. ceiling

storage/
bonus room
8' 8" h. ceiling

mud room

vest.

up

ski stor.
8' 8" h. ceiling

## Plan HPT840054

**Price Code:** C4
**Bedrooms:** 3  **Bathrooms:** 3½
**First Floor:** 2,146 sq. ft.
**Second Floor:** 952 sq. ft.
**Total:** 3,098 sq. ft.
**Lower-Level Entry:** 187 sq. ft.
**Width:** 52'-0"  **Depth:** 65'-4"

Tall windows wrap this noble exterior with dazzling details and allow plenty of natural light inside. A wraparound porch sets a casual but elegant pace for the home, with space for rockers and swings. Well-defined formal rooms are placed just off the foyer. A host of French doors opens the great room to an entertainment porch and, of course, inspiring views. Even formal meals take on the ease and comfort of a mountain region in the stunning open dining room. Nearby, a gourmet kitchen packed with amenities serves any occasion.

This new-age contemporary design features two floors full of comfortable modern amenities. An abundance of porch space encourages outdoor activities. A raised front porch welcomes you inside to a foyer accessing the main living area and a computer room illuminated by an arched window. The kitchen/eating area accesses a side porch. The formal dining room overlooks a wraparound back porch. This home is designed with a basement foundation.

## Plan HPT840056

**Price Code:** A4
**Bedrooms:** 3  **Bathrooms:** 2½
**First Floor:** 1,100 sq. ft.
**Second Floor:** 970 sq. ft.
**Total:** 2,070 sq. ft.
**Width:** 46'-0"  **Depth:** 46'-0"

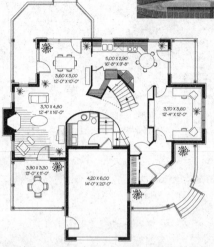

## Plan HPT840055

**Price Code:** A3
**Bedrooms:** 2  **Bathrooms:** 2½
**First Floor:** 1,143 sq. ft.
**Second Floor:** 651 sq. ft.
**Total:** 1,794 sq. ft.
**Bonus Space:** 651 sq. ft.
**Width:** 32'-0"  **Depth:** 57'-0"

This traditional country cabin is a vacationer's dream. An elegant entryway extends into the foyer where the two-story great room visually expands the lofty interior. This room provides a warming fireplace and offers built-in cabinetry. The dining room opens through double doors to the veranda on the left side on the plan. Upstairs, a vaulted ceiling enhances the master suite.

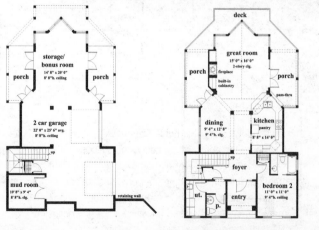

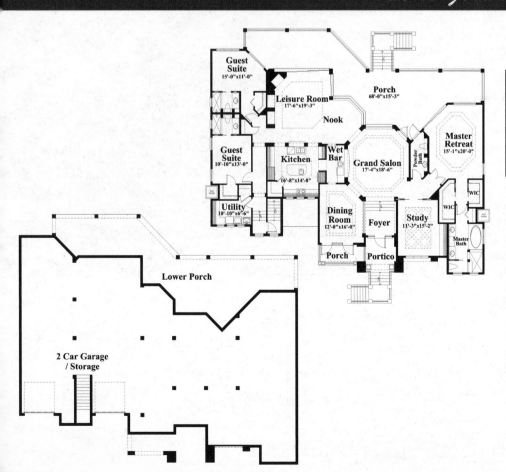

**Guest Suite**
15'-0"x11'-0"

**Leisure Room**
17'-6"x19'-3"

**Nook**

**Porch**
68'-0"x15'-3"

**Guest Suite**
10'-10"x13'-0"

**Kitchen**

**Wet Bar**

**Grand Salon**
17'-4"x18'-6"

**Master Retreat**
15'-1"x20'-0"

**Powder Bath**

16'-8"x14'-8"

**Utility**
10'-10"x6'-6"

**Dining Room**
12'-0"x16'-0"

**Foyer**

**Study**
11'-3"x15'-2"

**WIC**

**WIC**

**Master Bath**

**Porch**

**Portico**

**Lower Porch**

**2 Car Garage / Storage**

## Plan HPT840057

**Price Code:** C4
**Bedrooms:** 3 **Bathrooms:** 3½
**Square Footage:** 3,074
**Width:** 77'-0" **Depth:** 66'-8"

With a rugged stone-and-siding facade, this neighborhood-friendly home sets the pace with timeless character. A stately portico presents a warm welcome, while a mid-level foyer eases the transition to the elevated grand salon. Interior vistas extend throughout the living area, made even more inviting by rows of graceful arches and stunning wide views. In the gourmet kitchen, wide counters and a walk-in pantry surround a food-preparation island that sports a vegetable sink. A rambling master suite includes a spacious bath with a whirlpool tub and oversized shower.

## Plan HPT840058

**Price Code:** C3
**Bedrooms:** 4  **Bathrooms:** 4½
**First Floor:** 1,530 sq. ft.
**Second Floor:** 1,420 sq. ft.
**Third Floor:** 551 sq. ft.
**Total:** 3,501 sq. ft.
**Finished Basement:** 1,530 sq. ft.
**Width:** 45'-0"  **Depth:** 60'-8"

A massive stone chimney, clapboard siding and a copper-seam roof define this rugged exterior—and a well-arranged interior allows outdoor views in every room. The formal dining room links with an open gourmet kitchen through a butler's pantry, while a study leads to a computer room. Upstairs, each of two secondary bedrooms boasts a private bath, and the master suite features a sitting bay.

## Plan HPT840059

**Price Code:** A3
**Bedrooms:** 3  **Bathrooms:** 2
**First Floor:** 1,342 sq. ft.
**Second Floor:** 511 sq. ft.
**Total:** 1,853 sq. ft.
**Width:** 44'-0"  **Depth:** 40'-0"

Matchstick details and a careful blend of stone and siding lend a special style and spirit to this stately retreat. Multi-pane windows take in the scenery and deck out the refined exterior of this cabin-style home. An open foyer shares its natural light with the great room—a bright reprieve filled with its own outdoor light. Dinner guests may wander from the coziness of the hearth space into the crisp night air through lovely French doors.

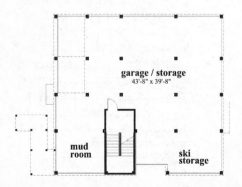

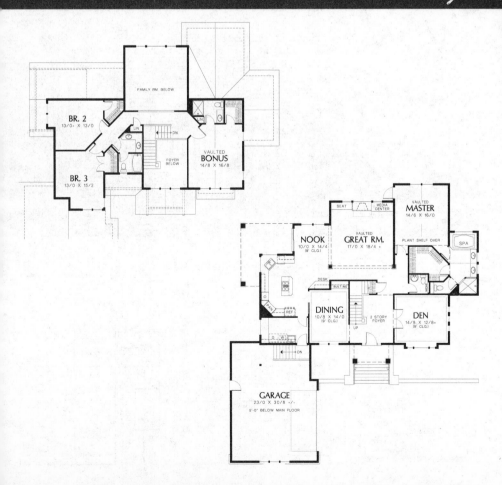

## Plan HPT840060

**Price Code:** C1
**Bedrooms:** 4  **Bathrooms:** 3½
**First Floor:** 2,005 sq. ft.
**Second Floor:** 689 sq. ft.
**Total:** 2,694 sq. ft.
**Bonus Room:** 356 sq. ft.
**Width:** 68'-0"  **Depth:** 73'-6"

Shingles and stone combine to present a highly attractive facade on this spacious three-bedroom home. The Craftsman-style influence is very evident and adds charm. The two-story foyer is flanked by a large, yet cozy den on the right and on the left, beyond the staircase, is the formal dining room with built-ins. The vaulted great room also offers built-ins, as well as a fireplace. The U-shaped kitchen will surely please the gourmet of the family with its planning desk, corner sink, cooktop island and plenty of counter and cabinet space.

## Plan HPT840061

**Price Code:** C2
**Bedrooms:** 4 **Bathrooms:** 3½
**First Floor:** 1,760 sq. ft.
**Second Floor:** 1,360 sq. ft.
**Total:** 3,120 sq. ft.
**Bonus Room:** 542 sq. ft.
**Width:** 75'-0" **Depth:** 63'-4"

Shed dormers set above wood siding, shutters and a wraparound porch lend an unmistakable country style to this three-bedroom home. Inside, the foyer introduces a study on the right and the dining area on the left. Note the kitchen's cooktop island/serving bar open to the great room. Three bedrooms and an optional fourth bedroom reside on the second floor. The master suite enjoys a fireplace, sunlit sitting room and walk-in closet.

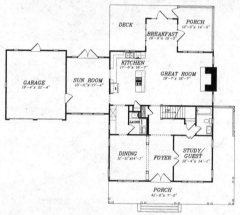

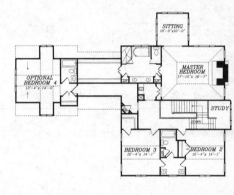

## Plan HPT840062

**Price Code:** C1
**Bedrooms:** 3 **Bathrooms:** 2½
**First Floor:** 1,825 sq. ft.
**Second Floor:** 1,020 sq. ft.
**Total:** 2,845 sq. ft.
**Width:** 49'-8" **Depth:** 57'-0"

A flagstone-decorated covered porch opens through French doors to a foyer where stone walls lead into the casual dining/great room area. This room is graced with a two-story ceiling and fireplace, as well as three sets of French doors opening to the rear porch. The master bedroom includes a sitting area, walk-in closet, linen closet and many other luxuries.

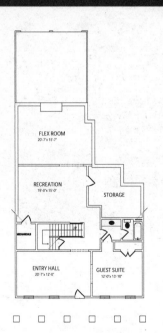

FLEX ROOM
20'-7"x15'-7"

RECREATION
19'-0"x15'-0"

STORAGE

MECHANICAL

ENTRY HALL
20'-7"x12'-0"

GUEST SUITE
12'-0"x13'-10"

GARAGE
19'-8"x19'-1"
*MAY BE DETACHED
OR SIDE LANE ENTRY

REAR COURTYARD

GREAT ROOM
19'-8"x16'0"
TWO STORY CEILING

BRKFST AREA

SITTING AREA

KITCHEN
19'-8"x10'-0"

LAUNDRY

POWDER ROOM

UP

MASTER SUITE
15'-3"x20'-3"

WALK-IN CLOSET

WALK-IN CLOSET

DINING
14'-2"x12'-4"

FOYER

MASTER BATH

PORCH

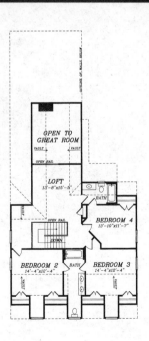

OUTLINE OF WALK BELOW

OPEN TO GREAT ROOM

VAULT    VAULT

OPEN RAIL

LOFT
13'-8"x15'-5"

BATH

OPEN RAIL

BEDROOM 4
13'-10"x11'-7"

DOWN

BEDROOM 2
14'-4"x12'-4"

BATH

BEDROOM 3
14'-4"x12'-4"

## Plan HPT840063

**Price Code:** C1
**Bedrooms:** 4 **Bathrooms:** 3½
**First Floor:** 1,630 sq. ft.
**Second Floor:** 1,198 sq. ft.
**Total:** 2,828 sq. ft.
**Finished Basement:** 1,630 sq. ft.
**Width:** 36'-0" **Depth:** 78'-0"

Three dormers and pillars aligning along the front porch set this home apart from the rest. The steep side-gabled rooflines offer an aura of sophistication. The foyer is flanked by the dining room and the master suite. A sitting area and private access to the rear courtyard make this elegant master suite a retreat within a retreat. Space is plentiful in the kitchen—just to the rear of the great room, which is adorned by a fireplace. The dining room is brightened by the large window overlooking the porch. Three bedrooms, two bathrooms and a loft complete the second floor.

## Plan HPT840064

**Price Code:** C3
**Bedrooms:** 4  **Bathrooms:** 3½
**First Floor:** 1,804 sq. ft.
**Second Floor:** 1,041 sq. ft.
**Total:** 2,845 sq. ft.
**Width:** 59'-10"  **Depth:** 71'-0"

There's a feeling of old Charleston in this stately home—particularly on the quiet side porch that wraps around the kitchen and breakfast room. The interior of this home revolves around a spacious great room with a welcoming fireplace. The left wing is dedicated to the master suite, which boasts wide views of the rear property. This home is designed with a basement foundation.

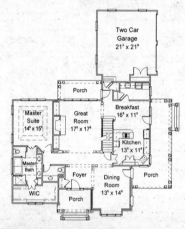

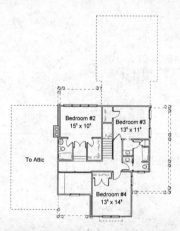

## Plan HPT840065

**Price Code:** C3
**Bedrooms:** 3  **Bathrooms:** 3½
**First Floor:** 1,930 sq. ft.
**Second Floor:** 755 sq. ft.
**Total:** 2,685 sq. ft.
**Bonus Room:** 488 sq. ft.
**Width:** 46'-6"  **Depth:** 71'-0"

This home boasts a townhouse silhouette with a country-style facade—ideal for a narrow lot. Massive columns anchor a full porch to the New England-style elevation. Inside, the formal dining room opens from the two-story foyer. The island kitchen offers plenty of space for cooking and overlooks the casual breakfast room. The family room features a fireplace. This home is designed with a walkout basement foundation.

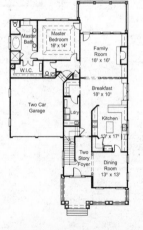

## Plan HPT840066

**Price Code:** C4
**Bedrooms:** 4 **Bathrooms:** 3½
**First Floor:** 1,532 sq. ft.
**Second Floor:** 1,846 sq. ft.
**Total:** 3,378 sq. ft.
**Width:** 63'-4" **Depth:** 65'-0"

An intriguing mix of stone and siding adds character to this home, which gives the impression of a small cottage that was added to as the family grew. The great room features a stone hearth and opens to the breakfast room, which provides access to the rear deck and the side porch. The kitchen includes an island cooktop counter and ample work space. The master suite dominates the second floor, providing a splendid bath with a tray ceiling and a spacious walk-in closet. This home is designed with a basement foundation.

Master Bath

W.I.C.

Bedroom No.4
14⁶ x 14⁹

Master Suite
22⁹ x 14⁹

Bedroom No.3
14³ x 11⁹

Bedroom No.2
14⁶ x 12⁹

Two Car Garage
23⁰ x 23⁰

Deck

Great Room
20⁰ x 14⁹

Breakfast
14⁹ x 13⁹

Porch

Kitchen
12⁹ x 13⁶

Porch Cochère

Study
14³ x 11⁹

Foyer

Dining Room
14³ x 12⁶

## Plan HPT840067

**Price Code:** C3
**Bedrooms:** 4  **Bathrooms:** 2½
**First Floor:** 1,326 sq. ft.
**Second Floor:** 1,254 sq. ft.
**Total:** 2,580 sq. ft.
**Bonus Room:** 230 sq. ft.
**Width:** 55'-4"  **Depth:** 57'-6"

This shingle-style home is a rustic yet elegant design that does not reveal itself fully at first glance. Double French doors at the entrance lead to a magnificent gallery hall and winding staircase. Stunning columns define the formal dining room, while French doors open to the front porch. Upstairs, a charming master bedroom includes a fireplace. This home is designed with a basement foundation.

## Plan HPT840068

**Price Code:** C4
**Bedrooms:** 5  **Bathrooms:** 4½
**First Floor:** 1,512 sq. ft.
**Second Floor:** 1,746 sq. ft.
**Total:** 3,258 sq. ft.
**Width:** 63'-6"  **Depth:** 62'-6"

This engaging design blends the clean, sharp edges of the sophisticated shingle style with relaxed cottage details such as dovecote gables and flower boxes. The rear of the plan takes advantage of rows of windows, allowing great views. The great room, with built-in bookshelves and a fireplace, opens to the kitchen and breakfast room, where a door leads to the deck. This home is designed with a walkout basement foundation.

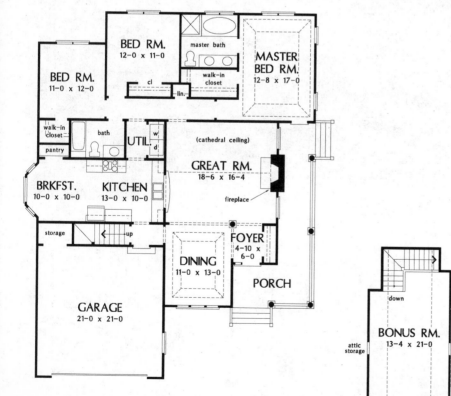

## Plan HPT840069

**Price Code:** A4
**Bedrooms:** 3  **Bathrooms:** 2
**Square Footage:** 1,687
**Bonus Room:** 333 sq. ft.
**Width:** 48'-8"  **Depth:** 59'-4"

This traditional home blends characteristics of the folk houses of the national movement with the Cape Cod homes of the Colonial Revival period—note the shed-roofed porch that wraps from the foyer to the master suite at the rear. The formal dining room, to the left of the foyer, boasts a tray ceiling as does the master bedroom. A decorative column opens the dining room to the foyer and the great room, where the majesty of the cathedral ceiling draws focus to the fireplace flanked by windows. The well-equipped kitchen serves the sunny breakfast nook and dining room with ease.
©2000 Donald A. Gardner, Inc.

BED RM.
12-0 x 11-0

master bath

MASTER
BED RM.
12-8 x 17-0

BED RM.
11-0 x 12-0

walk-in
closet

cl

walk-in
closet

lin.

bath

UTIL.

w
d

(cathedral ceiling)

pantry

GREAT RM.
18-6 x 16-4

fireplace

BRKFST.
10-0 x 10-0

KITCHEN
13-0 x 10-0

storage

up

FOYER
4-10 x
6-0

DINING
11-0 x 13-0

GARAGE
21-0 x 21-0

PORCH

down

BONUS RM.
13-4 x 21-0

attic
storage

attic
storage

## Plan HPT840070

**Price Code:** C1
**Bedrooms:** 5  **Bathrooms:** 4
**First Floor:** 1,438 sq. ft.
**Second Floor:** 1,464 sq. ft.
**Total:** 2,902 sq. ft.
**Width:** 52'-0"  **Depth:** 64'-6"

Nothing on a home says "Americana" like a pediment and covered porch detailing. Step into the two-story foyer and be formally introduced to the dining room on the left and the living room on the right. The two-story family room features a central fireplace. Five bedrooms, including a luxurious master suite, complete this plan. Please specify basement or crawlspace foundation when ordering.

## Plan HPT840071

**Price Code:** A4
**Bedrooms:** 4  **Bathrooms:** 3
**First Floor:** 1,321 sq. ft.
**Second Floor:** 1,070 sq. ft.
**Total:** 2,391 sq. ft.
**Width:** 63'-2"  **Depth:** 50'-8"

Touches of Victoriana add a whisper of the grace of yesteryear to this captivating home. The foyer separates a den from the formal living and dining rooms. The living room has a cozy fireplace; the dining room overlooks the rear sun deck. The hearth room and breakfast room form one large gathering area that is served handily by an island kitchen. Four bedrooms occupy the second floor.

**QUOTE ONE®**
Cost to build? See page 246
to order complete cost estimate
to build this house in your area!

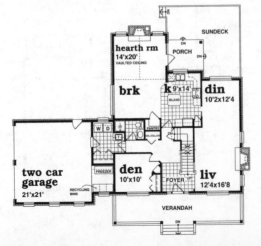

MR. BATH & DRSG.

MR. BEDROOM
16'-10" x 12'-10"

LIN

WIC

DN

BEDROOM
11'-2" x 11'-8"

LINEN

BEDROOM
10'-2" x 12'-10"

BATH

## Plan HPT840072

**Price Code:** A4
**Bedrooms:** 3  **Bathrooms:** 2½
**First Floor:** 1,229 sq. ft.
**Second Floor:** 939 sq. ft.
**Total:** 2,168 sq. ft.
**Width:** 74'-4"  **Depth:** 41'-4"

There's no place like home-sweet-home with this country farmhouse. The wraparound porch is great for outdoor enjoyment. The spacious floor plan features a formal dining room right off the entrance foyer and a nearby living room. Not only does the massive family room have access to the rear patio, but it also enjoys a cozy fireplace and is open to the angled kitchen with plenty of counter and cabinet space. A laundry and lavatory room are found nearby with quick access to the garage. The extravagant master bedroom shares the second floor with two additional family bedrooms.

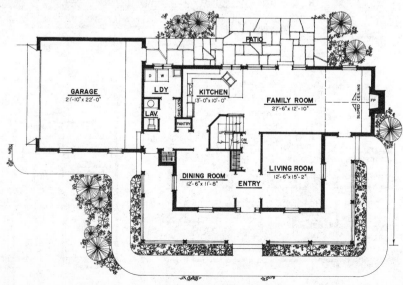

GARAGE
21'-10" x 22'-0"

PATIO

D  W

LDY

KITCHEN
13'-0" x 10'-0"

SHELVES

PANTRY

LAV.

UP

DN

FAMILY ROOM
27'-6" x 12'-10"

SLOPED CEILING

FP

DINING ROOM
12'-6" x 11'-8"

ENTRY

LIVING ROOM
12'-6" x 15'-2"

## Plan HPT840073

**Price Code:** C1
**Bedrooms:** 4 **Bathrooms:** 2½
**First Floor:** 1,530 sq. ft.
**Second Floor:** 1,268 sq. ft.
**Total:** 2,798 sq. ft.
**Bonus Room:** 354 sq. ft.
**Width:** 60'-0" **Depth:** 53'-0"

This contemporary farmhouse is enhanced by Colonial-style charm. Symmetry and a covered front porch dazzle the facade. Inside, the combined living and dining area is warmed by a fireplace. A casual den is found to the front left of the plan, while the family room, kitchen and bayed nook are located to the rear. Four family bedrooms are located upstairs, along with a bonus room located just above the garage.

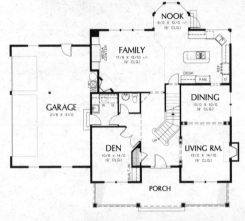

## Plan HPT840074

**Price Code:** C1
**Bedrooms:** 4 **Bathrooms:** 2½
**First Floor:** 1,317 sq. ft.
**Second Floor:** 1,216 sq. ft.
**Total:** 2,533 sq. ft.
**Width:** 65'-0" **Depth:** 44'-0"

Country elegance combined with a well-planned interior make this a perfect family home. The kitchen and breakfast nook serve as the hub of the first-floor plan. On the right are the living room and formal dining room; on the left is the family room. Fireplaces warm both the living room and the family room.

**Quote One®**

Cost to build? See page 246 to order complete cost estimate to build this house in your area!

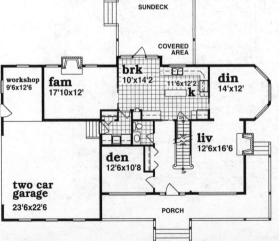

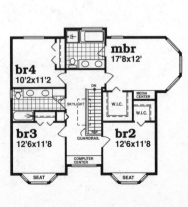

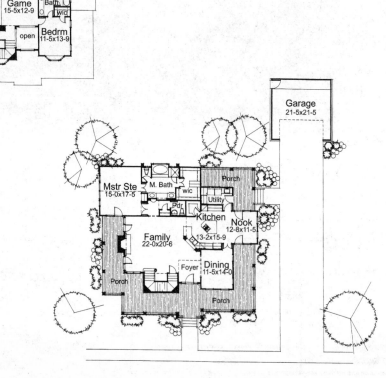

Bedrm
11-5x13-6
wic
wic
Bath
Game
15-5x12-9
Bath
wic
Bedrm
12-0x14-10
open
Bedrm
11-5x13-9

Garage
21-5x21-5

Mstr Ste
15-0x17-5
M. Bath
wic
Porch
Pdr
Utility
Kitchen
Nook
12-8x11-5
Family
22-0x20-6
13-2x15-9
Porch
Dining
11-5x14-0
Foyer
Porch
Porch

## Plan HPT840075

**Price Code:** C1
**Bedrooms:** 4  **Bathrooms:** 3½
**First Floor:** 1,920 sq. ft.
**Second Floor:** 1,032 sq. ft.
**Total:** 2,952 sq. ft.
**Width:** 58'-0"  **Depth:** 55'-6"

This country-style farmhouse boasts a range of well-planned amenities. A wraparound porch encourages outdoor entertaining. Inside, the foyer opens to a formal dining room and a family room warmed by a fireplace. The island kitchen opens to a nook and features efficient storage space. The master bedroom provides a private bath and double walk-in closet. Three family bedrooms reside upstairs, along with two baths and the family game room. Please specify basement, crawlspace or slab foundation when ordering.

## Plan HPT840077

**Price Code:** A4
**Bedrooms:** 3  **Bathrooms:** 2½
**First Floor:** 1,306 sq. ft.
**Second Floor:** 1,118 sq. ft.
**Total:** 2,424 sq. ft.
**Width:** 52'-0"  **Depth:** 46'-8"

The traditional charm of this family home offers a distinct American flavor. Horizontal siding and a quaint wrap-around front porch are sure signs of country styling. To the left of the foyer, the home office is a quiet retreat. To the right, a combined living and dining room area is found at the front of the home. This home is designed with a basement foundation.

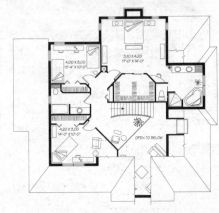

## Plan HPT840076

**Price Code:** A4
**Bedrooms:** 4  **Bathrooms:** 2½
**First Floor:** 1,472 sq. ft.
**Second Floor:** 861 sq. ft.
**Total:** 2,333 sq. ft.
**Width:** 52'-8"  **Depth:** 51'-0"

Three separate porches highlight this traditional two-story farmhouse. The foyer opens to the living room and the dining room with a sweeping staircase between the two. The dining room accesses one of the rear porches while the sun room has access to the front porch. The U-shaped kitchen is tucked in the rear where a snack bar offers space for a quick meal. This home is designed with a basement foundation.

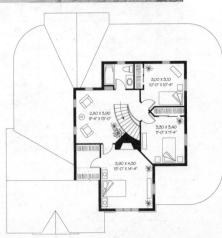

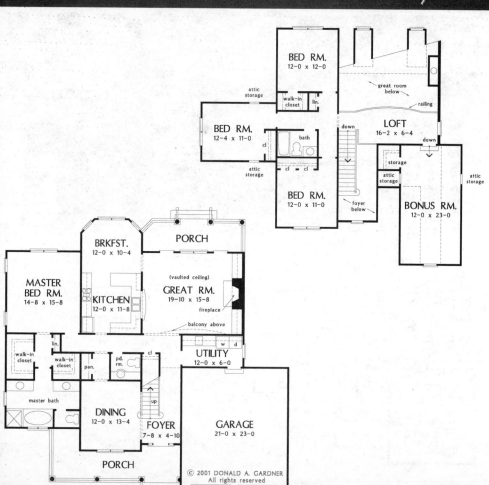

## Plan HPT840327

**Price Code:** C1
**Bedrooms:** 4  **Bathrooms:** 2½
**First Floor:** 1,667 sq. ft.
**Second Floor:** 803 sq. ft.
**Total:** 2,470 sq. ft.
**Bonus Space:** 318 sq. ft.
**Width:** 52'-4"  **Depth:** 57'-0"

Country accents and farmhouse style enhance the façade of this lovely two-story home. The first floor provides a formal dining room and great room warmed by a fireplace. The kitchen connects to a breakfast bay—perfect for casual morning meals. The first-floor master suite includes two walk-in closets and a private bath. Upstairs, a loft overlooks the two-story great room. Three second-floor bedrooms share a hall bath. The bonus room above the garage is great for a home office or guest suite.

BED RM. 12-0 x 12-0

attic storage

walk-in closet  lin.

great room below

railing

BED RM. 12-4 x 11-0

cl

bath

down

LOFT 16-2 x 6-4

down

attic storage

cl  cl

storage

storage

attic storage

attic storage

BED RM. 12-0 x 11-0

foyer below

BONUS RM. 12-0 x 23-0

BRKFST. 12-0 x 10-4

PORCH

MASTER BED RM. 14-8 x 15-8

KITCHEN 12-0 x 11-8

(vaulted ceiling)

GREAT RM. 19-10 x 15-8

fireplace

balcony above

walk-in closet

walk-in closet

lin.

pd. rm.

pan.

cl

UTILITY 12-0 x 6-0

w  d

master bath

DINING 12-0 x 13-4

FOYER 7-8 x 4-10

up

GARAGE 21-0 x 23-0

PORCH

## Plan HPT840078

**Price Code:** C3
**Bedrooms:** 5 **Bathrooms:** 3
**First Floor:** 1,385 sq. ft.
**Second Floor:** 1,195 sq. ft.
**Total:** 2,580 sq. ft.
**Width:** 48'-0" **Depth:** 49'-0"

This traditional home would fit perfectly into the scenic New England countryside. A covered front porch welcomes you into a two-story foyer flanked on either side by formal living and dining rooms. The two-story family room is warmed by a cozy fireplace. The handy kitchen features a serving bar to the breakfast room. Please specify basement or crawlspace foundation when ordering.

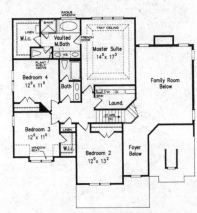

## Plan HPT840079

**Price Code:** C3
**Bedrooms:** 4 **Bathrooms:** 3½
**First Floor:** 2,665 sq. ft.
**Second Floor:** 1,081 sq. ft.
**Total:** 3,746 sq. ft.
**Width:** 88'-0" **Depth:** 52'-6"

This lovely plan steps into the future with an exterior mix of brick, stone and cedar siding. With a large front porch, the home appears as if it should be located in a quaint oceanfront community. Comfortable elegance coupled with modern-day amenities and nostalgic materials makes this home a great choice. The large great room and hearth room/breakfast area offer grand views to the rear yard, where a large deck complements outdoor activities.

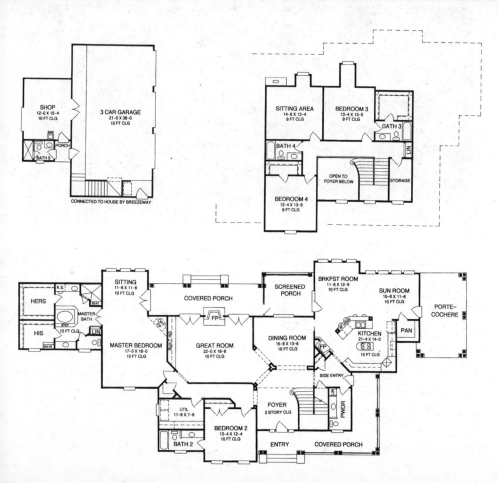

SHOP
12-0 X 15-4
10 FT CLG

3 CAR GARAGE
21-0 X 38-0
10 FT CLG

PORCH

BATH 5

CONNECTED TO HOUSE BY BREEZEWAY

SITTING AREA
14-8 X 13-4
9 FT CLG

BEDROOM 3
13-4 X 13-0
9 FT CLG

BATH 3

BATH 4

LIN

OPEN TO
FOYER BELOW

STORAGE

BEDROOM 4
13-4 X 13-6
9 FT CLG

HERS

K.S.

SEAT

MASTER
BATH
10 FT CLG

HIS

SHELF

LIN

SITTING
11-6 X 11-6
10 FT CLG

COVERED PORCH

FP

SCREENED
PORCH

BRKFST ROOM
11-8 X 12-6
10 FT CLG

SUN ROOM
15-8 X 11-8
10 FT CLG

PORTE-
COCHERE

MASTER BEDROOM
17-0 X 18-0
10 FT CLG

BUILT-INS

GREAT ROOM
22-0 X 16-6
10 FT CLG

DINING ROOM
15-6 X 13-6
10 FT CLG

KITCHEN
21-4 X 14-0
10 FT CLG

PAN

FP

SIDE ENTRY

UTIL
11-6 X 7-6

FOYER
2 STORY CLG

LIN

PWDR

BEDROOM 2
13-4 X 12-4
10 FT CLG

BATH 2

ENTRY

COVERED PORCH

## Plan HPT840080

**Price Code:** L1
**Bedrooms:** 4  **Bathrooms:** 5½
**First Floor:** 3,120 sq. ft.
**Second Floor:** 1,083 sq. ft.
**Total:** 4,203 sq. ft.
**Width:** 118'-1"  **Depth:** 52'-2"

The blending of natural materials and a nostalgic farmhouse look gives this home its unique character. Inside, a sophisticated floor plan includes all the amenities demanded by today's upscale family. Three large covered porches—one on the front and two on the rear—provide outdoor entertaining areas. The kitchen features a built-in stone fireplace visible from the breakfast and sun rooms. The master suite includes a large sitting area and a luxurious bath. Upstairs, two additional bedrooms and a large game room will please family and guests. Please specify crawlspace or slab foundation when ordering.

## Plan HPT840082

**Price Code:** C2
**Bedrooms:** 3 **Bathrooms:** 2½
**First Floor:** 1,788 sq. ft.
**Second Floor:** 639 sq. ft.
**Total:** 2,427 sq. ft.
**Bonus Room:** 235 sq. ft.
**Width:** 59'-0" **Depth:** 51'-0"

Shingle siding and quaint shutters open this three-bedroom plan. The interior revolves around a vaulted great room, which opens to a formal dining room. The island kitchen easily serves the breakfast area and the dining room. A vaulted study sits to the front of the first floor; the master suite resides in the back. Please specify basement or crawlspace foundation when ordering.

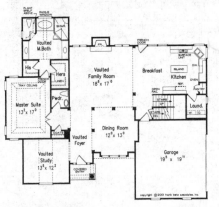

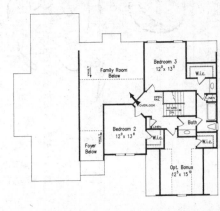

## Plan HPT840081

**Price Code:** C2
**Bedrooms:** 3 **Bathrooms:** 2½
**First Floor:** 1,615 sq. ft.
**Second Floor:** 565 sq. ft.
**Total:** 2,180 sq. ft.
**Bonus Room:** 471 sq. ft.
**Width:** 52'-0" **Depth:** 51'-4"

Shutters and stonework warmly accent the exterior of this three-bedroom home. Inside, a V-shaped serving bar in the kitchen views both the grand room and the breakfast nook. The master suite features a sitting room. A bridge above the foyer leads to two secondary bedrooms sharing a full bath. The bonus room upstairs provides room to grow. Please specify basement or crawlspace foundation when ordering.

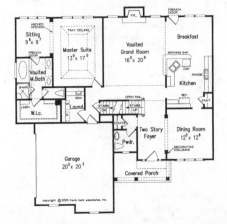

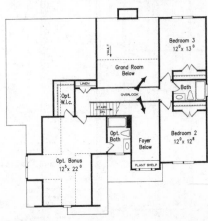

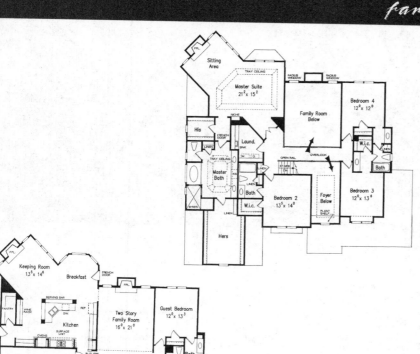

## Plan HPT840083

**Price Code:** L1
**Bedrooms:** 5 **Bathrooms:** 4½
**First Floor:** 1,999 sq. ft.
**Second Floor:** 2,046 sq. ft.
**Total:** 4,045 sq. ft.
**Width:** 66'-4" **Depth:** 64'-0"

This luxury farmhouse design is reserved for the hardworking home-owner who seeks a relaxing retreat. A front covered porch that wraps around the side adds a country accent to the exterior. Inside, a study and formal dining room flank the two-story foyer. A guest suite is placed to the right of the two-story family room, warmed by a fireplace. The kitchen is open to the nook and casual keeping room. A three-car garage is located nearby. Upstairs, the master suite features a hearth-warmed sitting room, private bath and two large walk-in closets. Please specify basement or crawl-space foundation when ordering.

## Plan HPT840085

**Price Code:** C2
**Bedrooms:** 4  **Bathrooms:** 2½
**First Floor:** 1,036 sq. ft.
**Second Floor:** 1,295 sq. ft.
**Total:** 2,331 sq. ft.
**Width:** 47'-0"  **Depth:** 42'-8"

A covered stoop around this home's entryway is defined by columns. The dining room, great room, morning room and kitchen comprise the first level of this home. Three family bedrooms and a master suite are located on the second level. Please specify basement, crawlspace or slab foundation when ordering.

*farmhouses & ranches*

## Plan HPT840084

**Price Code:** C2
**Bedrooms:** 4  **Bathrooms:** 2½
**First Floor:** 2,141 sq. ft.
**Second Floor:** 923 sq. ft.
**Total:** 3,064 sq. ft.
**Width:** 65'-0"  **Depth:** 56'-6"

A stone-and-siding exterior, arched windows and multiple gables create an exquisite appearance for this transitional home. Dual French doors with high arch-topped windows across the rear of the great room and a warm fireplace decorate this captivating gathering space with warmth and light. The breakfast room delivers a panoramic view in three directions and creates a sun-room effect for the family eating area.

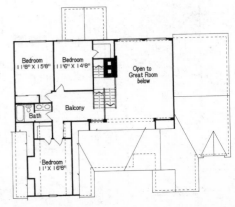

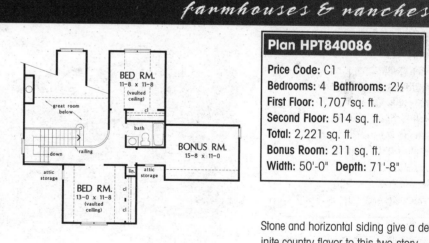

© 2001 Donald A. Gardner, Inc.

## Floor Plan

**PORCH**

**BRKFST.**
11-8 x 11-8

**PORCH**

fireplace

**GREAT RM.**
17-6 x 16-0

**KITCHEN**
11-8 x 12-0

**MASTER BED RM.**
15-6 x 14-8
(cathedral ceiling)

pan.

balcony above

up

pd. rm.

cl

cl

**FOYER**
5-8 x 13-4

**DINING**
11-8 x 13-0

**UTIL.**
6-0 x 10-0

walk-in closet

walk-in closet

master bath

w

d

**BED RM./ STUDY**
11-8 x 12-0

**PORCH**

© 2001 DONALD A. GARDNER
All rights reserved

**GARAGE**
21-0 x 21-0

storage

**BED RM.**
11-8 x 11-8
(vaulted ceiling)

cl

great room below

down

railing

bath

**BONUS RM.**
15-8 x 11-0

attic storage

lin.

attic storage

**BED RM.**
13-0 x 11-8
(vaulted ceiling)

cl

cl

## Plan HPT840086

**Price Code:** C1
**Bedrooms:** 4  **Bathrooms:** 2½
**First Floor:** 1,707 sq. ft.
**Second Floor:** 514 sq. ft.
**Total:** 2,221 sq. ft.
**Bonus Room:** 211 sq. ft.
**Width:** 50'-0"  **Depth:** 71'-8"

Stone and horizontal siding give a definite country flavor to this two-story home. The front study makes an ideal guest room with the adjoining powder room. The formal dining room is accented with decorative columns that define its perimeter. The great room boasts a fireplace, built-ins and a magnificent view of the backyard beyond one of two rear porches. The master suite boasts two walk-in closets and a private bath. Two bedrooms share a full bath on the second floor.

## Plan HPT840088

**Price Code:** C3
**Bedrooms:** 4  **Bathrooms:** 2½ + ½
**First Floor:** 2,025 sq. ft.
**Second Floor:** 1,726 sq. ft.
**Total:** 3,751 sq. ft.
**Width:** 76'-8"  **Depth:** 76'-4"

Here is a fieldstone farmhouse that has its roots in the rolling countryside of Pennsylvania. Based on the Pottsgrove home in Pottstown, which was built in 1752, it also features the popular pent roof of that era and shows the types of additions that came as the size of the family fortune increased. Two chimneys support five fireplaces. The simple elegance of Georgian design is evident in many interior details.

*farmhouses & ranches*

## Plan HPT840087

**Price Code:** C3
**Bedrooms:** 2  **Bathrooms:** 1½
**Units A & AR**
**First Floor:** 554 sq. ft.
**Second Floor:** 460 sq. ft.
**Total:** 1,014 sq. ft.
**Unit B**
**Square Footage:** 936 sq. ft.
**Width:** 46'-10"  **Depth:** 66'-2"

This unique Northwestern multi-family design features three separate apartment units. Units A and AR offer two floors of livability. The first floors provide a living room with a fireplace, a kitchen/dining area and an outdoor patio. Upstairs, each of the bedrooms has a walk-in closet, and they share a bath. Unit B is a one-story apartment, which enters from an outdoor porch into the living room, warmed by a fireplace.

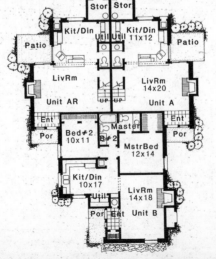

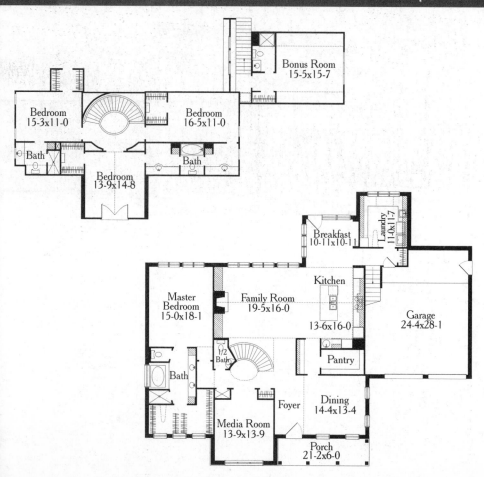

Bonus Room
15-5x15-7

Bedroom
15-3x11-0

Bedroom
16-5x11-0

Bath

Bath

Bedroom
13-9x14-8

Breakfast
10-11x10-11

Laundry
11-0x11-7

Kitchen
13-6x16-0

Master
Bedroom
15-0x18-1

Family Room
19-5x16-0

Garage
24-4x28-1

1/2
Bath

Bath

Pantry

Foyer

Dining
14-4x13-4

Media Room
13-9x13-9

Porch
21-2x6-0

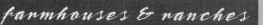

## Plan HPT840089

**Price Code:** C3
**Bedrooms:** 4  **Bathrooms:** 4½
**First Floor:** 2,458 sq. ft.
**Second Floor:** 1,483 sq. ft.
**Total:** 3,941 sq. ft.
**Bonus Room:** 240 sq. ft.
**Width:** 76'-6"  **Depth:** 61'-8"

This stunning four-bedroom home offers an exciting facade that combines stone and stucco. The foyer opens to a grand and elegant circular staircase that rises to a circular overlook. Magnificent views to the rear are beheld from the family, breakfast and utility rooms in addition to the master suite. In the era of electronics, the library has become the media room where full-length windows adorn the front wall. The master suite is on the first floor with three additional bedrooms upstairs—note the Jack-and-Jill bath on the right. Additional space is found above the two-car garage for future development.

## Plan HPT840091

**Price Code:** L1
**Bedrooms:** 4 **Bathrooms:** 3½
**First Floor:** 2,647 sq. ft.
**Second Floor:** 1,237 sq. ft.
**Total:** 3,884 sq. ft.
**Width:** 72'-3" **Depth:** 74'-6"

A perfect porch announces a subdued entry and provides an inviting introduction to this home. The leaded-glass entry leads to a two-story foyer that's enhanced by a stairwell with a wrought-iron railing. An ultra-elegant grand room sports a fireplace framed by French doors. This home is designed with a walkout basement foundation.

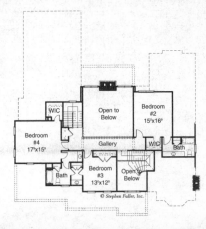

## Plan HPT840090

**Price Code:** A3
**Bedrooms:** 3 **Bathrooms:** 2½
**First Floor:** 1,320 sq. ft.
**Second Floor:** 433 sq. ft.
**Total:** 1,753 sq. ft.
**Width:** 51'-11" **Depth:** 50'-0"

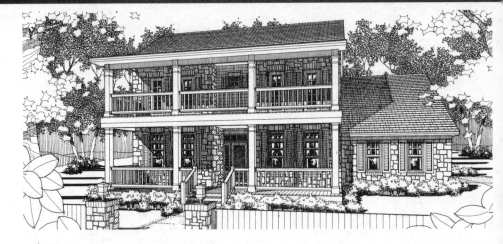

Truly a sight to behold, this home borrows elements from the Colonial styling of the South. Flagstone enhances the facade, while a two-story porch brings out the uniqueness of the design. Enter through the foyer to find a dining room, hearth-warmed great room and kitchen/nook area; the nook opens to a rear porch. Please specify basement, crawlspace or slab foundation when ordering.

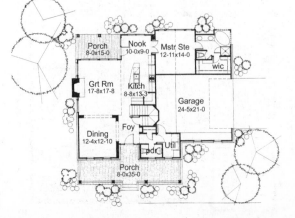

**Quote One®**

Cost to build? See page 246
to order complete cost estimate
to build this house in your area!

### Plan HPT840092

**Price Code:** L2
**Bedrooms:** 4 **Bathrooms:** 3½
**First Floor:** 2,086 sq. ft.
**Second Floor:** 2,040 sq. ft.
**Total:** 4,126 sq. ft.
**Width:** 66'-0" **Depth:** 68'-4"

This lovely stone farmhouse, reminiscent of the solid, comfortable homes once prevalent throughout America, will fit any region or neighborhood. The foyer leads to the formal rooms, including a spacious library. The family room and breakfast room have beam ceilings and open to the kitchen. On the second floor are four bedrooms, including a guest room with a private bath. The master suite has a fireplace and a fine bath with a whirlpool tub. A covered veranda leads to a side yard and invites enjoyment of the outdoors.

## Plan HPT840094

**Price Code:** A4
**Bedrooms:** 4  **Bathrooms:** 2½
**Square Footage:** 2,261
**Width:** 82'-0"  **Depth:** 54'-0"

A wonderful combination of textures, trim and windows fronts this attractive single-story design with an attached three-car garage. A large covered porch opens to an entry gallery flanked by a formal dining room and study or optional fourth bedroom. Ahead is a great room with a vaulted ceiling, fieldstone fireplace and access to an outdoor patio. The U-shaped kitchen opens to a large breakfast room which in turn opens to the patio.

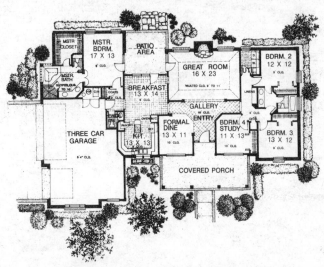

## Plan HPT840093

**Price Code:** A3
**Bedrooms:** 3  **Bathrooms:** 2½
**Square Footage:** 1,991
**Width:** 60'-0"  **Depth:** 57'-6"

This charming design is accented with an array of country complements. The front porch welcomes you inside to a foyer flanked on either side by a dining room and study. The family room features a fireplace and views of the rear deck. The island kitchen easily serves the breakfast nook. Please specify basement, crawlspace or slab foundation when ordering.

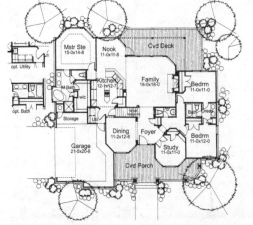

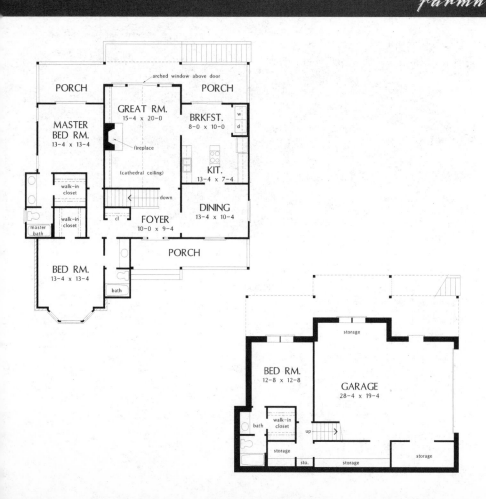

© 1991 Donald A. Gardner Architects, Inc.

B-NATHAN

## Plan HPT840095

**Price Code:** A4
**Bedrooms:** 2  **Bathrooms:** 2
**Square Footage:** 1,528
**Finished Basement:** 394 sq. ft.
**Width:** 45'-8"  **Depth:** 51'-1"

A covered front porch, dormers and gables, and a stone and siding exterior lend warmth and charm to this comfortable home. Ideal for sloping lots, this plan offers a basement which adds a third bedroom with a bath, plenty of storage, and a two-car garage. The heart of this home is a spacious great room that features a dramatic cathedral ceiling and a fireplace flanked by built-ins. The full-length back porch is accessed by the great room, breakfast area and master suite. Note that each bedroom has its own generous bath and walk-in closet. ©1991 Donald A. Gardner Architects, Inc.

PORCH

GREAT RM.
15-4 x 20-0

PORCH

arched window above door

BRKFST.
8-0 x 10-0

MASTER BED RM.
13-4 x 13-4

fireplace

walk-in closet

(cathedral ceiling)

KIT.
13-4 x 7-4

walk-in closet

master bath

DINING
13-4 x 10-4

down

FOYER
10-0 x 9-4

cl

BED RM.
13-4 x 13-4

bath

PORCH

BED RM.
12-8 x 12-8

GARAGE
28-4 x 19-4

storage

bath

walk-in closet

up

storage

sto.

storage

storage

## Plan HPT840096

**Price Code:** C1
**Bedrooms:** 2 **Bathrooms:** 2½
**Square Footage:** 1,997
**Bonus Room:** 310 sq. ft.
**Width:** 64'-4" **Depth:** 63'-0"

The hub of this charming plan is the spacious kitchen with an island and serving bar. The nearby breakfast nook accesses the greenhouse with its wall of windows and three large skylights. A built-in media center beside a warming fireplace is the focal point of the family room. Bedroom 2 shares a full bath with the den/study. Please specify basement, crawlspace or slab foundation when ordering.

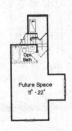

## Plan HPT840097

**Price Code:** C1
**Bedrooms:** 3 **Bathrooms:** 2
**Square Footage:** 1,616
**Bonus Room:** 362 sq. ft.
**Width:** 64'-0" **Depth:** 55'-0"

Shingles and open gables accentuate the familiar and loved country home. Inside, the split-bedroom plan provides seclusion for the master suite. Featuring a grand bath and walk-in closet, the master suite also enjoys a stepped ceiling. Open great and dining rooms share access to the spacious kitchen. Bedrooms 1 and 2 share a full bath.

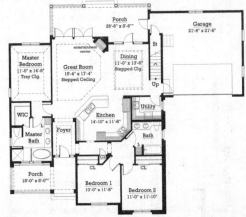

## Plan HPT840098

**Price Code:** C1
**Bedrooms:** 3 **Bathrooms:** 2
**Square Footage:** 1,526
**Bonus Room:** 336 sq. ft.
**Width:** 65'-0" **Depth:** 54'-6"

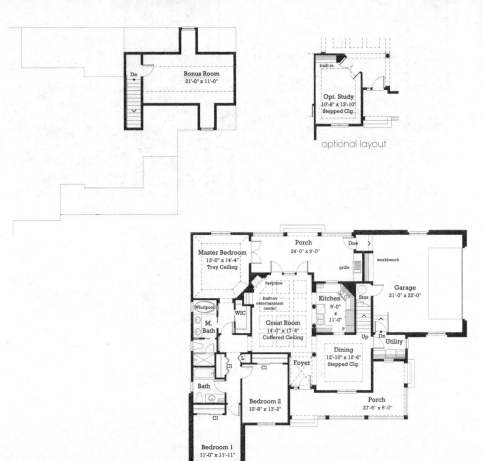

Bonus Room
21'-0" x 11'-0"

Dn

built-in

Opt. Study
10'-8" x 13'-10"
Stepped Clg.

optional layout

Master Bedroom
13'-0" x 14'-4"
Tray Ceiling

Porch
24'-0" x 9'-0"

Dn

workbench

grille

Garage
21'-0" x 22'-0"

fireplace

built-in entertainment center

Kitchen
9'-0" x 11'-0"

Stor.

Whirlpool

WIC

M. Bath

Great Room
14'-0" x 17'-6"
Coffered Ceiling

P

Up

Dn

Utility

C1

L

Dining
12'-10" x 12'-6"
Stepped Clg.

Bath

Foyer

C1

C1

Bedroom 2
10'-8" x 13'-2"

Porch
27'-6" x 6'-0"

C1

Bedroom 1
11'-0" x 11'-11"

This quaint and contemporary farm-house offers a wealth of amenities and options. A wrapping front porch welcomes you inside where formal rooms are the first to greet family and guests alike. A corner fireplace, built-ins and access to the rear porch enhance the great room. The master suite offers a whirlpool tub and a walk-in closet. Two additional family bedrooms offer ample closet space and share a hall bath. A compact kitchen, utility room and garage complete the first floor. The bonus room is great for a fourth bedroom or home office.

## Plan HPT840100

**Price Code:** C2
**Bedrooms:** 3 **Bathrooms:** 2½
**Square Footage:** 1,989
**Bonus Room:** 274 sq. ft.
**Width:** 81'-0" **Depth:** 50'-0"

This classic one-story farmhouse is a delight for any family. The front covered porch welcomes you inside. The formal dining room and great room create a spacious first impression. The kitchen easily serves the bayed nook. The master suite features two walk-in closets. The spacious rear porch provides a place for outdoor entertaining. Please specify basement or crawlspace foundation when ordering.

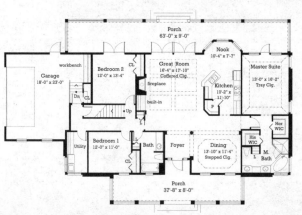

## Plan HPT840099

**Price Code:** C2
**Bedrooms:** 3 **Bathrooms:** 2½
**Square Footage:** 2,555
**Width:** 70'-6" **Depth:** 76'-6"

This amenity-filled country cottage is an attractive addition to any neighborhood. Shingles and a front covered porch enhance the facade, while inside a study and dining room flank the foyer. The great room features a fireplace, built-ins and three sets of double doors to the rear porch. The master suite provides back-porch access, two walk-in closets and a private master bath. Two additional bedrooms are located behind the garage.

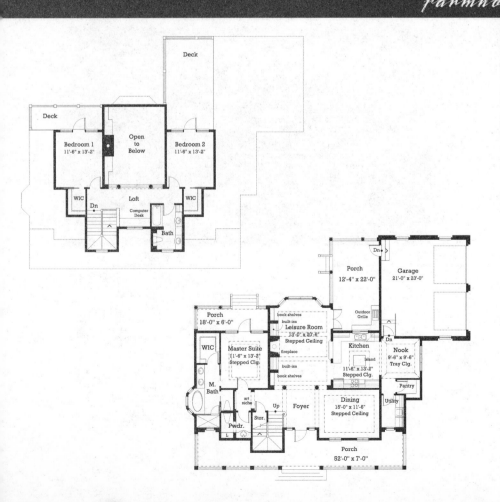

Deck

Deck

Bedroom 1
11'-6" x 13'-2"

Open
to
Below

Bedroom 2
11'-6" x 13'-2"

WIC

Loft

WIC

Dn

Computer
Desk

Bath

Porch
12'-4" x 22'-0"

Garage
21'-0" x 23'-0"

Dn

Porch
18'-0" x 6'-0"

book shelves
built-ins
**Leisure Room**
13'-0" x 20'-8"
Stepped Ceiling
fireplace
built-ins
book shelves

Outdoor
Grille

Kitchen
11'-6" x 13'-2"
Stepped Clg.

island

Dn

Nook
9'-6" x 9'-6"
Tray Clg.

WIC

Master Suite
11'-6" x 13'-2"
Stepped Clg.

M.
Bath

art
niche

Up

Foyer

Dining
15'-0" x 11'-6"
Stepped Ceiling

Pantry

Utility

Pwdr.

Stor.

Porch
52'-0" x 7'-0"

## Plan HPT840101

**Price Code:** C2
**Bedrooms:** 3  **Bathrooms:** 2½
**First Floor:** 1,493 sq. ft.
**Second Floor:** 676 sq. ft.
**Total:** 2,169 sq. ft.
**Width:** 70'-0"  **Depth:** 55'-8"

Matchstick trim and arch-top windows create plenty of curb appeal with this attractive design. A spacious leisure room with a stepped ceiling highlights the heart of the home. To the left of the plan, a rambling master suite boasts access to a private porch. The formal dining room adjoins the gourmet kitchen, which features a breakfast nook and a walk-in pantry. French doors lead out to the rear porch and an outdoor kitchen. The first-floor master suite features a private bath and walk-in closet. Please specify basement or crawlspace foundation when ordering.

GARAGE

BEDROOM
10-0 X 11-0

BEDROOM
10-0 X 11-0

BREAKFAST

KITCHEN

GREAT ROOM
17-6 X 23-0

MASTER
BEDROOM
13-0 X 15-0

## Plan HPT840103

**Price Code:** A3
**Bedrooms:** 3 **Bathrooms:** 2
**Square Footage:** 1,660
**Width:** 46'-0" **Depth:** 75'-0"

A lovely gazebo adorns the front porch of this one-story country home and complements the other perfect details that distinguish this home from others of its size and configuration. Inside, the living areas are clustered to the right of the plan: the great room with a fireplace, the sunny breakfast nook and the kitchen with a peninsular work area.

## Plan HPT840102

**Price Code:** A3
**Bedrooms:** 3 **Bathrooms:** 1½
**First Floor:** 960 sq. ft.
**Second Floor:** 841 sq. ft.
**Total:** 1,801 sq. ft.
**Width:** 36'-0" **Depth:** 30'-0"

This quaint Victorian cottage is ideal for any countryside setting. A wrapping porch with a gazebo-style sitting area enhances the exterior, while interior spaces are open to each other. The kitchen with a snack bar is open to both the dining area and the living room area. The second floor offers three family bedrooms and a pampering bath. This home is designed with a basement foundation.

4,20 X 4,20
14'-0" X 14'-0"

6,20 X 4,10
20'-8" X 13'-8"

3,90 X 4,50
13'-0" X 15'-0"

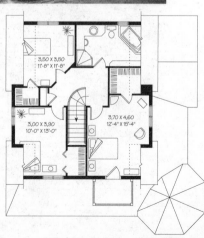

3,50 X 3,50
11'-8" X 11'-8"

3,00 X 3,90
10'-0" X 13'-0"

3,70 X 4,60
12'-4" X 15'-4"

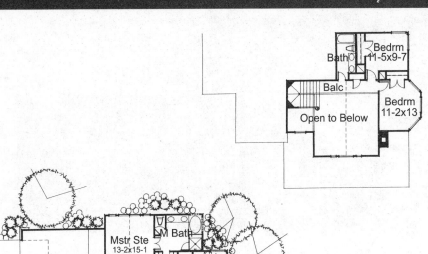

## Plan HPT840104

**Price Code:** A3
**Bedrooms:** 3 **Bathrooms:** 2½
**First Floor:** 1,450 sq. ft.
**Second Floor:** 448 sq. ft.
**Total:** 1,898 sq. ft.
**Width:** 59'-11" **Depth:** 47'-6"

This Country-style farmhouse features a facade complemented with classic Victorian accents. The wrapping front porch accesses the entry foyer and bayed dining room. The living room and study reside to the front of the plan, while the secluded master bedroom is located at the rear. Master amenities include a private bath and roomy walk-in closet. An island kitchen and two-car garage complete the first floor. Please specify basement, crawlspace or slab foundation when ordering.

## Plan HPT840105

**Price Code:** A4
**Bedrooms:** 3 **Bathrooms:** 2
**Square Footage:** 2,198
**Width:** 84'-8" **Depth:** 59'-0"

This striking ranch has an eye-catching exterior with a breathtaking interior. A twelve-foot ceiling welcomes you into the foyer and gives you access to a hallway on the right along with a full view of the stunning great room. The hallway leads to three bedrooms and a bathroom. The master bedroom is sure to please with its cathedral ceiling, two walk-in closets and elaborate private bath.

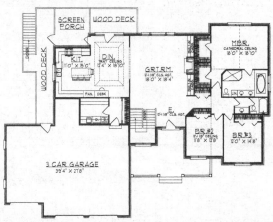

## Plan HPT840328

**Price Code:** C1
**Bedrooms:** 3 **Bathrooms:** 2½
**Square Footage:** 2,330
**Bonus Room:** 364 sq. ft.
**Width:** 62'-3" **Depth:** 60'-6"

Quaint and simple, this country home with front dormers will charm the whole neighborhood. Inside, the foyer is flanked by a formal dining room and a study. A cathedral ceiling enlarges the great room, which is warmed by a fireplace flanked by built-ins. The master suite is located to the right and includes two walk-in closets and a private bath. ©2001 Donald A. Gardner, Inc.

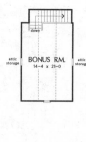

© 2001 Donald A. Gardner, Inc.

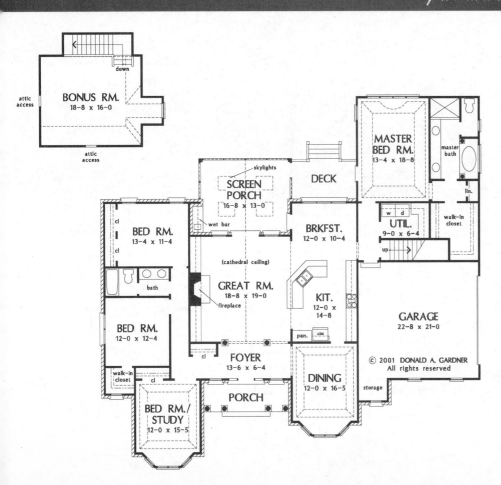

**BONUS RM.**
18-8 x 16-0

attic access

down

attic access

**BED RM.**
13-4 x 11-4

cl
cl

bath

**BED RM.**
12-0 x 12-4

walk-in closet

cl

**BED RM./ STUDY**
12-0 x 15-5

**PORCH**

**FOYER**
13-6 x 6-4

cl

**GREAT RM.**
18-8 x 19-0

fireplace

(cathedral ceiling)

wet bar

**SCREEN PORCH**
16-8 x 13-0

skylights

**DECK**

**BRKFST.**
12-0 x 10-4

**KIT.**
12-0 x 14-8

pan.

dw

**DINING**
12-0 x 16-5

storage

**MASTER BED RM.**
13-4 x 18-8

master bath

lin.

**UTIL.**
9-0 x 6-4

w d

walk-in closet

up

**GARAGE**
22-8 x 21-0

© 2001 DONALD A. GARDNER
All rights reserved

## Plan HPT840106

**Price Code:** C1
**Bedrooms:** 4  **Bathrooms:** 2
**Square Footage:** 2,461
**Bonus Room:** 397 sq. ft.
**Width:** 71'-2"  **Depth:** 67'-2"

Great outdoor living spaces define this plan—and comfortable amenities reside throughout the interior. An open foyer extends vistas and views through the great room to the screened porch and beyond. Family bedrooms share a hall bath on the left side of the plan. A flex room to the front of the plan converts to a study, guest room or home office. A garden tub and separate vanities highlight the master retreat. A bonus room is available for future use—perfect for an additional bedroom, storage or a playroom.

## Plan HPT840107

**Price Code:** C1
**Bedrooms:** 3 **Bathrooms:** 2
**Square Footage:** 1,604
**Bonus Room:** 316 sq. ft.
**Width:** 57'-0" **Depth:** 59'-0"

This traditional cottage plan offers a simple one-story design with a bonus room for flexible use. A wrapping front porch welcomes you inside to a formal living room warmed by a fireplace. The island kitchen is open to the dining room. The rear screened porch is vaulted and provides space for brisk entertaining at seasonal times of the year. Three family bedrooms and a garage complete the first floor.

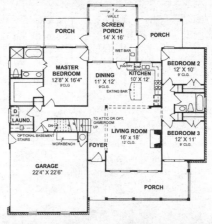

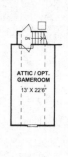

## Plan HPT840108

**Price Code:** A4
**Bedrooms:** 3 **Bathrooms:** 2
**Square Footage:** 1,904
**Width:** 55'-2" **Depth:** 50'-5"

Columns and a hipped roof give this traditional home a taste of Colonial style. Just off the foyer are two family bedrooms to the left, while a formal dining room is to the right. The great room enjoys a cathedral ceiling and fireplace and is open to the breakfast area with a bay window and the gourmet kitchen. ©2000 Donald A. Gardner, Inc.

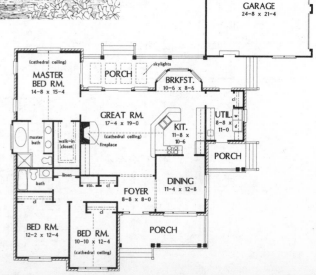

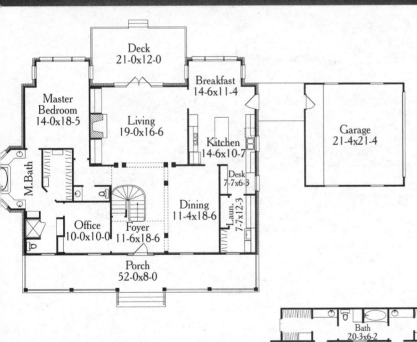

Deck
21-0x12-0

Breakfast
14-6x11-4

Master
Bedroom
14-0x18-5

Living
19-0x16-6

Garage
21-4x21-4

M.Bath

Kitchen
14-6x10-7

Desk
7-7x6-3

Office
10-0x10-0

Foyer
11-6x18-6

Dining
11-4x18-6

Laun.
7-7x12-3

Porch
52-0x8-0

Bath
20-3x6-2

Open to
Below

Bedroom
12-2x15-7

Bedroom
11-2x15-7

Balcony

## Plan HPT840109

**Price Code:** C2
**Bedrooms:** 3  **Bathrooms:** 2½
**First Floor:** 2,109 sq. ft.
**Second Floor:** 896 sq. ft.
**Total:** 3,005 sq. ft.
**Width:** 90'-4"  **Depth:** 56'-4"

This American classic boasts a full-length covered porch and a two-car garage with a connecting breezeway. The U-shaped staircase creates a lasting first impression as the focal point of the foyer. The formal dining room and the living room are defined by decorative columns for an open effect. French doors in the living room lead to the rear deck. The master suite offers a sunny bedroom, a private bath with a garden tub, and direct access to the office. Please specify basement, crawlspace or slab foundation when ordering.

## Plan HPT840111

**Price Code:** A4
**Bedrooms:** 3  **Bathrooms:** 2½
**First Floor:** 1,437 sq. ft.
**Second Floor:** 531 sq. ft.
**Total:** 1,968 sq. ft.
**Width:** 51'-4"  **Depth:** 41'-6"

This sophisticated country home is economical and cozy, yet it has all the amenities of a larger plan. From the wraparound porch to the vaulted great room, this floor plan provides space for family togetherness, as well as personal privacy. The secluded master suite contains two spacious walk-in closets, double lavatories and a garden tub. ©2000 Donald A. Gardner, Inc.

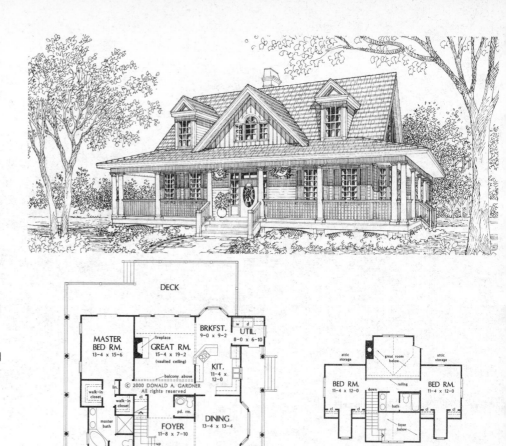

## Plan HPT840110

**Price Code:** C1
**Bedrooms:** 4  **Bathrooms:** 3
**First Floor:** 1,743 sq. ft.
**Second Floor:** 555 sq. ft.
**Total:** 2,298 sq. ft.
**Bonus Room:** 350 sq. ft.
**Width:** 77'-11"  **Depth:** 53'-2"

A lovely arch-top window and a wrap-around porch set off this country exterior. Inside, the formal dining room opens off the foyer, which leads to a spacious great room. This living area has a fireplace and access to a screened porch with a cathedral ceiling. Bay windows allow natural light into the breakfast area and formal dining room. The master suite has a spacious bath. ©1997 Donald A. Gardner Architects, Inc.

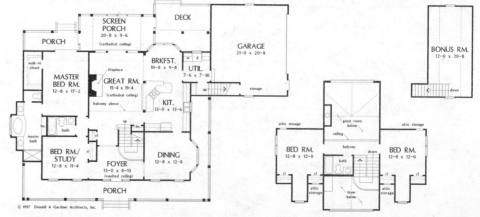

© 1994 Donald A. Gardner Architects, Inc.

B. NATHAN

master bath

walk-in closet

great room below

railing

**BED RM.**
12-8 x 11-0

cl

bath

lin.

cl

**MASTER BED RM.**
12-8 x 17-8

down

**BED RM.**
12-8 x 11-0

foyer below

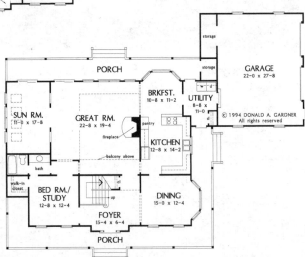

storage

**PORCH**

storage

**GARAGE**
22-0 x 27-8

**BRKFST.**
10-8 x 11-2

**UTILITY**
8-8 x 11-0

w   d

d

**SUN RM.**
11-0 x 17-8

**GREAT RM.**
22-8 x 19-4

pantry

fireplace

**KITCHEN**
12-8 x 14-2

© 1994 Donald A. Gardner
All rights reserved

balcony above

bath

walk-in closet

cl

**BED RM./ STUDY**
12-8 x 12-4

up

**DINING**
15-0 x 12-4

**FOYER**
15-4 x 6-4

**PORCH**

### Plan HPT840112

**Price Code:** C1
**Bedrooms:** 4  **Bathrooms:** 3
**First Floor:** 1,821 sq. ft.
**Second Floor:** 956 sq. ft.
**Total:** 2,777 sq. ft.
**Width:** 77'-0"  **Depth:** 58'-8"

With its long wraparound porches and expansive informal living spaces stretching across the back, this farmhouse projects a graceful, relaxed attitude. Nine-foot ceilings on the first level with a vaulted ceiling in the great room, ventilating skylights in the sun room, a two-level foyer, and bay windows combine to make this home feel more like 3,000 square feet. The first-level bedroom can double as a study, while the master bedroom upstairs features double vanities and a large walk-in closet.

## Plan HPT840114

**Price Code:** A4
**Bedrooms:** 3  **Bathrooms:** 2½
**First Floor:** 2,281 sq. ft.
**Balcony Hall:** 112 sq. ft.
**Total:** 2,393 sq. ft.
**Future Space:** 912 sq. ft.
**Width:** 60'-0"  **Depth:** 71'-0"

Dormers and doubled columns on the front porch give this traditional home a grand entrance. The living room right at the center of the floor plan includes a cozy fireplace and accesses the rear screened porch. The island kitchen enjoys a pass-through to the eating area, which features a built-in china cabinet. The lavish master bedroom boasts a relaxing sitting area. Please specify crawlspace or slab foundation when ordering.

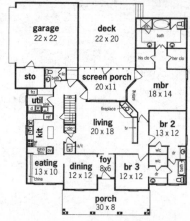

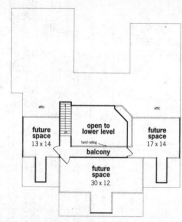

## Plan HPT840113

**Price Code:** A3
**Bedrooms:** 3  **Bathrooms:** 2
**Square Footage:** 1,932
**Bonus Room:** 342 sq. ft.
**Future Space:** 820 sq. ft.
**Width:** 66'-0"  **Depth:** 72'-0"

This elegant and modern farmhouse is enhanced by a range of interior amenities and exterior details. Double doors from the front covered porch welcome you inside to the formal living room warmed by a fireplace. The kitchen easily serves the formal dining room and casual eating nook. The master bedroom is located to rear of plan for privacy. Please specify crawlspace or slab foundation when ordering.

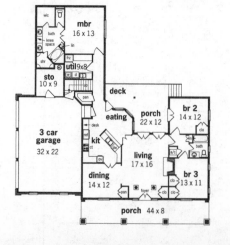

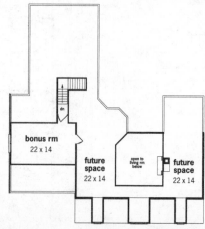

## Plan HPT840115

**Bedrooms:** 3 **Bathrooms:** 2
**Square Footage:** 1,692
**Bonus Room:** 358 sq. ft.
**Width:** 54'-0" **Depth:** 56'-6"

This cozy country cottage is enhanced with a front-facing planter box above the garage and a charming covered porch. The foyer leads to a vaulted great room, complete with a fireplace and radius windows. Decorative columns complement the entrance to the dining room, as does a decorative arch. On the left side of the plan resides the master suite, which is resplendent with amenities including a vaulted sitting room, tray ceiling, French doors to the vaulted full bath and an arched opening to the sitting room. On the right side, two additional bedrooms share a full bath. Please specify basement or crawlspace foundation when ordering.

### Floor Plan

SHWR.

LINEN

Vaulted M.Bath

W.i.c.

RADIUS WINDOW

FPL

RADIUS WINDOW

Breakfast

Bedroom 3
11³ x 11⁰

PLANT SHELF ABOVE

SERVING BAR

PANTRY

REF.

LINEN

FRENCH DOOR

Vaulted Great Room
15⁰ x 20⁰
14'-6" CLG. HT.

Kitchen

DW.

RANGE

Bath

Master Suite
15⁰ x 13²

TRAY CLG.

DECORATIVE COLUMN

COATS

ARCHED OPG.

VAULT

STAIRS UP

ARCHED OPG.

Foyer
14'-6" CLG. HT.

Dining Room
11⁰ x 12⁴
12'-0" CLG. HT.

Bedroom 2
11⁰ x 11⁰

Sitting Room

VAULT

W. D.

Laund.

STAIRS TO OPT. BSMT.

Covered Porch

Garage
20⁵ x 22²

### Optional Bonus

STAIRS DN

OPEN RAIL

Opt. Bonus
12⁵ x 20⁹

## Plan HPT840117

**Price Code:** C1
**Bedrooms:** 4  **Bathrooms:** 2½
**Square Footage:** 2,413
**Bonus Room:** 417 sq. ft.
**Width:** 78'-8"  **Depth:** 57'-8"

Dormers set above a charming porch and a beautiful entry door with arched transoms lend eye appeal to this wonderful four-bedroom design. The foyer leads to the dining room to the right and a bedroom or study to the left—both featuring exciting ceiling treatments. The hearth-warmed great room shares an open area with the island kitchen and bayed breakfast nook.
©2001 Donald A. Gardner, Inc.

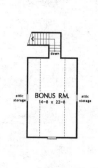

## Plan HPT840116

**Price Code:** A4
**Bedrooms:** 3  **Bathrooms:** 2½
**First Floor:** 2,281 sq. ft.
**Balcony Hall:** 112 sq. ft.
**Total:** 2,393 sq. ft.
**Future Space:** 866 sq. ft.
**Width:** 60'-0"  **Depth:** 71'-0"

A most welcoming porch is detailed with double-columned pillars and tall shuttered windows. The foyer introduces the dining room on the left and living room straight ahead. A corner fireplace and built-in entertainment center makes the living room a casual and formal space. Please specify crawlspace or slab foundation when ordering.

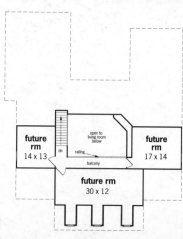

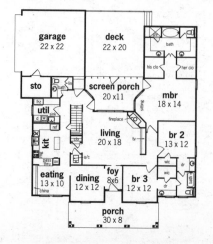

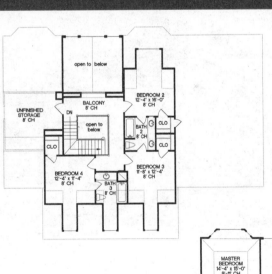

## Plan HPT840118

**Price Code:** C3
**Bedrooms:** 4 **Bathrooms:** 3½
**First Floor:** 1,907 sq. ft.
**Second Floor:** 908 sq. ft.
**Total:** 2,815 sq. ft.
**Bonus Room:** 183 sq. ft.
**Width:** 64'-8" **Depth:** 51'-0"

Dormers and transom windows lend charm to this Colonial design. Inside, columns define the formal dining room to the right of the foyer, while the study to the left of the foyer is accessed by double doors. The vaulted family room offers a corner fireplace. A bay window, large closet and spacious private bath highlight the first-floor master suite; a bay window also decorates the breakfast area. Upstairs are three family bedrooms, all with walk-in closets, and two full baths. Please specify basement or slab foundation when ordering.

## Plan HPT840120

**Price Code:** C1
**Bedrooms:** 4 **Bathrooms:** 3
**First Floor:** 2,069 sq. ft.
**Second Floor:** 767 sq. ft.
**Total:** 2,836 sq. ft.
**Width:** 87'-2" **Depth:** 55'-0"

A sheltering porch both front and back opens the living spaces to the outdoors. The formal dining room, to the left of the foyer, is near the U-shaped kitchen for ease of service. The sun room offers a casual eating space and is separated from the great room by the split-descending staircase. Please specify basement, crawlspace or slab foundation when ordering.

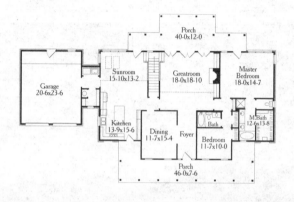

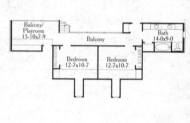

## Plan HPT840119

**Price Code:** A3
**Bedrooms:** 3 **Bathrooms:** 2
**Square Footage:** 1,727 sq. ft.
**Bonus Room:** 563 sq. ft.
**Width:** 52'-9" **Depth:** 66'-2"

This traditional country home features an array of family-friendly amenities. Triple dormers and a covered front porch enhance the exterior. The great room is warmed by a fireplace and is open to the dining area and kitchen. Three family bedrooms complete the main level, along with a rear porch and two-car garage. A bonus room easily converts to a home office. Please specify basement, crawlspace or slab foundation when ordering.

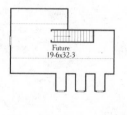

Laun.
9-6x6-8

Basement Stair
Location

## Plan HPT840121

**Price Code:** C1
**Bedrooms:** 4  **Bathrooms:** 2½
**Square Footage:** 2,925
**Width:** 83'-0"  **Depth:** 76'-2"

Storage
20-3x6-2

3 Bay Garage
20-3x30-1

Owner's
Bedroom
16-1x17-9

Porch
19-9x7-0

Morning Area
15-0x14-0

Bath

Laundry
12-0x7-10

Greatroom
20-8x19-6

Breakfast
15-0x12-2

Bedroom
11-7x13-2

Bath

1/2
Bath

Kitchen
13-9x12-0

Bedroom
12-10x12-1

Bedroom
11-10x12-0

Foyer

Dining
11-10x14-6

Porch
32-0x6-0

Symmetry and style color the facade of this four-bedroom home. Magnificent views beyond the triplet of French doors in the great room are visible upon entering the foyer. The formal dining room is conveniently situated near the galley kitchen that adjoins the breakfast area. Both the morning area and the great room enjoy the warmth of a fireplace. Three bedrooms on the left share a full bath. The master suite boasts a sun-filled bedroom, a lavish bath and a large walk-in closet. Please specify basement, crawlspace or slab foundation when ordering.

*farmhouses & ranches*

## Plan HPT840122

Price Code: A3
Bedrooms: 3 Bathrooms: 2
Square Footage: 1,936
Width: 62'-0" Depth: 68'-0"

This traditional ranch-style home is enhanced by graceful Southern accents. A front covered porch welcomes you inside to a foyer that introduces a formal dining room and living room brightened by skylights. The master suite provides a skylit bath and a roomy walk-in closet. Two additional family bedrooms are located on the opposite side of the home and share a hall bath. The rear deck provides plenty of outdoor entertainment options. Please specify crawlspace or slab foundation when ordering.

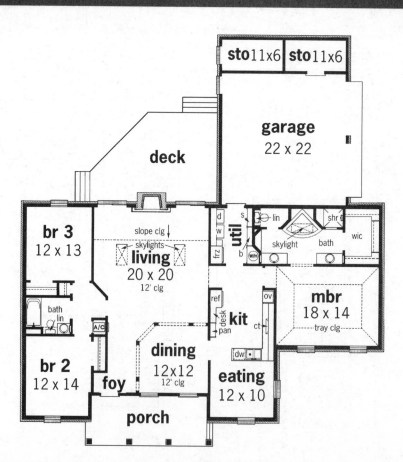

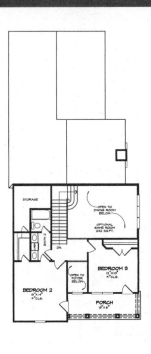

## Plan HPT840123

**Price Code:** A3
**Bedrooms:** 3 **Bathrooms:** 2½
**First Floor:** 1,347 sq. ft.
**Second Floor:** 537 sq. ft.
**Total:** 1,884 sq. ft.
**Width:** 32'-10" **Depth:** 70'-10"

This old-fashioned townhome design features an attractive two-story floor plan. Two front covered porches enhance the traditional facade. Inside, the foyer introduces an island kitchen that overlooks the dining room. A formal two-story living room, located at the rear of the plan, is warmed by a fireplace. The first-floor master suite enjoys a private bath and huge walk-in closet. A powder room, laundry room and two-car garage complete the first floor. Upstairs, two secondary bedrooms—one with a walk-in closet—share a full hall bath. Bedroom 3 features a private balcony overlooking the front property.

This home, as shown in the photograph, may differ from the actual blueprints.
For more detailed information, please check the floor plans carefully.

## Plan HPT840124

**Price Code:** C4
**Bedrooms:** 3  **Bathrooms:** 4½
**First Floor:** 1,781 sq. ft.
**Second Floor:** 2,199 sq. ft.
**Third Floor:** 604 sq. ft.
**Total:** 4,584 sq. ft.
**Width:** 53'-0"  **Depth:** 63'-2"

This attractive townhouse design offers three levels of comfortable family living. Two-story front covered porches enhance the exterior. The foyer on the main level is flanked on either side by formal living and dining rooms. The kitchen/breakfast area features an island workstation and a rear grilling porch. A quiet study and garage complete the main level. Upstairs, the master bedroom doubles in size with its hearth-warmed sitting area, which extends into the private bath past two walk-in closets. Bedrooms 2 and 3 share a Jack-and-Jill bath. An exercise room completes the second level. The third floor is reserved for the home office.

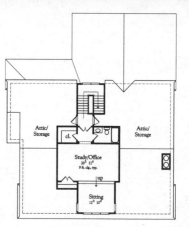

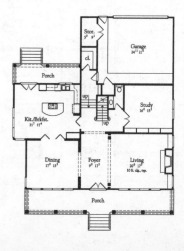

This home, as shown in the photograph, may differ from the actual blueprints.
For more detailed information, please check the floor plans carefully.

Photo by ©Looney Ricks Kiss Architects

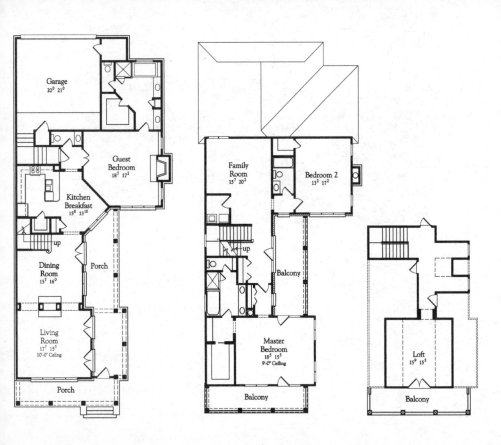

### Plan HPT840125

**Price Code:** C2
**Bedrooms:** 4  **Bathrooms:** 3½
**First Floor:** 1,613 sq. ft.
**Second Floor:** 1,383 sq. ft.
**Total:** 2,996 sq. ft.
**Loft:** 475 sq. ft.
**Width:** 24'-5"  **Depth:** 63'-8"

This stunning townhouse design is ideal for the urban narrow lot. The wrapping front porch complements the living areas of the main level. A two-sided fireplace warms the formal living and dining rooms. The U-shaped kitchen serves the breakfast room. A first-floor guest bedroom offers a fire-place, private bath and walk-in closet. Upstairs, the master bedroom is luxurious with private balcony access, walk-in closet space and a private bath. Bedroom 2 shares a hall bath with the second-floor family room. A third-floor loft is a nice option for future space, along with the balcony.

## Plan HPT840126

**Price Code:** A4
**Bedrooms:** 4  **Bathrooms:** 2½
**First Floor:** 1,061 sq. ft.
**Second Floor:** 1,263 sq. ft.
**Total:** 2,324 sq. ft.
**Width:** 50'-0"  **Depth:** 43'-0"

This stately two-story home is reminiscent of the Colonial era. The pedimented entry porch opens to shared living spaces on the first floor, including both a dining and living room to the front and a family room, kitchen and breakfast nook to the rear. Four bedrooms are featured on the second floor, including the grand master suite, which is enhanced by a tray ceiling. Please specify basement or crawlspace foundation when ordering.

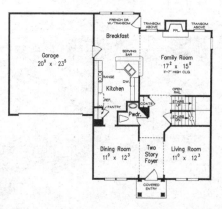

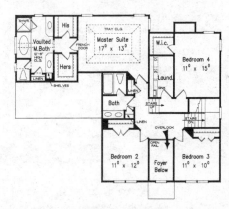

## Plan HPT840127

**Price Code:** C1
**Bedrooms:** 5  **Bathrooms:** 3½
**First Floor:** 1,286 sq. ft.
**Second Floor:** 1,675 sq. ft.
**Total:** 2,961 sq. ft.
**Width:** 35'-0"  **Depth:** 64'-0"

A Southern plantation comes to mind when looking at this two-story home complete with a porch and terrace. Formal elegance is the order of the day as you enter the foyer flanked by the living and dining rooms. The family room features a full window wall overlooking the deck. Rear stairs lead to the master suite, located over the garage. Please specify basement or slab foundation when ordering.

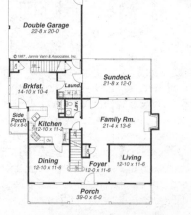

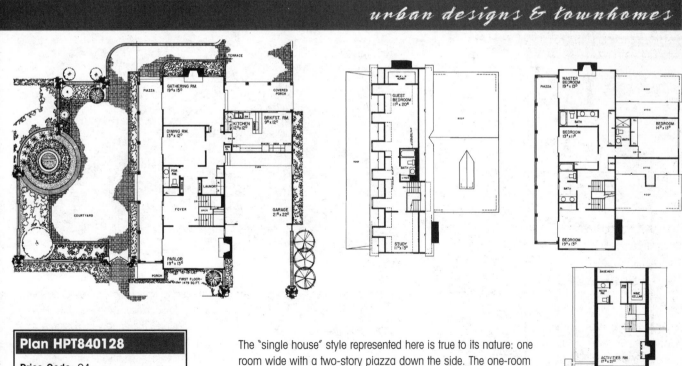

## Plan HPT840128

**Price Code:** C4
**Bedrooms:** 5 **Bathrooms:** 4½ + ½
**Main Level:** 1,479 sq. ft.
**Second Level:** 1,501 sq. ft.
**Third Level:** 912 sq. ft.
**Total:** 3,892 sq. ft.
**Finished Basement:** 556 sq. ft.
**Width:** 90'-0" **Depth:** 72'-0"

The "single house" style represented here is true to its nature: one room wide with a two-story piazza down the side. The one-room width allows for extra ventilation. The foyer opens to a parlor and, down the hall, a dining room and gathering room. The kitchen is located at the back of the wing created by the garage. A breakfast room here and another porch add to livability. The second floor is comprised of four bedrooms. A third floor holds a guest bedroom and a study. The basement holds a hearth-warmed activities room, a powder room, and a wine cellar.

Box-paneled shutters add a touch of class to this townhouse design—a home that is simply the ultimate in comfort and style. A winding staircase highlights a refined foyer that sets the pace for the entire home. Fireplaces warm the formal and casual rooms, which can accommodate all occasions.

## Plan HPT840129

**Price Code:** C3
**Bedrooms:** 3 **Bathrooms:** 2½
**First Floor:** 1,587 sq. ft.
**Second Floor:** 1,191 sq. ft.
**Total:** 2,778 sq. ft.
**Width:** 21'-8" **Depth:** 93'-8"

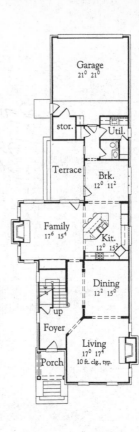

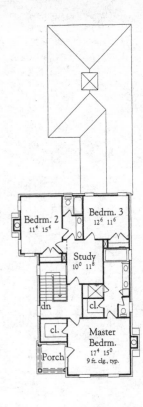

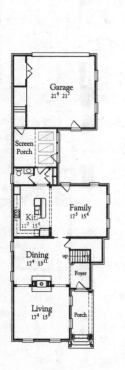

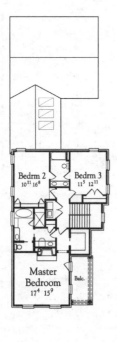

## Plan HPT840130

**Price Code:** A4
**Bedrooms:** 3 **Bathrooms:** 2½
**First Floor:** 1,239 sq. ft.
**Second Floor:** 1,087 sq. ft.
**Total:** 2,326 sq. ft.
**Width:** 29'-10" **Depth:** 46'-11"

This traditional urban townhouse, reminiscent of styles seen in the northeastern Colonial cities, expresses a stately architecture. The narrow-lot design enjoys two stories of livability. A two-sided fireplace warms the formal living and dining rooms. The island kitchen opens up to the casual family room. A brisk screened porch leads to the garage. Upstairs, the master suite features a fireplace, private bath and walk-in closet. Bedrooms 2 and 3 share a Jack-and-Jill bath.

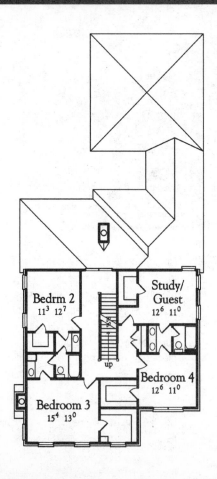

Bedrm 2
11³ 12⁷

Study/ Guest
12⁶ 11⁰

up

Bedroom 4
12⁶ 11⁰

Bedroom 3
15⁴ 13⁰

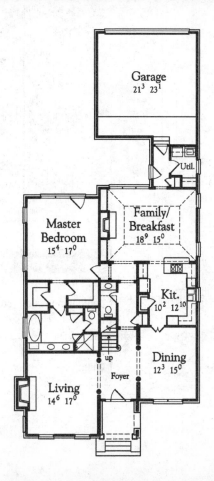

Garage
21³ 23¹

Util.

Master Bedroom
15⁴ 17⁰

Family/ Breakfast
18⁹ 15⁰

Kit.
10² 12¹⁰

up

Dining
12³ 15⁰

Living
14⁶ 17⁰

Foyer

## Plan HPT840131

Price Code: C2
Bedrooms: 5  Bathrooms: 3½
First Floor: 1,827 sq. ft.
Second Floor: 1,209 sq. ft.
Total: 3,036 sq. ft.
Width: 40'-0"
Depth: 84'-11"

The stately facade of this traditional townhouse design encloses two levels of amenity-filled livability. Formal living and dining rooms flank the foyer—the living room is warmed by a fireplace. The kitchen easily serves the family/breakfast room, also warmed by a fireplace. The first-floor master suite features two walk-in closets and a private whirlpool bath. A utility room and two-car garage complete the first floor. Upstairs, four additional bedrooms boast their own walk-in closets. Bedrooms 2 and 3 share a bath, while Bedroom 4 shares a bath with the guest room/study.

## Plan HPT840133

**Price Code:** C1
**Bedrooms:** 4 **Bathrooms:** 4
**First Floor:** 1,267 sq. ft.
**Second Floor:** 1,219 sq. ft.
**Total:** 2,486 sq. ft.
**Width:** 44'-1" **Depth:** 70'-4"

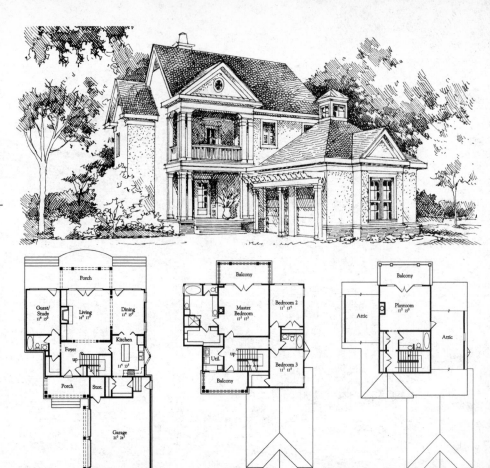

The stately design of this narrow-lot townhouse is enhanced by gracious Colonial accents. The first floor offers front and rear porches, a living room warmed by a fireplace, a dining room served by the kitchen, a guest room/study, hall bath and garage with storage. The second floor holds a sumptuous master suite with a private balcony. The third level features a playroom and attic storage.

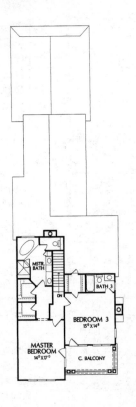

## Plan HPT840132

**Price Code:** C3
**Bedrooms:** 3 **Bathrooms:** 3½
**First Floor:** 1,660 sq. ft.
**Second Floor:** 943 sq. ft.
**Total:** 2,603 sq. ft.
**Width:** 30'-10" **Depth:** 102'-10"

Grand arch-top windows set off the lovely facade of this gently French design, and promote the presence of natural light within. The open formal rooms blend traditional style with supreme comfort, with a centered fireplace and French doors to the covered porch. A secluded study or secondary bedroom has a splendid bath with a dressing area and a walk-in closet. Upstairs, an additional bedroom has its own door to the covered balcony.

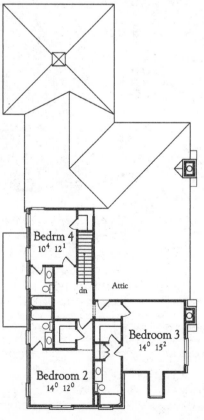

**Garage**
22⁴ 21⁰

**Breakfast/Family**
23¹⁰ 17⁴

**Kit.**
14⁶ 17⁴

Utility

up

**Dining**
15³ 13¹

**Living**
15³ 19¹

**Master Bedroom**
14⁰ 18⁰

Porch

**Bedrm 4**
10⁴ 12¹

dn    Attic

**Bedroom 3**
14⁰ 15²

**Bedroom 2**
14⁰ 12⁰

## Plan HPT840134

**Price code:** C2
**Bedrooms:** 4  **Bathrooms:** 4½
**First Floor:** 2,074 sq. ft.
**Second Floor:** 994 sq. ft.
**Total:** 3,068 sq. ft.
**Width:** 40'-4"  **Depth:** 86'-4"

This stately look of this two-story townhouse is further enhanced with French-European style. A covered front porch welcomes you inside, where the living room warmed by a fireplace extends into the formal dining room. The kitchen offers an island/snack counter that serves the breakfast/family room, warmed by a second fireplace. The first-floor master suite is located to the front of the plan and includes a private bath and two walk-in closets. A garage and utility room complete the first floor. Three additional bedrooms reside upstairs—each has its own walk-in closet and private bath.

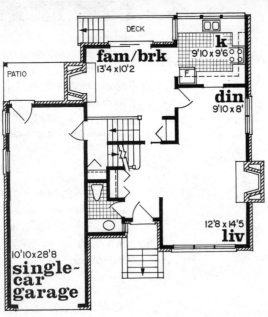

DECK

**k**
9'10 x 9'6

**fam/brk**
13'4 x 10'2

PATIO

**din**
9'10 x 8'

10'10 x 28'8
**single-car garage**

12'8 x 14'5
**liv**

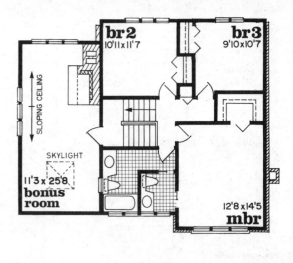

**br2**
10'11 x 11'7

**br3**
9'10 x 10'7

SLOPING CEILING

SKYLIGHT

11'3 x 25'8
**bonus room**

12'8 x 14'5
**mbr**

**Plan HPT840135**

Price Code: A2
Bedrooms: 3  Bathrooms: 1½ + ½
First Floor: 737 sq. ft.
Second Floor: 736 sq. ft.
Total: 1,473 sq. ft.
Bonus Room: 313 sq. ft.
Width: 36'-5"  Depth: 42'-0"

Ideally suited for a narrow frontage lot, this home features a facade of stucco, brick and wood trimming, reminiscent of Tudor styling. The weather-protected entry opens to a large living and dining room. The efficient kitchen features a pass-through counter to the dining room. The family room, with its adjoining breakfast room, has a sliding glass door to the rear deck. The bonus room, featuring a vaulted ceiling, skylights and fireplace, provides an additional 313 square feet of living space. The master bedroom boasts a spacious walk-in closet and two-piece ensuite.

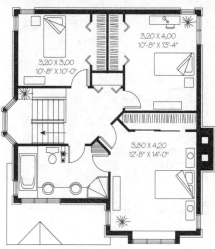

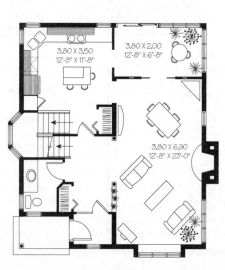

3,20 X 4,00
10'-8" X 13'-4"

3,20 X 3,00
10'-8" X 10'-0"

3,80 X 4,20
12'-8" X 14'-0"

3,80 X 3,50
12'-8" X 11'-8"

3,80 X 2,00
12'-8" X 6'-8"

3,80 X 6,90
12'-8" X 23'-0"

## Plan HPT840136

**Price Code:** C1
**Bedrooms:** 3  **Bathrooms:** 1½
**First Floor:** 788 sq. ft.
**Second Floor:** 732 sq. ft.
**Total:** 1,520 sq. ft.
**Width:** 28'-0"  **Depth:** 32'-0"

This narrow-lot design is enhanced by various contemporary and European elements. A living/dining room combination enjoys the warmth of a central fireplace, just to the right of the entry. The island snack-bar kitchen easily serves both the dining area and back porch. A powder room and hall closet complete the first floor. Three bedrooms upstairs, including a spacious master suite, share a hall bath with dual-vanity sinks. This home is designed with a basement foundation.

## Plan HPT840138

**Price Code:** A3
**Bedrooms:** 2 **Bathrooms:** 2½
**First Floor:** 993 sq. ft.
**Second Floor:** 642 sq. ft.
**Total:** 1,635 sq. ft.
**Width:** 28'-0" **Depth:** 44'-0"

This modern three-level home is just right for a young family. The main level features a study, kitchen, dining room, laundry and two-story living room with a corner fireplace. A rear patio makes summertime grilling fun. The master bedroom is vaulted and features a double-bowl vanity bath and walk-in closet. Bedroom 2 offers its own full bath as well. The basement level boasts a spacious garage and storage area.

## Plan HPT840137

**Price Code:** A3
**Bedrooms:** 3 **Bathrooms:** 2½
**First Floor:** 897 sq. ft.
**Second Floor:** 740 sq. ft.
**Total:** 1,637 sq. ft.
**Width:** 30'-0" **Depth:** 42'-6"

With a garage on the ground level, this home takes a much smaller footprint and is perfect for narrow lots. Take a short flight of stairs up to the entry, which opens to a receiving hall and then to the living and dining combination. Upstairs are two family bedrooms sharing a full bath and the vaulted master suite, with a private bath and two walk-in closets.

(VAULTED)
**MASTER**
13/6 X 12/0

BUILT-INS

DN

OPEN TO
BELOW

(VAULTED)
**BR. 2**
12/0 X 10/2

**DINING**
11/0 X 12/6
(12' CLG.)

**LIVING**
13/6 X 12/0
(9' CLG.)

BUILT-INS

UP    DN.

REF

UP

PAN.

W. D.

BUILT-INS    BUILT-INS

**STUDY**
12/0 X 10/2+
(9' CLG.)

DN.

CRAWLSPACE

**GARAGE**
19/0 X 23/2

A mixture of materials and modern styling offers a lovely home plan for the small family. The main level provides formal living and dining rooms as well as a kitchen area. The quiet study may be converted to an additional bedroom as space is needed. A laundry and powder room are located nearby. The vaulted master bedroom boasts a private bath with a double-bowl vanity and a walk-in closet. Bedroom 2 provides its own bath.

**Plan HPT840139**

**Price Code:** A3
**Bedrooms:** 2 **Bathrooms:** 2½
**First Floor:** 1,005 sq. ft.
**Second Floor:** 620 sq. ft.
**Total:** 1,625 sq. ft.
**Width:** 30'-0" **Depth:** 44'-6"

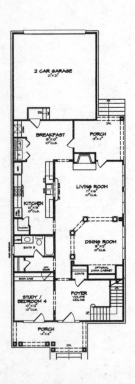

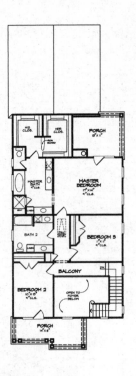

This design proves that a narrow-lot home can still provide luxury! The two front porches can be accessed by French doors through the study and the upper bedroom. The elegant dining room offers built-in cabinetry that's perfect for storing china. The breakfast room and living room, with a fireplace, open to a back porch. The second-floor balcony overlooks the generous foyer.

## Plan HPT840140

**Price Code:** A4
**Bedrooms:** 3 **Bathrooms:** 3
**First Floor:** 1,311 sq. ft.
**Second Floor:** 1,136 sq. ft.
**Total:** 2,447 sq. ft.
**Width:** 29'-10" **Depth:** 79'-4"

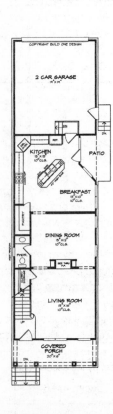

## Plan HPT840141

**Price Code:** C1
**Bedrooms:** 3 **Bathrooms:** 2½
**First Floor:** 911 sq. ft.
**Second Floor:** 1,029 sq. ft.
**Total:** 1,940 sq. ft.
**Width:** 20'-10" **Depth:** 75'-10"

This aesthetically pleasing home has a well-balanced floor plan that starts with the two covered porches that make up the facade. Floor-to-ceiling windows brighten the front rooms, which focus on the see-through fireplace at the center. Nearby, a gourmet kitchen with a pantry and island looks out to the side patio. Upstairs, a built-in desk allows for study.

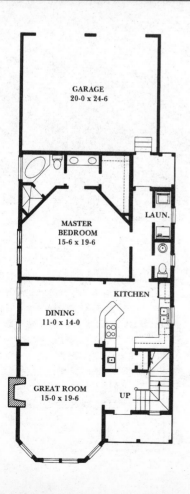

GARAGE
20-0 x 24-6

MASTER
BEDROOM
15-6 x 19-6

LAUN.

KITCHEN

DINING
11-0 x 14-0

GREAT ROOM
15-0 x 19-6

UP

BEDROOM
11-6 x 14-0

DOWN

BEDROOM
13-6 x 15-0

### Plan HPT840142

**Price Code:** A3
**Bedrooms:** 3  **Bathrooms:** 3½
**First Floor:** 1,340 sq. ft.
**Second Floor:** 651 sq. ft.
**Total:** 1,991 sq. ft.
**Width:** 30'-0"  **Depth:** 74'-0"

Charm abounds with a delightful porch, gable detailing and an ornamented chimney on this captivating Victorian home. This design is perfect for a narrow lot or first-time homeowners. The fireplace brings warmth to all gatherings in the great room that also boasts a lovely bay window. The angled kitchen offers a snack bar for casual dining when the formal dining area is too much. The uniquely shaped master suite is secluded on the first floor for privacy while two bedroom suites—each with a private bath—occupy the second floor.

## Plan HPT840143

**Price Code:** C1
**Bedrooms:** 3 **Bathrooms:** 2½
**First Floor:** 1,440 sq. ft.
**Second Floor:** 1,515 sq. ft.
**Total:** 2,955 sq. ft.
**Width:** 39'-2" **Depth:** 69'-5"

This attractive two-story townhouse is not only ideal for a narrow lot, but for the family shopping for the most modern amenities. A front covered porch welcomes you inside. Formal living and dining rooms are located across from the casual island kitchen and breakfast room. The rear porch and deck are great for entertaining or outdoor grilling. Fireplaces are found in the living room and second-floor master bedroom.

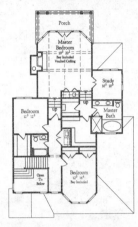

## Plan HPT840144

**Price Code:** L1
**Bedrooms:** 4 **Bathrooms:** 3½
**Main Level:** 1,531 sq. ft.
**Second Level:** 1,307 sq. ft.
**Total:** 2,838 sq. ft.
**Guest Suite:** 664 sq. ft.
**Width:** 70'-0" **Depth:** 40'-0"

From a lovely covered front porch to a classic rear veranda, this three-story Folk Victorian offers the finest in modern floor plans. The formal living areas are set off by a family room which connects the main house to the service areas. The laundry has room for not only a washer and dryer but also a freezer and sewing area. The second floor holds three bedrooms and two full baths.

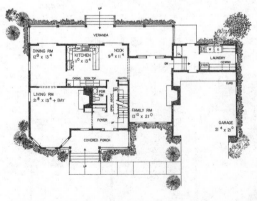

MASTER
12/0 X 13/0

MASTER
12/0 X 13/0

BR. 3
10/8 X 10/0

BR. 3
10/8 X 10/0

DN.    DN.

FOYER
BELOW

FOYER
BELOW

BR. 2
11/0 X 11/8

BR. 2
11/0 X 11/8

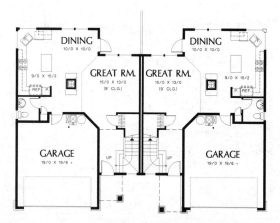

DINING
10/0 X 10/0

DINING
10/0 X 10/0

9/0 X 15/2

GREAT RM.
15/0 X 13/0
(9' CLG)

GREAT RM.
15/0 X 13/0
(9' CLG)

9/0 X 15/2

REF  P

P  REF

GARAGE
19/0 X 19/6

UP    UP

GARAGE
19/0 X 19/6

## Plan HPT840145

**Price Code:** C4
**Bedrooms:** 3  **Bathrooms:** 2½
**Units A/B:**
**First Floor:** 709 sq. ft.
**Second Floor:** 801 sq. ft.
**Total:** 1,510 sq. ft.
**Width:** 60'-0"  **Depth:** 42'-0"

With charming European accents, this dazzling duplex home offers style and comfortable livability. Mirror-image floor plans are offered inside the units, accessed from two first-floor entries. The foyer leads into a great room—great for casual or formal family gatherings. The island kitchen opens to a dining area. A powder room and two-car garage complete the first floor. Upstairs, the master suite provides a private shower bath and walk-in closet. Bedrooms 2 and 3 share a full hall bath between them.

## Plan HPT840147

**Price Code** C1
**Bedrooms:** 4 **Bathrooms:** 3½
**First Floor:** 1,439 sq. ft.
**Second Floor:** 1,402 sq. ft.
**Total:** 2,841 sq. ft.
**Width:** 48'-0" **Depth:** 74'-0"

This charming narrow-lot Victorian home is reminiscent of suburban New England homes of an earlier era. A front porch welcomes you inside to formal living and dining rooms flanking the foyer. The island kitchen easily serves the breakfast room. The hearth-warmed great room is located at the rear. Upstairs, the master suite is complemented by a private bath and double walk-in closet. Three additional bedrooms also reside on the second floor.

Symmetrical bay windows adorn this amazing four-bedroom Victorian design. A fabulous two-story foyer with a curving stair to the second floor introduces the comfortable interior of this home. A guest suite sits conveniently to the left in a bay window. Enjoy a multitude of views during dinner in the bayed dining room to the right of the foyer. Nearby, the angled kitchen features a serving bar facing the breakfast room and window views of the backyard.

## Plan HPT840146

**Price Code:** C2
**Bedrooms:** 4 **Bathrooms:** 4½
**First Floor:** 1,614 sq. ft.
**Second Floor:** 1,447 sq. ft.
**Total:** 3,061 sq. ft.
**Width:** 52'-0" **Depth:** 76'-0"

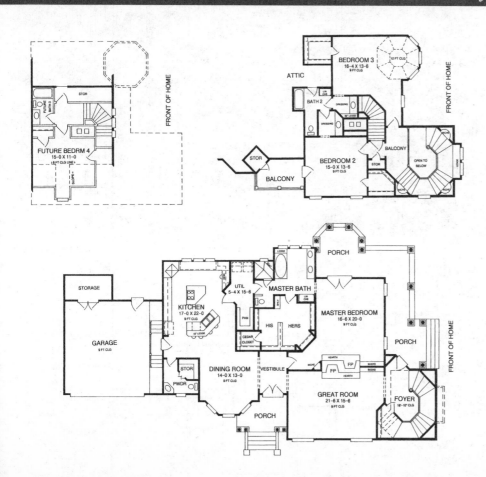

**FUTURE BEDRM 4**
15-0 X 11-0

STOR

BATH

FRONT OF HOME

**BEDROOM 3**
16-4 X 13-6
9 FT CLG

ATTIC

BATH 2

**BEDROOM 2**
15-0 X 13-6
9 FT CLG

STOR

BALCONY

OPEN TO BELOW

FRONT OF HOME

STORAGE

**KITCHEN**
17-0 X 22-0

UTIL
5-4 X 15-6

**MASTER BATH**

HIS HERS

CEDAR CLOSET

**GARAGE**
9 FT CLG

STOR

PWDR

**DINING ROOM**
14-0 X 13-0
9 FT CLG

VESTIBULE

**MASTER BEDROOM**
16-6 X 20-0
9 FT CLG

FP FP

**GREAT ROOM**
21-6 X 15-6
9 FT CLG

PORCH

PORCH

**FOYER**
18-10 CLG

FRONT OF HOME

PORCH

## Plan HPT840148

**Price Code:** C2
**Bedrooms:** 3  **Bathrooms:** 2½
**First Floor:** 2,194 sq. ft.
**Second Floor:** 870 sq. ft.
**Total:** 3,064 sq. ft.
**Bonus Space:** 251 sq. ft.
**Width:** 50'-11"  **Depth:** 91'-2"

With equally appealing front and side entrances, a charming Victorian facade invites entry into this stunning home. The foyer showcases the characteristic winding staircase and opens to the large great room with a masonry fireplace. An enormous kitchen features a cooktop island and a breakfast bar large enough to seat four. A lovely bay window distinguishes the nearby dining room. The master suite with a masonry fireplace is located on the first floor. The second floor contains two bedrooms—one with access to the outdoor balcony on the side of the home. Please specify crawlspace or slab foundation when ordering.

## Plan HPT840150

**Price Code:** C4
**Bedrooms:** 4  **Bathrooms:** 4
**First Floor:** 2,193 sq. ft.
**Second Floor:** 1,136 sq. ft.
**Total:** 3,329 sq. ft.
**Width:** 41'-6"  **Depth:** 71'-4"

This farmhouse is far from old-fashioned with a computer room/library and future game room designed into the second floor. Two wrapping porches grace the exterior, offering expanded outdoor living spaces. The breakfast nook, dining and family rooms radiate off the central island kitchen. The study/bedroom at the front is situated with an adjacent full bath making this ideal for a guest room.

## Plan HPT840149

**Price Code:** C4
**Bedrooms:** 4  **Bathrooms:** 4
**First Floor:** 2,236 sq. ft.
**Second Floor:** 1,208 sq. ft.
**Total:** 3,444 sq. ft.
**Width:** 42'-6"  **Depth:** 71'-4"

This spacious home offers a front porch and second-floor balcony as well as a wraparound porch in the rear. The elegant foyer, with its grand staircase, is flanked by the dining room on the left and the study on the right. The island kitchen adjoins the family room and the sunny breakfast nook. The master suite, with an elaborate private bath, is secluded in the back for privacy.

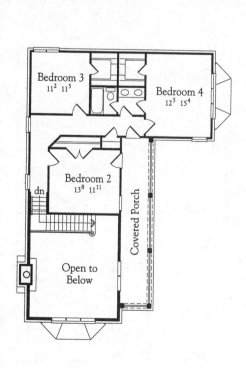

Bedroom 3
11² 11⁵

Bedroom 4
12⁵ 15⁴

Bedroom 2
13⁸ 11¹¹

dn

Covered Porch

Open to Below

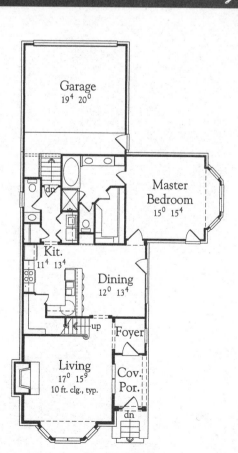

Garage
19⁴ 20⁰

Master Bedroom
15⁰ 15⁴

dn

Kit.
11⁴ 13⁴

Dining
12⁰ 13⁴

up

Foyer

Living
17⁰ 15⁹
10 ft. clg., typ.

Cov. Por.

dn

## Plan HPT840151

**Price Code:** C2
**Bedrooms:** 4  **Bathrooms:** 2½
**First Floor:** 1,369 sq. ft.
**Second Floor:** 856 sq. ft.
**Total:** 2,225 sq. ft.
**Width:** 36'-2"  **Depth:** 71'-6"

The lovely facade of this new-neighborhood home is beautifully decorated with a double portico. A front bay window provides a stunning accent to the traditional exterior, while allowing natural light within. The formal living room features a fireplace and opens to the dining room, which leads outdoors. The gourmet kitchen has a walk-in pantry. The master suite is a relaxing space that includes a sitting bay, access to the side grounds, walk-in closet and soothing bath. A winding staircase offers an overlook to the living room.

## Plan HPT840152

**Price Code:** C4
**Bedrooms:** 4  **Bathrooms:** 3
**First Floor:** 1,742 sq. ft.
**Second Floor:** 1,624 sq. ft.
**Total:** 3,366 sq. ft.
**Width:** 42'-10"  **Depth:** 77'-0"

Elegant Southern living is the theme of this seaside townhouse. The narrow-lot design allows for comfortable urban living. Inside, the living room is warmed by a fireplace, while the island kitchen serves the breakfast room and casual den. A first-floor guest bedroom is located at the front of the design. The dining room is reserved for more formal occasions. Upstairs, the gracious master suite features a private second-floor porch, two walk-in closets and a private bath. Two additional bedrooms share a hall bath on this floor.

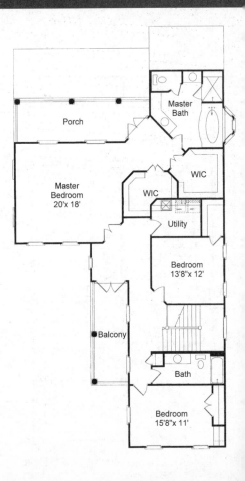

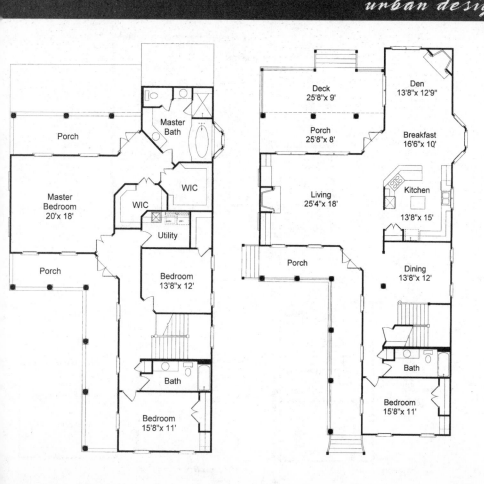

Porch

Master
Bath

Master
Bedroom
20'x 18'

WIC

WIC

Utility

Porch

Porch

Bedroom
13'8"x 12'

Bath

Bedroom
15'8"x 11'

Deck
25'8"x 9'

Porch
25'8"x 8'

Living
25'4"x 18'

Porch

Den
13'8"x 12'9"

Breakfast
16'6"x 10'

Kitchen
13'8"x 15'

Dining
13'8"x 12'

Bath

Bedroom
15'8"x 11'

## Plan HPT840153

**Price Code:** C4
**Bedrooms:** 4 **Bathrooms:** 3
**First Floor:** 1,742 sq. ft.
**Second Floor:** 1,624 sq. ft.
**Total:** 3,366 sq. ft.
**Width:** 42'-10" **Depth:** 77'-6"

Porches abound upon this grand, two-story home—perfect for nature enthusiasts. The first floor holds the entertaining spaces with the island kitchen acting as a hub around which all activity revolves. The den, with a cozy corner fireplace, and the breakfast nook are ideal for more intimate situations. On the second floor, the master suite pampers with a luxurious bath and a private porch. Two additional bedrooms share a full bath on this floor while the first-floor bedroom works well as a guest bedroom.

## Plan HPT840154

**Price Code:** A4
**Bedrooms:** 3  **Bathrooms:** 2½
**First Floor:** 1,096 sq. ft.
**Second Floor:** 1,108 sq. ft.
**Total:** 2,204 sq. ft.
**Width:** 56'-0"  **Depth:** 38'-0"

This traditional family home boasts an array of European accents that enhance the exterior, while modern amenities are found inside. The entry-way provides a coat closet, while first-floor rooms are arranged around a central staircase. A two-story living room is found to the left, while a laundry room and garage are placed to the right. The snack-bar kitchen easily serves the family sitting room and the dining area. Upstairs, the master bedroom offers a walk-in closet and private bath, while two additional bedrooms with walk-in closets share a hall bath. This home is designed with a basement foundation.

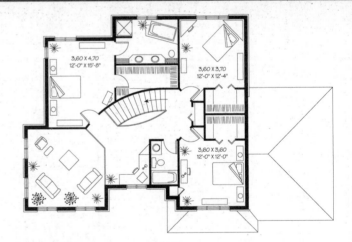

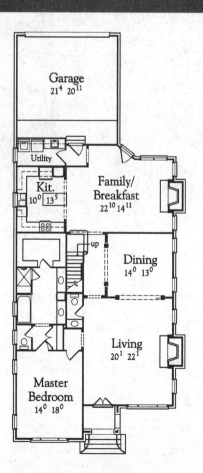

## Garage
21⁴ 20¹¹

Utility

Kit.
10⁰ 13⁵

Family/
Breakfast
22¹⁰ 14¹¹

up

Dining
14⁰ 13⁰

Living
20¹ 22¹

Master
Bedroom
14⁰ 18⁰

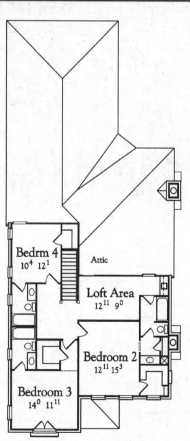

Bedrm 4
10⁴ 12¹

Attic

Loft Area
12¹¹ 9⁰

Bedroom 2
12¹¹ 15³

Bedroom 3
14⁰ 11¹¹

### Plan HPT840155

**Price Code:** C2
**Bedrooms:** 4  **Bathrooms:** 4½
**First Floor:** 1,927 sq. ft.
**Second Floor:** 1,093 sq. ft.
**Total:** 3,020 sq. ft.
**Width:** 34'-2"  **Depth:** 84'-1"

This stately Colonial-style home expresses an interesting mix of early-American architecture and French influences. Enter inside, where a cozy hearth warms the formal living room. The island kitchen serves the family/ breakfast room and formal dining room with ease. The first-floor master suite views the front of the property and offers a private bath and walk-in closet. This level is completed by a two-car garage, located just behind the utility room. Each of the three bedrooms upstairs provides a walk-in closet and private bath—they share the second level with a comfortable loft area.

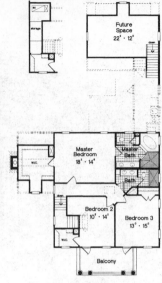

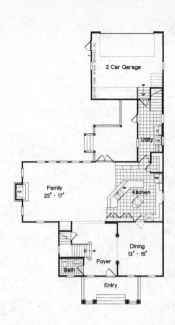

## Plan HPT840156

**Price Code:** C1
**Bedrooms:** 3 **Bathrooms:** 2½
**First Floor:** 1,447 sq. ft.
**Second Floor:** 1,423 sq. ft.
**Total:** 2,870 sq. ft.
**Bonus Space:** 264 sq. ft.
**Width:** 45'-0" **Depth:** 80'-0"

This grand home delights with its beautiful Greek Revival facade. The foyer opens to the family room with its window wall and fireplace. The angled kitchen is sure to please with its proximity to the laundry room. Upstairs is the master suite, designed to pamper with a delightful private bath and walk-in closet.

## Plan HPT840157

**Price Code:** C2
**Bedrooms:** 4 **Bathrooms:** 3½
**First Floor:** 1,536 sq. ft.
**Second Floor:** 1,498 sq. ft.
**Total:** 3,034 sq. ft.
**Width:** 48'-0" **Depth:** 32'-0"

This grand facade is adorned with majestic pillars and delightful quoins. The covered porch leads into the foyer which is flanked by the dining and living rooms. The L-shaped kitchen features an island and connects to the breakfast nook. The second floor is dedicated to the sleeping quarters, which include three family bedrooms and a master suite.

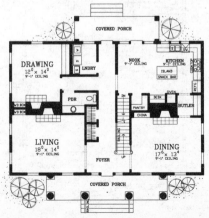

QUOTE ONE®
Cost to build? See page 246
to order complete cost estimate
to build this house in your area!

## Plan HPT840158

**Price Code:** C3
**Bedrooms:** 4 **Bathrooms:** 2½
**First Floor:** 1,373 sq. ft.
**Second Floor:** 1,552 sq. ft.
**Total:** 2,925 sq. ft.
**Width:** 64'-6" **Depth:** 51'-2"

This luxurious farmhouse is an old-world plantation style filled with modern-day amenities. Classic columns add drama to the facade, while a wide front porch welcomes you inside. Double doors open into a foyer flanked by formal living and dining rooms. The leisure room is a cozy retreat offering a warm fireplace flanked by built-ins and topped by a stepped ceiling. The gourmet island kitchen opens to a nook and provides a storage pantry. Upstairs, a loft overlooks the foyer and two-story living room. Please specify basement or crawlspace foundation when ordering.

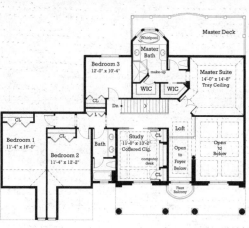

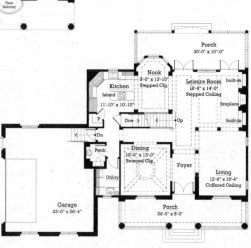

## Plan HPT840159

**Price Code:** C1
**Bedrooms:** 3 **Bathrooms:** 2
**Square Footage:** 2,791
**Width:** 84'-0" **Depth:** 54'-0"

This stately country home is a quaint mix of Colonial style and romantic French flavor. Inside, formal living and dining rooms flank the entry foyer. Two sets of double doors open from the family room onto the rear patio. A romantic courtyard is placed to the far right of the plan, just beyond the family bedrooms. A three-car garage with an extra storage room offers plenty of space. Please specify basement or crawlspace foundation when ordering.

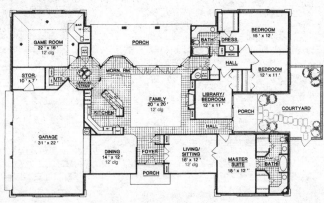

This elegant Colonial design boasts many European influences such as the stucco facade, corner quoins and arched windows. The foyer is flanked by a formal dining room and a study, which converts to an additional bedroom. Straight ahead, the great room features a fireplace and built-ins. This home is designed with a basement foundation.

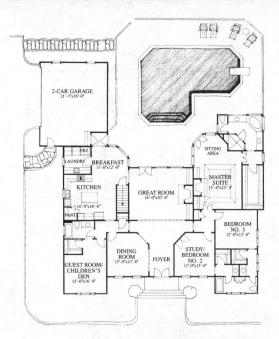

## Plan HPT840160

**Price Code:** C2
**Bedrooms:** 3 **Bathrooms:** 3
**Square Footage:** 2,785
**Width:** 72'-0" **Depth:** 73'-0"

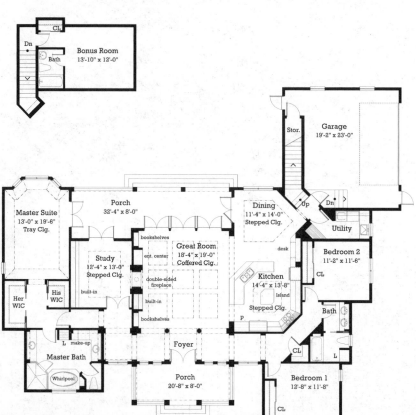

Bonus Room
13'-10" x 12'-0"

Dn

CL

Bath

Garage
19'-2" x 23'-0"

Stor.

Up

Dn

Dining
11'-4" x 14'-0"
Stepped Clg.

Utility

Master Suite
13'-0" x 19'-6"
Tray Clg.

Porch
32'-4" x 8'-0"

Study
12'-4" x 13'-0"
Stepped Clg.

bookshelves

ent. center

double-sided
fireplace

built-in

bookshelves

Great Room
18'-4" x 19'-0"
Coffered Clg.

Kitchen
14'-4" x 13'-8"
Stepped Clg.

desk

island

Bedroom 2
11'-2" x 11'-6"

CL

Bath

Her
WIC

His
WIC

built-in

make-up

Master Bath

Whirlpool

Foyer

Porch
20'-8" x 8'-0"

P

CL

L

CL

Bedroom 1
12'-8" x 11'-8"

CL

## Plan HPT840161

**Price Code:** C2
**Bedrooms:** 3 **Bathrooms:** 2
**Square Footage:** 2,454
**Bonus Room:** 256 sq. ft.
**Width:** 80'-6" **Depth:** 66'-0"

This traditional home offers a wide variety of modern amenities. The spacious foyer opens to the great room, which boasts built-in bookshelves, a wall of double doors to the rear porch and a double-sided fireplace shared with the study. To the far left, the master suite is enhanced by a bay window, His and Hers walk-in closets and a luxury whirlpool bath. The island cooktop kitchen serves the dining area with ease. Two additional family bedrooms share a hall bath. The bonus room above the garage is perfect for a home office or guest suite.

## Plan HPT840162

**Price Code:** L1
**Bedrooms:** 5 **Bathrooms:** 4
**First Floor:** 1,709 sq. ft.
**Second Floor:** 1,958 sq. ft.
**Total:** 3,667 sq. ft.
**Width:** 59'-4" **Depth:** 63'-6"

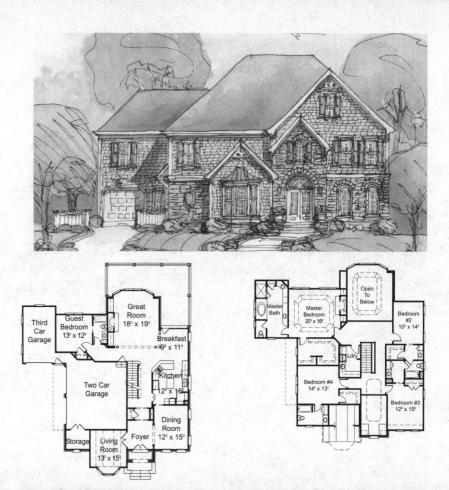

The charming exterior of this one-of-a-kind home features exquisite architectural details set off by a romantic massing and a warm blend of materials. The first floor provides a secluded guest room that offers private access to a full bath. Stunning formal rooms frame the foyer—a perfect arrangement for entertaining. To the rear of the plan, a spacious great room offers a fireplace and splendid views of the rear property. This home is designed with a walkout basement foundation.

## Plan HPT840163

**Price Code:** L1
**Bedrooms:** 5 **Bathrooms:** 4
**First Floor:** 2,068 sq. ft.
**Second Floor:** 1,788 sq. ft.
**Total:** 3,856 sq. ft.
**Width:** 64'-8" **Depth:** 71'-4"

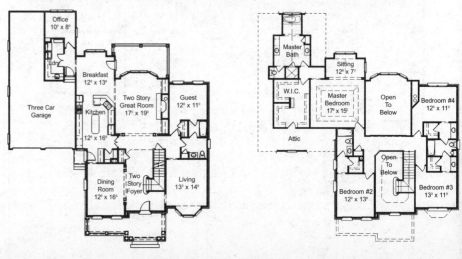

This heartwarming home has a traditional touch. The two-story foyer leads to either the formal dining room or to the living room which enjoys a bay window—perfect for outdoor views. The two-story great room enjoys a cozy fireplace with built-ins and is open to the island kitchen and the breakfast area. Three additional family bedrooms along with the master bedroom are found upstairs. This home is designed with a walkout basement foundation.

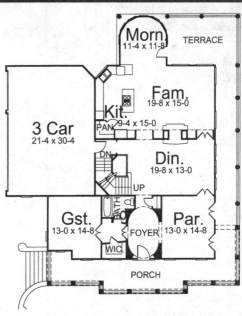

SCREEN
PORCH

M.
BATH

Sit.
11-4 x 15-0

Mstr.
15-2 x 15-0

WIC.

DN

LND.

Bdr.2
11-6 x 15-0

BATH

Bdr.4
13-0 x 14-8

Bdr.3
14-0 x 12-8

BATH

TERRACE

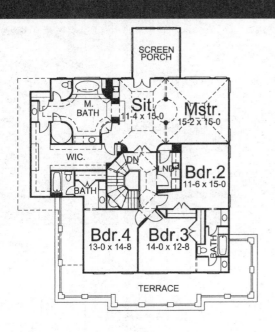

Morn.
11-4 x 11-8

TERRACE

3 Car
21-4 x 30-4

Kit.
9-4 x 15-0

PAN.

Fam.
19-8 x 15-0

DN

Din.
19-8 x 13-0

UP

Gst.
13-0 x 14-8

BATH

WIC.

FOYER

Par.
13-0 x 14-8

PORCH

This luxurious design boasts a classic Colonial silhouette with favorable coastal features. A wraparound porch on two stories offers breathtaking vistas. An oval foyer flanked by a guest suite and parlor welcomes you inside. A see-through fireplace warms the dining and family rooms. The island kitchen is open and provides a pantry and morning nook. A three-car garage completes the first floor. A circular staircase spirals to the second floor. Upstairs, Bedrooms 2 and 3 share a Jack-and-Jill bath, while Bedroom 4 features its own bath. The master suite is a pampering haven with a sitting area warmed by a fireplace.

### Plan HPT840164

**Price Code:** L1
**Bedrooms:** 4  **Bathrooms:** 4
**First Floor:** 1,681 sq. ft.
**Second Floor:** 1,935 sq. ft.
**Total:** 3,616 sq. ft.
**Width:** 58'-0"  **Depth:** 68'-10"

## Plan HPT840165

**Price Code:** L1
**Bedrooms:** 3 **Bathrooms:** 3½
**First Floor:** 2,682 sq. ft.
**Second Floor:** 847 sq. ft.
**Total:** 3,529 sq. ft.
**Bonus Room:** 770 sq. ft.
**Width:** 62'-8" **Depth:** 81'-8"

This formal, shingle-style home offers symmetry and elegance, starting with a grand entry porch. Inside, a balcony hall overlooks the family room and foyer. Double doors lead to a private study. An island highlights the kitchen, which is set between the dining and breakfast rooms. The two-story great room offers a fireplace and double-door access to the rear porch, also accessed by the sun room. This home is designed with a walkout basement foundation.

## Plan HPT840166

**Price Code:** C3
**Bedrooms:** 4 **Bathrooms:** 4
**First Floor:** 1,285 sq. ft.
**Second Floor:** 1,345 sq. ft.
**Total:** 2,630 sq. ft.
**Bonus Space:** 352 sq. ft.
**Width:** 59'-2" **Depth:** 51'-9"

Early American design contributes to this two-story home's attractive curb appeal. In the family room, a corner fireplace and built-ins reside along the left wall. The family room and kitchen, with a cooktop island and bayed breakfast area, share access to the backyard through French doors. Four bedrooms and a computer alcove complete the second floor. The master suite features a tray ceiling and a sumptuous private bath. Please specify basement or slab foundation when ordering.

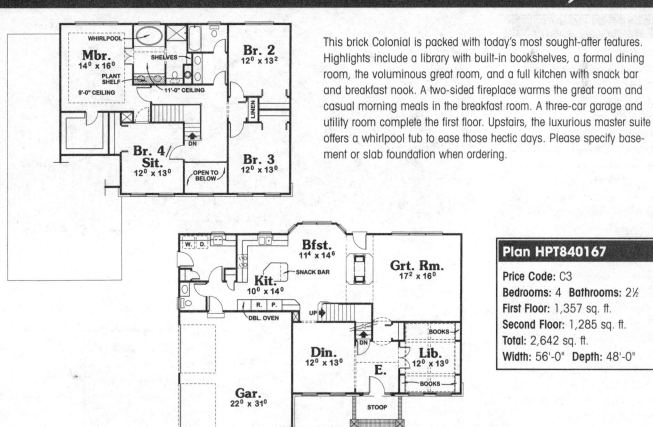

This brick Colonial is packed with today's most sought-after features. Highlights include a library with built-in bookshelves, a formal dining room, the voluminous great room, and a full kitchen with snack bar and breakfast nook. A two-sided fireplace warms the great room and casual morning meals in the breakfast room. A three-car garage and utility room complete the first floor. Upstairs, the luxurious master suite offers a whirlpool tub to ease those hectic days. Please specify basement or slab foundation when ordering.

**Plan HPT840167**

Price Code: C3
Bedrooms: 4  Bathrooms: 2½
First Floor: 1,357 sq. ft.
Second Floor: 1,285 sq. ft.
Total: 2,642 sq. ft.
Width: 56'-0"  Depth: 48'-0"

## Plan HPT840168

**Price Code:** C1
**Bedrooms:** 4  **Bathrooms:** 2½
**First Floor:** 1,365 sq. ft.
**Second Floor:** 1,288 sq. ft.
**Total:** 2,653 sq. ft.
**Width:** 61'-0"  **Depth:** 38'-0"

A regal hipped roof, Palladian window and double dormers add elegance to this Williamsburg Colonial. The foyer is flanked on the right by a dining room and on the left by a living room, both enhanced with tray ceilings. The sunken family room enjoys a fireplace and access to a rear deck. A cozy island kitchen leads to a bayed breakfast room. Upstairs, the master bedroom boasts two walk-in closets.

## Plan HPT840169

**Price Code:** C4
**Bedrooms:** 4  **Bathrooms:** 4½
**First Floor:** 2,130 sq. ft.
**Second Floor:** 973 sq. ft.
**Total:** 3,103 sq. ft.
**Width:** 78'-0"  **Depth:** 45'-4"

A Georgian influence gives this plan a sense of timelessness and prominence. An informal family area to the rear of the home features a bayed breakfast area, snack bar and raised hearth fireplace. The master bath offers a spa atmosphere with sloped ceiling, large windows and atrium door that lead outside.

## Plan HPT840170

**Price Code:** A4
**Bedrooms:** 3 **Bathrooms:** 2½
**Square Footage:** 2,311 sq. ft.
**Bonus Space:** 720 sq. ft.
**Width:** 74'-0" **Depth:** 50'-0"

This timeless Colonial design boasts both contemporary and classic elements. Double doors enter inside where formal living and dining rooms flank the foyer. The spacious family room boasts a cozy fireplace, built-ins and access to the rear sun deck. The first-floor master bedroom, brightened by a bay window, features a private bath and roomy walk-in closet. Two family bedrooms are placed just behind the two-car garage. Bedroom 4, a home office and storage space are all located on the second floor.

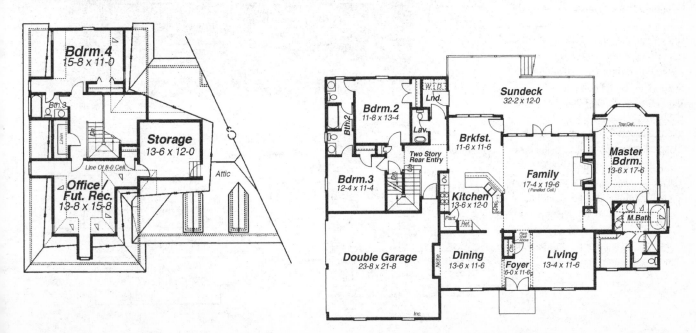

## Plan HPT840171

**Price Code:** C1
**Bedrooms:** 4 **Bathrooms:** 3½
**First Floor:** 1,341 sq. ft.
**Second Floor:** 1,591 sq. ft.
**Total:** 2,932 sq. ft.
**Width:** 64'-0" **Depth:** 38'-6"

A columned entry opens to the classic floor plan of this timeless and traditional home. Revealed beyond the foyer are formal living and dining rooms, plus a hearth-warmed family room. The island kitchen connects to a two-story breakfast room. Three family bedrooms and the master suite with a sitting room are on the second floor. Please specify basement or crawl-space foundation when ordering.

## Plan HPT840172

**Price Code:** C3
**Bedrooms:** 4 **Bathrooms:** 3½
**First Floor:** 2,194 sq. ft.
**Second Floor:** 973 sq. ft.
**Total:** 3,167 sq. ft.
**Bonus Room:** 281 sq. ft.
**Width:** 71'-11" **Depth:** 54'-4"

Practically symmetrical, this country home enjoys a spacious covered porch both front and back. The formal dining room has clipped corners, creating an elegant octagon which is a repeated pattern in the tray ceilings of the master bedroom and master bath. The efficient kitchen is placed between the breakfast bay and the dining room. The great room offers a balcony overlook, a fireplace and a window wall that accesses the rear porch. ©2001 Donald A. Gardner, Inc.

## Plan HPT840173

**Price Code:** C2
**Bedrooms:** 3 **Bathrooms:** 2½
**First Floor:** 2,270 sq. ft.
**Second Floor:** 685 sq. ft.
**Total:** 2,955 sq. ft.
**Bonus Room:** 563 sq. ft.
**Width:** 75'-1" **Depth:** 53'-6"

Hipped rooflines, sunburst windows and French-style shutters are the defining elements of this home's exterior. Inside, the foyer is flanked by the dining room and the study. Further on, the lavish great room can be entered through two stately columns, and is complete with a fireplace, built-in shelves, a vaulted ceiling and views to the rear patio. The island kitchen easily accesses a pantry area, includes a desk and flows into the bayed breakfast area. The first-floor master bedroom enjoys a fireplace, two walk-in closets and an amenity-filled private bath.

## Plan HPT840175

Price Code: C4
Bedrooms: 4 Bathrooms: 5½
First Floor: 2,314 sq. ft.
Second Floor: 1,828 sq. ft.
Total: 4,142 sq. ft.
Width: 64'-0" Depth: 54'-3"

This Early American Colonial home—perfect for a New England setting—displays a charming floor plan. Inside, fireplaces warm both the dining room and the study, which flank the foyer on either side. Three sets of double doors open to the rear yard and illuminate the great room, which is also warmed by a grand hearth. The breakfast room is set between the kitchen and keeping room. The master bedroom resides upstairs.

*colonials & history houses*

## Plan HPT840174

Price Code: C3
Bedrooms: 4 Bathrooms: 3½
First Floor: 2,138 sq. ft.
Second Floor: 988 sq. ft.
Total: 3,126 sq. ft.
Width: 67'-0" Depth: 54'-0"

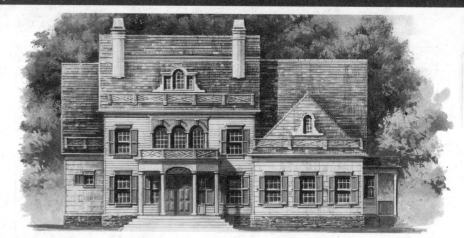

With all the quaint character of the New England coast, this remarkable Colonial design features all the drama of the past with the all the amenities of the future. A portico welcomes you inside to a foyer flanked on either side by a parlor and formal dining room. The two-story grand room and keeping room share a see-through fireplace.

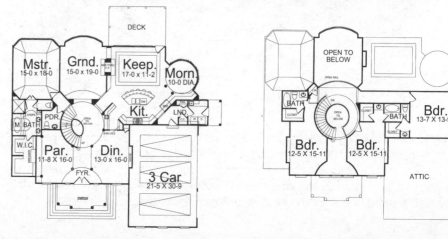

RECREATION ROOM
21'-0"x 21'-0"

GUEST SUITE
13'-0" x 13'-0"

STUDY
12'-7" x 17'-7"

GARAGE
21'-4" x 19'-4"

GREAT ROOM
21'-7" x 14'-7"

PORCH
38'-10" x 8'-0"

BREAKFAST AREA
13'-3" x 13'-10"

KITCHEN
11'-3" x 16'-3"

STUDY
13'-4" x 13'-4"

DINING
13'-4" x 18'-8"

FOYER

PORCH

MASTER BEDROOM
21'-7" x 15'-0"

PORCH
38'-10" x 8'-0"

WALK-IN CLOSET

BEDROOM 2
13'-4" x 13'-4"

BEDROOM 3
13'-4" x 13'-4"

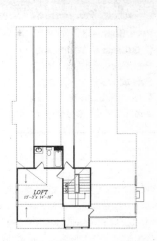

LOFT
13'-3" x 14'-10"

---

**Plan HPT840176**

**Price Code:** C3
**Bedrooms:** 4  **Bathrooms:** 5
**First Floor:** 1,590 sq. ft.
**Second Floor:** 1,525 sq. ft.
**Loft:** 500 sq. ft.
**Total:** 3,615 sq. ft.
**Lower Floor:** 1,590 sq. ft.
**Width:** 36'-0"  **Depth:** 58'-4"

---

This stately plan is ideal for a narrow lot. It is adorned with an eyebrow dormer, French-style shutters and fine brick detailing. The porch leads into a long foyer, flanked on the right by a dining room and on the left by a study. The great room at the rear of the plan, away from the noise of traffic, boasts a fireplace and access to the porch. The kitchen leads to a bayed breakfast area, which looks out to the side porch. The second level is home to the master bedroom. A loft occupies the third level.

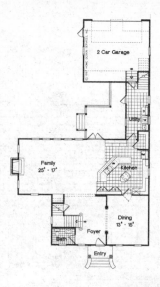

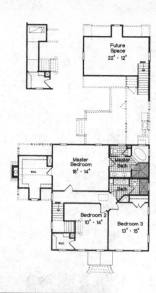

Shutters, a pedimented porch and an oval Adamesque window in a second pediment above combine to create a classic Colonial facade on this two-story home. The family room is the heart of this home with a fireplace and a window wall that opens to the covered porch for indoor/outdoor entertaining. The master suite with a huge walk-in closet and private bath shares the upper level with two additional bedrooms.

## Plan HPT840178

**Price Code:** C1
**Bedrooms:** 3 **Bathrooms:** 2½
**First Floor:** 1,447 sq. ft.
**Second Floor:** 1,169 sq. ft.
**Total:** 2,616 sq. ft.
**Bonus Space:** 264 sq. ft.
**Width:** 45'-4" **Depth:** 80'-0"

## Plan HPT840177

**Price Code:** C3
**Bedrooms:** 5 **Bathrooms:** 3
**First Floor:** 1,341 sq. ft.
**Second Floor:** 1,299 sq. ft.
**Total:** 2,640 sq. ft.
**Width:** 50'-0" **Depth:** 42'-6"

Stately Colonial accents and classic symmetry enhance the facade of this two-story design. Inside, the two-story foyer is flanked by formal living and dining rooms. The two-story family room is warmed by a cozy fireplace. The kitchen with a pantry and serving bar easily serves the bayed breakfast room, which features a French door to the backyard. Please specify basement or crawl-space foundation when ordering.

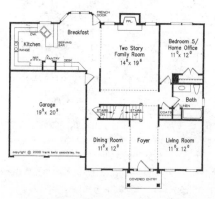

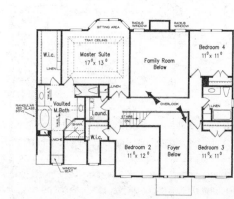

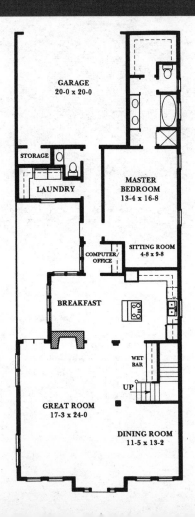

GARAGE
20-0 x 20-0

STORAGE

LAUNDRY

MASTER
BEDROOM
13-4 x 16-8

COMPUTER/
OFFICE

SITTING ROOM
4-8 x 9-8

BREAKFAST

WET
BAR

UP

GREAT ROOM
17-3 x 24-0

DINING ROOM
11-5 x 13-2

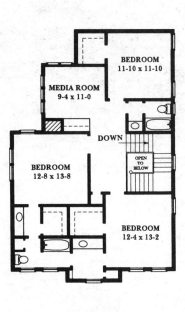

BEDROOM
11-10 x 11-10

MEDIA ROOM
9-4 x 11-0

DOWN

BEDROOM
12-8 x 13-8

OPEN
TO
BELOW

BEDROOM
12-4 x 13-2

## Plan HPT840179

**Price Code:** C1
**Bedrooms:** 4 **Bathrooms:** 3½
**First Floor:** 1,767 sq. ft.
**Second Floor:** 1,079 sq. ft.
**Total:** 2,846 sq. ft.
**Width:** 30'-0" **Depth:** 82'-0"

With its formal symmetry, balanced proportion and classical detailing, this Georgian design will maintain its appeal for those who value timeless architecture. Once inside, its open floor plan will entice those who realize that modern families enjoy a different lifestyle. The entrance is open to a spacious great room and formal dining room. The column-encircled stairway wraps itself around a built-in wet bar, with easy access to kitchen, dining and living areas of the home. A computer/desk area is located between the kitchen and the first-floor master suite. This roomy master suite contains a secluded and separate sitting area. A second-floor media room will provide additional living space.

## Plan HPT840180

**Price Code:** C4
**Bedrooms:** 5 **Bathrooms:** 3½
**First Floor:** 2,125 sq. ft.
**Second Floor:** 1,106 sq. ft.
**Total:** 3,231 sq. ft.
**Width:** 52'-0" **Depth:** 84'-0"

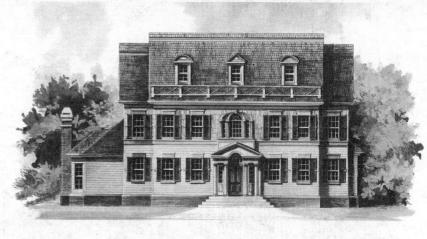

This northeastern Colonial design features an impressive family-oriented layout. The front porch welcomes you inside to a foyer flanked on either side by a formal dining room and a library warmed by a fireplace. Past the cascading staircase, the grand room is enhanced by a fireplace with flanking built-ins. From here, double doors open onto a rear veranda. A fireplace warms the combined keeping and morning room, which connects to the kitchen.

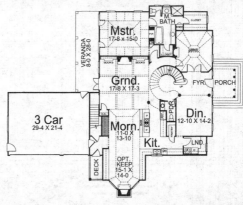

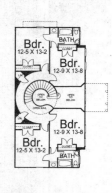

*colonials & history houses*

## Plan HPT840181

**Price Code:** C2
**Bedrooms:** 4 **Bathrooms:** 3½
**First Floor:** 1,565 sq. ft.
**Second Floor:** 1,839 sq. ft.
**Total:** 3,404 sq. ft.
**Width:** 78'-8" **Depth:** 34'-0"

The formal brick facade of this classic Colonial design is impressive with an equally impressive interior layout. Formal living and dining rooms flank the entry foyer. The island kitchen is open to both the breakfast nook and hearth-warmed family room. A three-car garage completes the first floor. Upstairs, the master bedroom features a private fireplace, master bath and two walk-in closets. Bedrooms 2 and 3 share a hall bath, while Bedroom 4 offers a private bath.

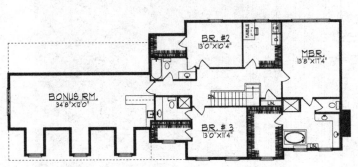

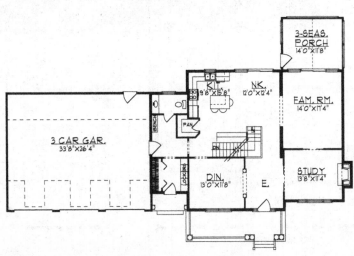

## Plan HPT840182

**Price Code:** C1
**Bedrooms:** 3  **Bathrooms:** 3½
**First Floor:** 1,365 sq. ft.
**Second Floor:** 1,336 sq. ft.
**Total:** 2,701 sq. ft.
**Width:** 82'-0"  **Depth:** 44'-0"

This impressive Colonial design sings of timeless elegance and modern amenities. A front covered porch adds a country accent to the exterior. Inside, a formal dining room and a study warmed by a fireplace flank the entry. The island snack-bar kitchen is open to both the breakfast nook and family room. A three-season porch is attached at the rear of the plan. A three-car garage and laundry room complete the first floor. Upstairs, the master bedroom features a private bath and walk-in closet. Bedrooms 2 and 3 boast their own walk-in closets and private baths. The bonus room is great for a family recreation room or home office.

## Plan HPT840184

**Price Code:** C3
**Bedrooms:** 4 **Bathrooms:** 3½ + ½
**First Floor:** 1,923 sq. ft.
**Second Floor:** 1,106 sq. ft.
**Total:** 3,029 sq. ft.
**Width:** 64'-0" **Depth:** 47'-4"

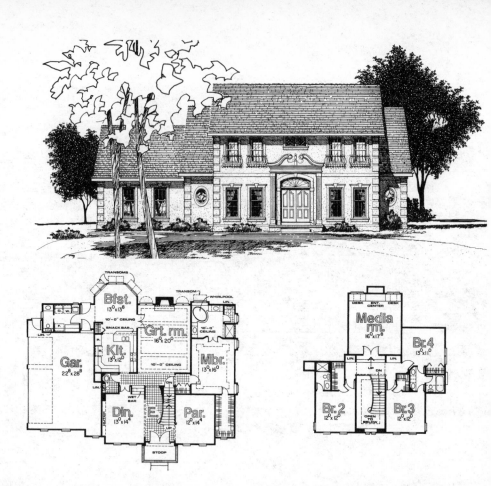

Fluted columns and decorative moldings present a grand entrance. A volume entry with a flared staircase opens to the formal dining room and parlor. The comfortable great room with its boxed-beam ceiling and a raised-hearth fireplace is brightened by arched transom windows. The master suite includes a large walk-in closet and a spacious bath with a whirlpool tub.

## Plan HPT840183

**Price Code:** C1
**Bedrooms:** 3 **Bathrooms:** 2½
**First Floor:** 1,346 sq. ft.
**Second Floor:** 1,320 sq. ft.
**Total:** 2,666 sq. ft.
**Width:** 44'-0" **Depth:** 30'-0"

A stone facade and classical symmetry shape the exterior of this lovely European cottage. Steps lead up to a charming front entrance. The entranceway makes way for a foyer with a coat closet. A professional home office is located to the right. To the left of the foyer, a warming fireplace is set between the open living and dining rooms—perfect for formal entertaining or casual family occasions. This home is designed with a basement foundation.

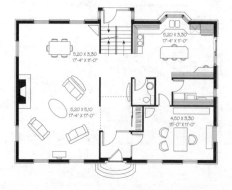

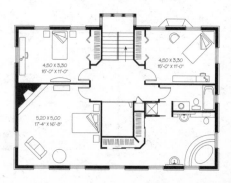

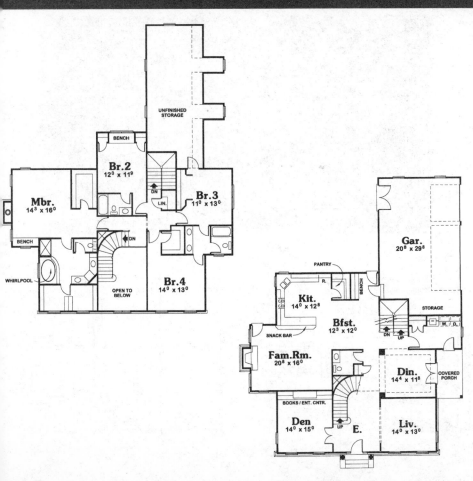

## Plan HPT840185

**Price Code:** C3
**Bedrooms:** 4  **Bathrooms:** 3½
**First Floor:** 1,892 sq. ft.
**Second Floor:** 1,530 sq. ft.
**Total:** 3,422 sq. ft.
**Bonus Space:** 497 sq. ft.
**Width:** 54'-8"  **Depth:** 68'-0"

This northeastern Colonial home possesses a distinct New England flavor, enhanced by a formal symmetrical design. Inside, the entry is flanked by a formal living room and a relaxing den. The formal dining room opens through double doors to a side covered porch. The kitchen, open to the breakfast and family rooms, features a snack bar. A fireplace warms the family room on cold winter nights. A garage and laundry room complete the first floor. Upstairs, the master suite enjoys a private bath and two walk-in closets. Three additional family bedrooms also reside on the second floor. Please specify basement or block foundation when ordering.

## Plan HPT840186

**Price Code:** C2
**Bedrooms:** 4  **Bathrooms:** 3
**First Floor:** 1,252 sq. ft.
**Second Floor:** 1,112 sq. ft.
**Total:** 2,364 sq. ft.
**Width:** 50'-0"  **Depth:** 46'-0"

This traditional two-story cottage is perfect for a narrow lot. Colonial elements enhance the exterior, while modern amenities are abundant inside. The two-story foyer opens to the formal dining room and vaulted grand room warmed by a fireplace. The kitchen easily serves the casual breakfast room, which accesses the rear through a French door. Please specify basement or crawlspace foundation when ordering.

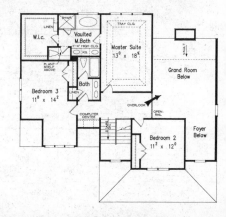

## Plan HPT840187

**Price Code:** C2
**Bedrooms:** 3  **Bathrooms:** 2½
**First Floor:** 1,784 sq. ft.
**Second Floor:** 478 sq. ft.
**Total:** 2,262 sq. ft.
**Bonus Space:** 336 sq. ft.
**Width:** 54'-0"  **Depth:** 54'-6"

This farmhouse-style, three-bedroom home holds a spacious floor plan. The vaulted family room joins the breakfast room and kitchen for everyday affairs, but is near a formal dining room for more special occasions. The master suite is on the first floor and opens to a sitting room or study. The master bath ensures a wonderful retreat. Please specify basement or crawlspace foundation when ordering.

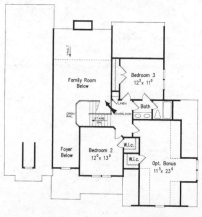

© Stephen Fuller, Inc.

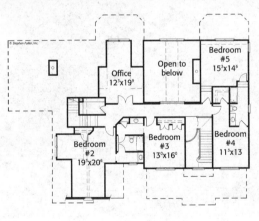

© Stephen Fuller, Inc.

**Office**
12³x19⁹

**Open to below**

**Bedroom #5**
15³x14⁶

**Bedroom #2**
19³x20⁶

**Bedroom #3**
13⁰x16⁰

**Bedroom #4**
11³x13

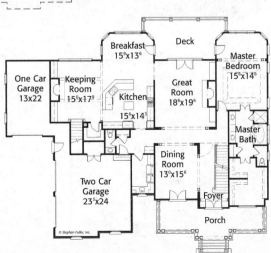

**Breakfast**
15⁹x13⁶

**Deck**

**Master Bedroom**
15⁶x14⁶

**One Car Garage**
13x22

**Keeping Room**
15⁰x17⁹

**Kitchen**
15⁵x14³

**Great Room**
18⁶x19⁶

**Master Bath**

**Two Car Garage**
23³x24

**Dining Room**
13⁰x15⁶

**Foyer**

**Porch**

© Stephen Fuller, Inc.

## Plan HPT840188

**Price Code:** C4
**Bedrooms:** 5 **Bathrooms:** 3½
**First Floor:** 2,628 sq. ft.
**Second Floor:** 1,775 sq. ft.
**Total:** 4,403 sq. ft.
**Width:** 79'-6" **Depth:** 72'-4"

With five bedrooms and a wonderful stone-and-siding exterior, this country home will satisfy every need. Two sets of French doors provide access to the dining room and foyer. The great room enjoys a warming fireplace and deck access. The kitchen, breakfast bay and keeping room feature an open floor plan. A charming sitting room in a bay window sets off the master bedroom. The master bath features a large walk-in closet, two-sink vanity, separate tub and shower and compartmented toilet. This home is designed with a walkout basement foundation.

## Plan HPT840189

**Price Code:** C2
**Bedrooms:** 4 **Bathrooms:** 3
**First Floor:** 1,220 sq. ft.
**Second Floor:** 963 sq. ft.
**Total:** 2,183 sq. ft.
**Width:** 50'-0" **Depth:** 45'-0"

This two-story traditional design features elegant early-American elements and a modern array of amenities within. The brick facade makes a stately first impression. Inside, the narrow two-story foyer is flanked by a home office on the right and a formal dining room on the left. With a hall bath located just next door, the home office easily converts to a first-floor bedroom. Please specify basement or crawlspace foundation when ordering.

## Plan HPT840190

**Price Code:** C2
**Bedrooms:** 4 **Bathrooms:** 2½
**First Floor:** 1,033 sq. ft.
**Second Floor:** 1,359 sq. ft.
**Total:** 2,392 sq. ft.
**Width:** 50'-0" **Depth:** 42'-6"

A shed dormer and a pedimented porch enhance the charm of this four-bedroom farmhouse. Inside, the first floor provides plenty of shared living space away from the second-floor sleeping zone. The nearby kitchen features a pantry, work island, pass-through to the family room and a sunny breakfast nook. A coffered ceiling adds elegance to the hearth-warmed family room. Please specify basement or crawlspace foundation when ordering.

## Plan HPT840191

**Price Code:** C3
**Bedrooms:** 4  **Bathrooms:** 3
**First Floor:** 2,028 sq. ft.
**Second Floor:** 558 sq. ft.
**Total:** 2,586 sq. ft.
**Bonus Space:** 272 sq. ft.
**Width:** 64'-10"  **Depth:** 61'-0"

Double columns and an arch-top clerestory window create an inviting entry to this fresh interpretation of traditional style. The two-story foyer features a decorative ledge—perfect for displaying a tapestry. Decorative columns and arches open to the formal dining room and to the octagonal great room, which provides a ten-foot tray ceiling. The kitchen looks over an angled counter to a breakfast bay that brings in the outdoors and shares a through-fireplace with the great room. Please specify basement, crawlspace or slab foundation when ordering.

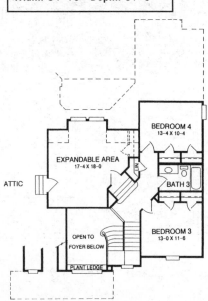

## Plan HPT840192

**Price Code:** A4
**Bedrooms:** 4  **Bathrooms:** 3
**Square Footage:** 2,453
**Width:** 48'-10"  **Depth:** 95'-6"

This quaint and traditional design is dazzled in Colonial simplicity, but enhanced with French charm. The front covered porch provides an abundance of windows looking in, accented with French shutters. Inside, a dining room and breakfast bay flank the kitchen. A fireplace warms the living room and accesses the rear covered porch. The master suite and Bedroom 2 are located on the first floor, while two other bedrooms are upstairs.

## Plan HPT840193

**Price Code:** C3
**Bedrooms:** 4  **Bathrooms:** 3½
**First Floor:** 2,588 sq. ft.
**Second Floor:** 1,578 sq. ft.
**Total:** 4,166 sq. ft.
**Width:** 78'-6"  **Depth:** 56'-6"

This Colonial Revival home offers a Cape Cod exterior with a covered front porch. Symmetry abounds with three dormers above three pairs of French doors with fanlights. The addition of a sun room on the left washes the interior with sunlight. The formal dining room has easy access to the country kitchen, where a fireplace adds atmosphere. Please specify basement, crawlspace or slab foundation when ordering.

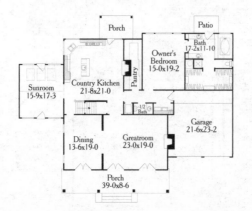

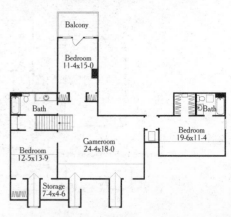

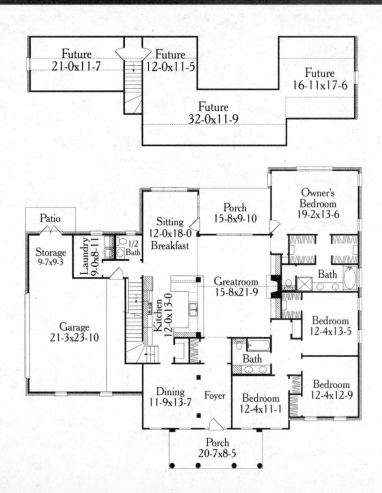

| Future 21-0x11-7 | Future 12-0x11-5 | |
| Future 32-0x11-9 | | Future 16-11x17-6 |

**Plan HPT840194**

Price Code: C1
Bedrooms: 4  Bathrooms: 2½
Square Footage: 2,636
Bonus Space: 1,132 sq. ft.
Width: 74'-5"  Depth: 64'-5"

This Colonial Revival adds a pedimented porch from the Georgian era for a stately effect. The side-loading garage keeps the facade fresh and symmetrical. Columns define the formal dining room while a butler's pantry connects it to the expansive kitchen. The sunny sitting/breakfast nook lies at the opposite end of the kitchen. The generous great room delights with a window wall, a fireplace and built-ins. A wealth of undeveloped space is available on the second floor for future use. Please specify basement, crawlspace or slab foundation when ordering.

## Plan HPT840195

**Price Code:** C1
**Bedrooms:** 4 **Bathrooms:** 2½
**First Floor:** 1,784 sq. ft.
**Second Floor:** 777 sq. ft.
**Total:** 2,561 sq. ft.
**Bonus Space:** 232 sq. ft.
**Width:** 60'-0" **Depth:** 51'-0"

This traditional Country home is a perfect semblance of old-fashioned style and modern features. Triple dormers and a front covered porch add country accents to the facade. A dining room and study flank the foyer. Vaulted ceilings enhance the great room and breakfast nook. The first-floor master bedroom is complete with two closets and a private bath. Three additional bedrooms and a bonus room reside upstairs.

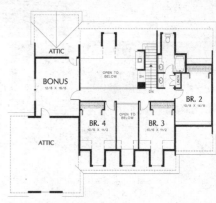

## Plan HPT840196

**Price Code:** C1
**Bedrooms:** 3 **Bathrooms:** 2½ + ½
**First Floor:** 1,588 sq. ft.
**Second Floor:** 1,101 sq. ft.
**Total:** 2,689 sq. ft.
**Width:** 66'-0" **Depth:** 48'-0"

Five dormers and a pair of chimneys add character to this magnificent country home. Here are two floors of excellent livability. The country kitchen will be the center for family activities with an island, a desk, a raised-hearth fireplace, a conversation area and sliding glass doors to the terrace. Adjacent to this area is the washroom and the laundry. Quieter areas are available in the living room and the library.

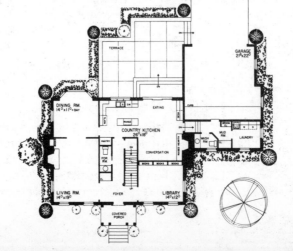

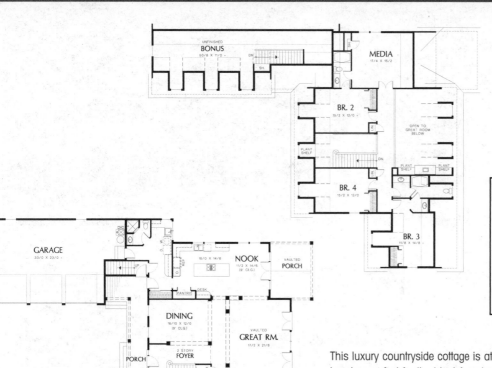

## Plan HPT840197

**Price Code:** C3
**Bedrooms:** 4  **Bathrooms:** 4½
**First Floor:** 2,513 sq. ft.
**Second Floor:** 1,421 sq. ft.
**Total:** 3,934 sq. ft.
**Width:** 72'-0"  **Depth:** 93'-0"

This luxury countryside cottage is at home in New England-style neighborhoods—perfect for the ideal American home. The foyer is flanked by a dining room and study. The great room is central, while the kitchen and breakfast nook are located to the left of the plan. A luxurious bath and roomy walk-in closet are featured in the master suite. Three additional bedrooms and a media room are upstairs. A bonus room is above the garage.

## Plan HPT840199

**Price Code:** A3
**Bedrooms:** 3 **Bathrooms:** 1½
**First Floor:** 886 sq. ft.
**Second Floor:** 868 sq. ft.
**Total:** 1,754 sq. ft.
**Width:** 32'-0" **Depth:** 28'-0"

Inside this lovely, New England-Colonial home, the foyer is flanked by a living room and cozy den. The kitchen features a snack bar and dining area. A utility room completes the first floor. Upstairs, three family bedrooms share a whirlpool bath. A bonus room—perfect for a guest suite or home office—is located above the detached garage. This home is designed with a basement foundation.

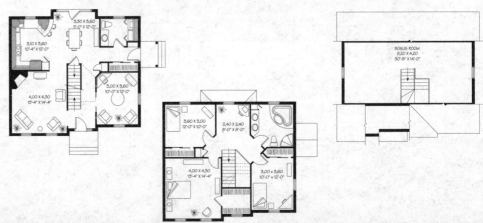

## Plan HPT840198

**Price Code:** C2
**Bedrooms:** 4 **Bathrooms:** 2½
**First Floor:** 1,386 sq. ft.
**Second Floor:** 1,171 sq. ft.
**Total:** 2,557 sq. ft.
**Width:** 58'-0" **Depth:** 41'-4"

Amenities for casual family living and entertaining abound in this attractive farmhouse. A charming, covered front porch makes for an inviting exterior. Inside, the two-story entry with a flared staircase opens to the formal dining and living rooms. A tray ceiling and a hutch complement the dining room. French doors connect the living room with the more informal family room for expanded entertaining space.

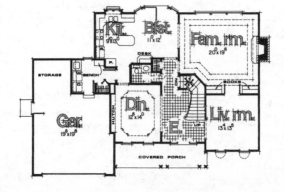

## Plan HPT840200

**Price Code:** C1
**Bedrooms:** 3  **Bathrooms:** 2½
**First Floor:** 1,278 sq. ft.
**Second Floor:** 1,390 sq. ft.
**Total:** 2,668 sq. ft.
**Bonus Room:** 203 sq. ft.
**Width:** 60'-0"  **Depth:** 44'-0"

A truly lavish master suite resides on the second floor of this complex two-story farmhouse. The recessed entry opens to the dining room and kitchen with the family room on the right. The massive wraparound porch can be accessed from the family room, living room and the sunny breakfast bay. The island kitchen is conveniently placed between the dining room and the well-equipped utility room. On the second floor, the master suite enjoys a fireplace, a pampering bath and access to the second-floor deck. This home is designed with a basement foundation.

## Plan HPT840201

**Price Code:** C1
**Bedrooms:** 5  **Bathrooms:** 3
**First Floor:** 1,258 sq. ft.
**Second Floor:** 1,568 sq. ft.
**Total:** 2,826 sq. ft.
**Width:** 57'-0"  **Depth:** 41'-0"

A beautiful brick exterior and lovely arching windows highlight this traditional family home. The spacious two-story foyer opens to a living area with a boxed-tray ceiling and a warming fireplace. The kitchen, which includes a pantry, is placed between the formal dining room and the casual breakfast area overlooking the rear patio deck. The left wing of the home offers a quiet home office that converts to a fifth family bedroom.

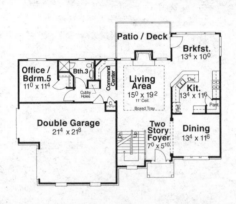

## Plan HPT840202

**Price Code:** C2
**Bedrooms:** 5  **Bathrooms:** 4
**First Floor:** 1,553 sq. ft.
**Second Floor:** 1,587 sq. ft.
**Total:** 3,140 sq. ft.
**Width:** 58'-0"  **Depth:** 40'-4"

An elegant covered porch spans the front of this house and draws attention to the muntin windows and brick detailing. A two-story foyer is flanked by a dining room on the right and a living room on the left. A spacious kitchen—with plenty of counter space—leads into a cozy breakfast area, which opens to the rear sun deck. The two-story family room boasts a fireplace and an abundance of windows.

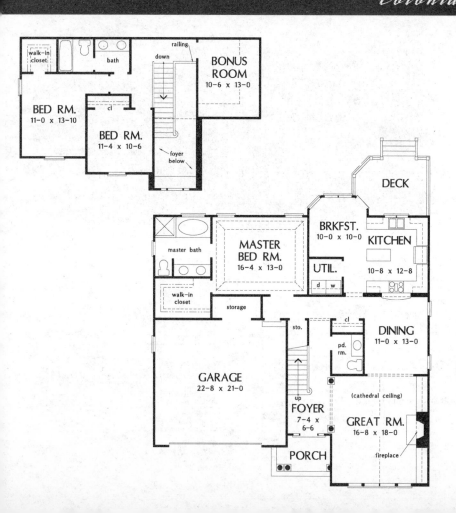

walk-in closet

bath

railing

down

BONUS ROOM
10-6 x 13-0

BED RM.
11-0 x 13-10

cl

BED RM.
11-4 x 10-6

foyer below

DECK

master bath

MASTER BED RM.
16-4 x 13-0

BRKFST.
10-0 x 10-0

KITCHEN
10-8 x 12-8

UTIL.
d   w

walk-in closet

storage

sto.

cl

DINING
11-0 x 13-0

pd. rm.

GARAGE
22-8 x 21-0

up

FOYER
7-4 x 6-6

GREAT RM.
16-8 x 18-0

(cathedral ceiling)

fireplace

PORCH

## Plan HPT840203

**Price Code:** C1
**Bedrooms:** 3  **Bathrooms:** 2½
**First Floor:** 1,475 sq. ft.
**Second Floor:** 540 sq. ft.
**Total:** 2,015 sq. ft.
**Bonus Room:** 151 sq. ft.
**Width:** 48'-0"  **Depth:** 48'-10"

Hints of European flavor accent the facade of this fine two-story home. The foyer opens directly to the right to the vaulted great room and nearby formal dining room. The breakfast room and island kitchen are to the back; the breakfast room opens to a rear deck. The master suite remains on the first level and holds a tray ceiling in the bedroom and a bath with separate tub and shower. Family bedrooms and a bonus room are on the second level.
©2000 Donald A. Gardner, Inc.

## Plan HPT840204

**Price Code:** C3
**Bedrooms:** 4 **Bathrooms:** 3½
**First Floor:** 1,878 sq. ft.
**Second Floor:** 886 sq. ft.
**Total:** 2,764 sq. ft.
**Width:** 67'-10" **Depth:** 56'-4"

This distinguished brick home with traditional stucco accents includes a spectacular, two-story foyer and grand room featuring a dramatic Palladian window. The grand room also opens to the kitchen and morning room. The master suite and morning room create matching bay wings to form a beautiful rear facade. A deck/terrace is accessible from both wings.

*colonials & history houses*

## Plan HPT840205

**Price Code:** C4
**Bedrooms:** 5 **Bathrooms:** 3½
**First Floor:** 2,637 sq. ft.
**Second Floor:** 1,534 sq. ft.
**Total:** 4,171 sq. ft.
**Width:** 112'-10" **Depth:** 46'-10"

From your first glimpse of this architectural wonder, you'll know it has been crafted in the classic Georgian tradition. The central entry foyer introduces the custom living inside: an exquisitely designed stairway with flanking formal dining room and living room (note fireplaces in each). The great room is sunken a step beyond the foyer and has its own fireplace and wet bar.

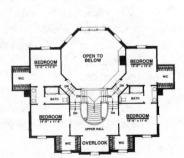

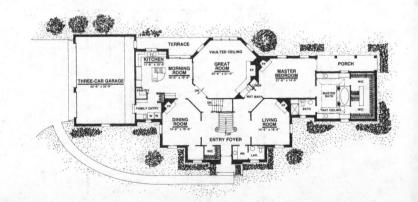

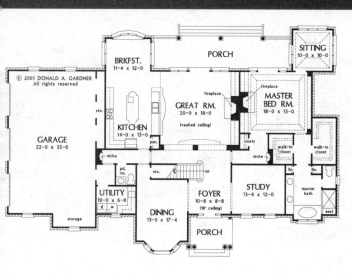

## Plan HPT840330

**Price Code:** C4
**Bedrooms:** 4 **Bathrooms:** 3½
**First Floor:** 2,511 sq. ft.
**Second Floor:** 1,062 sq. ft.
**Total:** 3,573 sq. ft.
**Bonus Room:** 465 sq. ft.
**Width:** 84'-11" **Depth:** 55'-11"

An abundance of windows and an attractive brick facade enhance the exterior of this traditional two-story home. Inside, a study and formal dining room flank either side of the two-story foyer. Fireplaces warm both the great room and first-floor master suite. The suite also provides a separate sitting room, two walk-in closets and a private bath. The island kitchen extends into the breakfast room. The second floor features three additional family bedrooms, two baths and a bonus room fit for a home office.

## Plan HPT840207

**Price Code:** C3
**Bedrooms:** 4 **Bathrooms:** 2½
**First Floor:** 2,126 sq. ft.
**Second Floor:** 914 sq. ft.
**Total:** 3,040 sq. ft.
**Bonus Space:** 564 sq. ft.
**Width:** 84'-8" **Depth:** 56'-0"

This traditional style home has an elegant glass entryway with a fanlight above the door. The dining area focuses on a bayed window and flows to the formal living room with fireplace and to the efficient island kitchen. The family room and breakfast area manage the family leisure time. The master suite has two walk-in closets and a whirlpool bath. Please specify basement or crawl-space foundation when ordering.

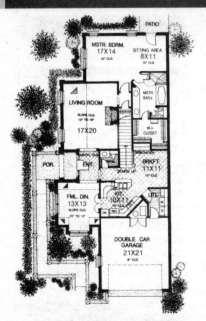

## Plan HPT840206

**Price Code:** C1
**Bedrooms:** 3 **Bathrooms:** 2½
**First Floor:** 1,689 sq. ft.
**Second Floor:** 672 sq. ft.
**Total:** 2,361 sq. ft.
**Width:** 34'-10" **Depth:** 75'-0"

Keystone lintels, corner quoins and a brick facade create classic elegance for this three-bedroom home. The vaulted side entrance introduces a formal dining room to the right and a welcoming living room with a fireplace to the left. Situated conveniently near the dining area, the kitchen features a serving bar, powder room and breakfast nook. The master suite enjoys a sumptuous master bath with a walk-in closet and a sitting room.

## Plan HPT840208

**Price Code:** C4
**Bedrooms:** 4 **Bathrooms:** 3½
**First Floor:** 2,813 sq. ft.
**Second Floor:** 1,091 sq. ft.
**Total:** 3,904 sq. ft.
**Width:** 85'-5" **Depth:** 74'-8"

Keystone lintels, an arched transom over the entry and sidelights spell classic design for this four-bedroom home. The tiled foyer offers entry to any room you choose, whether it be the secluded den with its built-in bookshelves, the formal dining room, the formal living room with its fireplace, wet bar and wall of windows, or the spacious rear family and kitchen area with its sunny breakfast nook. The master suite offers privacy on the first floor and features a sitting room with bookshelves, two walk-in closets and a private bath with a corner whirlpool tub. Upstairs, two family bedrooms share a bath and enjoy separate vanities.

## Plan HPT840210

**Price Code:** C3
**Bedrooms:** 4 **Bathrooms:** 3
**First Floor:** 2,861 sq. ft.
**Second Floor:** 783 sq. ft.
**Total:** 3,644 sq. ft.
**Bonus Space:** 232 sq. ft.
**Basement:** 709 sq. ft.
**Width:** 67'-10" **Depth:** 71'-8"

The stone and siding combination on the facade creates a country feeling when approaching this home. A large Palladian window sheds light on the two-story foyer and gallery below. There is plenty of living space throughout this amazing design. A sun room and covered rear porch create delightful opportunities for seasonal entertaining or relaxing near nature. The family room can be centered around the fireplace. Please specify basement or slab foundation when ordering.

## Plan HPT840209

**Price Code:** A3
**Bedrooms:** 3 **Bathrooms:** 2
**Square Footage:** 1,852
**Width:** 70'-0" **Depth:** 45'-0"

Shingles and vertical siding combine with multiple rooflines and gables on a hipped roof to create an eye-catching appeal for this three-bedroom home. All on one floor, this home provides plenty of room with ease of accessibility. Just inside the entry, the great room features a warming fireplace and a built-in media center. The dining room and island kitchen have an excellent view of this focal point in the great room.

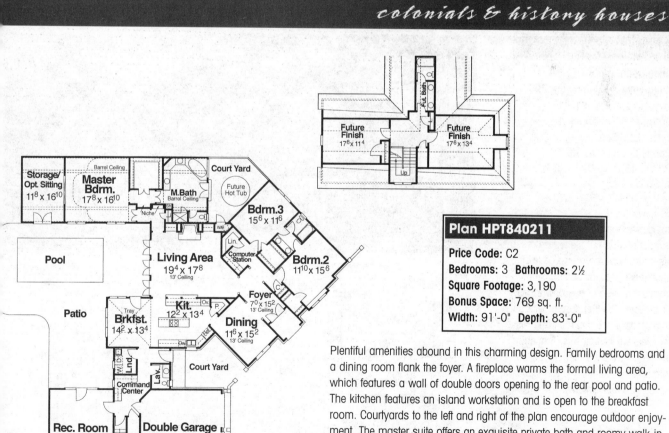

**Future Finish**
17⁸ x 11⁴

**Full Bath**

**Future Finish**
17⁶ x 13⁴

Up

Storage/ Opt. Sitting
11⁸ x 16¹⁰

Barrel Ceiling

**Master Bdrm.**
17⁸ x 16¹⁰

**M.Bath**
Barrel Ceiling

Court Yard

Future Hot Tub

Niche

**Bdrm.3**
15⁶ x 11⁶

W.I.C.

Lin.

**Living Area**
19⁴ x 17⁸
13' Ceiling

Computer Station

**Bdrm.2**
11¹⁰ x 15⁶

**Pool**

**Foyer**
7⁰ x 15²
13' Ceiling

C.

**Patio**

Tray

**Brkfst.**
14² x 13⁴

**Kit.**
12² x 13⁴

Ov.

P.

**Dining**
11⁶ x 15²
13' Ceiling

Ref.

Dw.

W./D.

Lnd.

**Command Center**

**Lav.**

Court Yard

**Rec. Room**
20² x 21⁴

**Double Garage**
23⁴ x 21⁴

Up

### Plan HPT840211

**Price Code:** C2
**Bedrooms:** 3 **Bathrooms:** 2½
**Square Footage:** 3,190
**Bonus Space:** 769 sq. ft.
**Width:** 91'-0" **Depth:** 83'-0"

Plentiful amenities abound in this charming design. Family bedrooms and a dining room flank the foyer. A fireplace warms the formal living area, which features a wall of double doors opening to the rear pool and patio. The kitchen features an island workstation and is open to the breakfast room. Courtyards to the left and right of the plan encourage outdoor enjoyment. The master suite offers an exquisite private bath and roomy walk-in closet. The two-car garage and recreation room are appealing additions to the floor plan. Optional space above the garage is reserved for future use.

## Plan HPT840212

**Price Code:** A4
**Bedrooms:** 4 **Bathrooms:** 3
**First Floor:** 1,865 sq. ft.
**Second Floor:** 565 sq. ft.
**Total:** 2,430 sq. ft.
**Bonus Space:** 425 sq. ft.
**Width:** 54'-0" **Depth:** 62'-4"

The rustic look of shingles against cut stone and siding presents a relaxing welcome to passersby. Inside, the formal dining room provides a triple view of the front property. The luxurious master suite opens from the vaulted grand room. Bedrooms 2 and 3 share a full bath upstairs. Please specify basement or crawlspace foundation when ordering.

## Plan HPT840213

**Price Code:** A3
**Bedrooms:** 3 **Bathrooms:** 2½
**First Floor:** 1,241 sq. ft.
**Second Floor:** 565 sq. ft.
**Total:** 1,806 sq. ft.
**Bonus Space:** 310 sq. ft.
**Width:** 45'-10" **Depth:** 57'-0"

Siding, shutters and a Palladian window set off with cut-stone trim adorn this lovely two-story home. A few highlights inside include the sunny breakfast nook and hearth-warmed great room. The first-floor master suite features a sumptuous bath and His and Hers walk-in closets. A handy laundry room leads into the two-car garage. Please specify basement or crawlspace foundation when ordering.

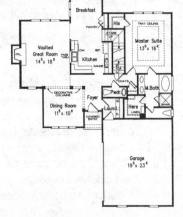

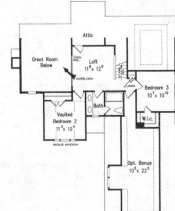

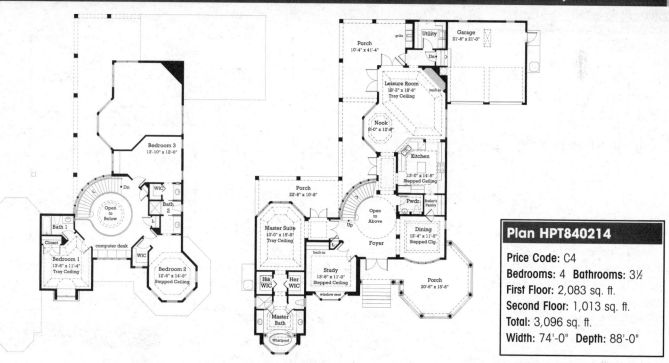

Porch
10'-4" x 41'-4"

Utility

Garage
21'-6" x 21'-0"

Dn

grille

Leisure Room
18'-2" x 18'-6"
Tray Ceiling

built-in

Nook
8'-0" x 12'-8"

Kitchen
13'-0" x 14'-6"
Stepped Ceiling

Bedroom 3
13'-10" x 12'-0"

Open to
Below

Dn

WIC

Bath
2

L

Bath 1

Closet

computer desk

WIC

Bedroom 1
13'-6" x 11'-4"
Tray Ceiling

Bedroom 2
12'-6" x 14'-9"
Stepped Ceiling

Porch
22'-6" x 10'-8"

Open to
Above

Up

Foyer

Pwdr.

Butler's
Pantry

Dining
12'-4" x 11'-6"
Stepped Clg.

Master Suite
13'-0" x 15'-8"
Tray Ceiling

built-in

L

Study
13'-6" x 11'-0"
Stepped Ceiling

Porch
20'-6" x 15'-6"

His
WIC

Her
WIC

window seat

Master
Bath

Whirlpool

### Plan HPT840214

**Price Code:** C4
**Bedrooms:** 4  **Bathrooms:** 3½
**First Floor:** 2,083 sq. ft.
**Second Floor:** 1,013 sq. ft.
**Total:** 3,096 sq. ft.
**Width:** 74'-0"  **Depth:** 88'-0"

This elegant and traditional farmhouse design combines rustic charm and Victorian accents. A circular front porch encourages outdoor entertaining. Inside, the foyer introduces a graceful curved staircase and is flanked by a formal dining room and study. A butler's pantry leads from the dining room to the island kitchen. The breakfast nook and family leisure room are located at the rear for casual enjoyment. The master suite is enchanting with His and Hers walk-in closets and a pampering whirlpool bath. Upstairs, Bedrooms 2 and 3 share a Jack-and-Jill bath, while another family bedroom provides its own bath. A garage, utility room and vast rear porch complete this plan.

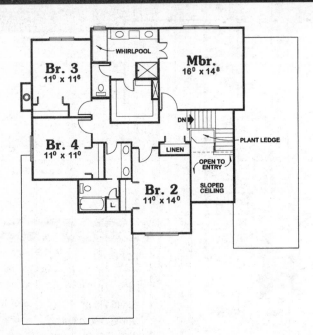

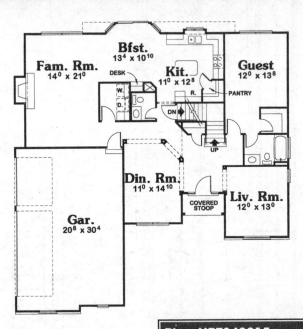

From its open gables to its steep rooflines, this home is a welcome addition to any neighborhood. Inside, architectural accents such as sturdy columns, built-ins, volume ceilings and lots of windows offer style and luxury. The gourmet kitchen features an island workstation, pantry storage and a bayed breakfast nook, opening to the hearth-warmed family room. Upstairs, the master bedroom offers a whirlpool bath and spacious walk-in closet. Three additional bedrooms on this level share a hall bath.

## Plan HPT840215

**Price Code:** C3
**Bedrooms:** 4   **Bathrooms:** 3½
**First Floor:** 1,582 sq. ft.
**Second Floor:** 1,170 sq. ft.
**Total:** 2,752 sq. ft.
**Width:** 53'-4"   **Depth:** 54'-4"

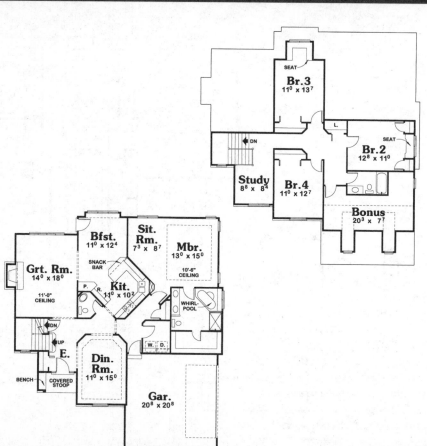

SEAT
**Br.3**
11⁰ x 13⁷

←DN

L.

SEAT

**Br.2**
12⁸ x 11⁰

**Study**
8⁸ x 8⁴

**Br.4**
11⁰ x 12⁷

**Bonus**
20³ x 7⁷

**Bfst.**
11⁰ x 12⁴

**Sit. Rm.**
7³ x 8⁷

**Mbr.**
13⁰ x 15⁰

10'-6"
CEILING

**Grt. Rm.**
14⁰ x 18⁰

11'-0"
CEILING

SNACK BAR

P.    **Kit.**
R.    11⁰ x 10²

WHIRL-
POOL

DN

UP

W. D.

E.

BENCH

COVERED
STOOP

**Din. Rm.**
11⁰ x 15⁰

**Gar.**
20⁸ x 20⁸

## Plan HPT840216

**Price Code:** C2
**Bedrooms:** 4  **Bathrooms:** 2½
**First Floor:** 1,554 sq. ft.
**Second Floor:** 867 sq. ft.
**Total:** 2,421 sq. ft.
**Bonus Space:** 240 sq. ft.
**Width:** 47'-8"  **Depth:** 52'-4"

This home is loaded with modern amenities that make it comfortable and functional. Sitting between the formal dining room and the breakfast nook, the 45-degree positioning of the U-shaped kitchen adds variety and spice to the layout of the first floor. The lavish master suite offers a large sitting area, walk-in closet, whirlpool tub, separate shower and double-sink vanity. The second-floor study provides a quiet work space, while quaint window seats in two of the family bedrooms offer additional sitting space for reflection and solitude.

## Plan HPT840217

**Price Code:** A4
**Bedrooms:** 3 **Bathrooms:** 2½
**First Floor:** 1,464 sq. ft.
**Second Floor:** 599 sq. ft.
**Total:** 2,063 sq. ft.
**Bonus Room:** 374 sq. ft.
**Width:** 50'-0" **Depth:** 48'-0"

Three shed dormers and a stone-faced gable draw attention to this plan. Inside, the vaulted grand room and U-shaped kitchen pivot around a pantry column. The master suite enjoys French-door access to the backyard. The master bath is vaulted and provides a spacious walk-in closet. Bedrooms 2 and 3 share a computer center upstairs. The bonus room is great for a home office, guest suite or playroom. Please specify basement or crawlspace foundation when ordering.

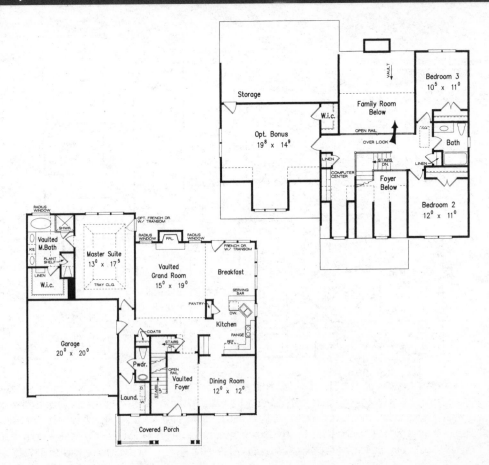

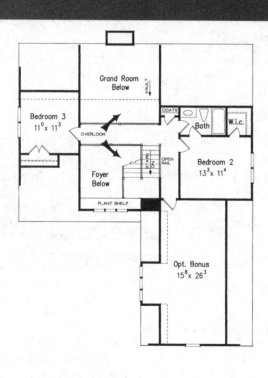

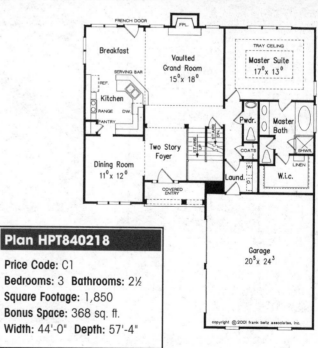

**Plan HPT840218**

**Price Code:** C1
**Bedrooms:** 3  **Bathrooms:** 2½
**Square Footage:** 1,850
**Bonus Space:** 368 sq. ft.
**Width:** 44'-0"  **Depth:** 57'-4"

This European design boasts a layout perfect for a narrow lot. A covered front porch welcomes you inside to a two-story foyer that leads to the vaulted great room. The kitchen with a pantry and serving bar easily serves the dining and breakfast rooms. The first-floor master suite is topped by a tray ceiling and includes a private bath with a walk-in closet. A laundry room leading to the two-car garage completes the first floor. Upstairs, two additional bedrooms are separated by a bridge overlook and share a hall bath. The optional bonus room is great for a home office, storage room or guest suite. Please specify basement or crawlspace foundation when ordering.

## Plan HPT840219

**Price Code:** C1
**Bedrooms:** 4 **Bathrooms:** 2½
**First Floor:** 2,079 sq. ft.
**Second Floor:** 796 sq. ft.
**Total:** 2,875 sq. ft.
**Width:** 63'-0" **Depth:** 68'-0"

This exquisite European cottage offers all the charm of the Old World. A beautiful courtyard announces your entry. The foyer is flanked by a dining room and study. The kitchen features a snack counter, while the nook extends double-door access to the three-season porch. The master suite includes a pampering private bath and walk-in closet. A three-car garage completes the first floor. Three family bedrooms reside upstairs.

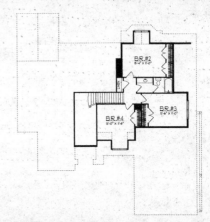

## Plan HPT840220

**Price Code:** C2
**Bedrooms:** 4 **Bathrooms:** 3½
**Square Footage:** 3,070
**Width:** 75'-0" **Depth:** 80'-4"

European grace surrounds this fine cottage home. The double-door entrance leads to a study and formal dining room, each opening to a tiled gallery. The living room is a wash in light from a wall of windows. The kitchen is within steps of the breakfast bay and family room. The family room features a extended-hearth fireplace and cathedral ceiling.

© Stephen Fuller, Inc.

**Bedroom Office** 12³ x 13³

**Bedroom #2** 14⁹ x 13⁰

**Media Room** 14⁰ x 10⁰

**Exercise** 8⁹ x 13⁹

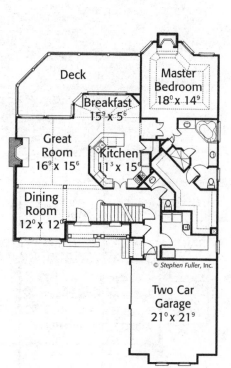

**Deck**

**Master Bedroom** 18⁰ x 14⁹

**Breakfast** 15⁹ x 5⁶

**Great Room** 16⁹ x 15⁶

**Kitchen** 11³ x 15⁶

**Dining Room** 12⁰ x 12⁰

© Stephen Fuller, Inc.

**Two Car Garage** 21⁰ x 21⁹

---

### Plan HPT840221

**Price Code:** C2
**Bedrooms:** 3 **Bathrooms:** 2½
**First Floor:** 1,746 sq. ft.
**Second Floor:** 651 sq. ft.
**Total:** 2,397 sq. ft.
**Width:** 50'-0" **Depth:** 75'-4"

At the heart of this home, a gourmet kitchen provides beautiful hardwood floors, a snack counter and a walk-in pantry. Double doors open to a gallery hall that leads to the formal dining room—an enchanting retreat for chandelier-lit evenings that provides a breathtaking view of the front yard. A classic great room—perfect for both formal and casual family gatherings, is warmed by a cozy fireplace and brightened by a wall of windows. The outdoor living area is spacious enough for grand events. The master suite is brightened by sweeping views of the backyard and a romantic fireplace just for two. This home is designed with a walkout basement foundation.

## Plan HPT840223

Price Code: C3
Bedrooms: 4   Bathrooms: 2½
First Floor: 1,369 sq. ft.
Second Floor: 1,239 sq. ft.
Total: 2,608 sq. ft.
Width: 49'-0"   Depth: 46'-4"

An elegant portico opens to the grand foyer where French doors lead to the living room/den. A formal dining room is located to the right of the foyer. A double-sided fireplace warms the family room and the hearth room that adjoins the island kitchen and morning nook. Upstairs, the master suite boasts a private bath with a garden tub and double-sink vanity as well as twin walk-in closets. Three additional bedrooms share a hall bath.

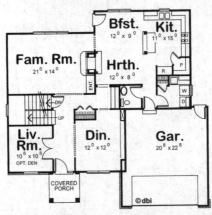

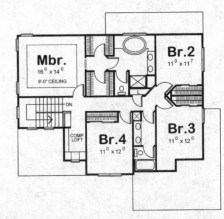

## Plan HPT840222

Price Code: C2
Bedrooms: 4   Bathrooms: 2½
First Floor: 1,538 sq. ft.
Second Floor: 727 sq. ft.
Total: 2,265 sq. ft.
Width: 48'-4"   Depth: 50'-0"

A multitude of windows welcomes in the warm summer breezes in this delightful two-story stucco home. The den/living room off the foyer offers privacy with French-door access. The great room adds elegance with columns and arches as well as a majestic fireplace. The master suite boasts a private bath and view of the backyard.

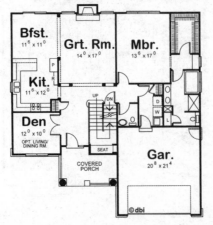

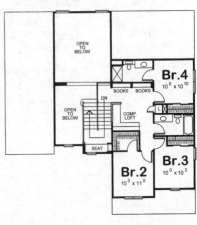

Multi-pane windows, shutters and shingle accents adorn the stucco facade of this wonderful French country home. Inside, the foyer introduces the hearth-warmed great room that features French-door access to the rear deck. The dining room, defined from the foyer and great room by columns, enjoys front-yard views. The master bedroom includes two walk-in closets, rear-deck access and a dual vanity bath. The informal living areas have an open plan. The box-bayed breakfast nook joins the cooktop-island kitchen and hearth-warmed family room. The second floor holds two bedrooms with walk-in closets, a study and an unfinished bedroom for future expansion.

**Plan HPT840224**

Price Code: C3
Bedrooms: 3  Bathrooms: 2½
First Floor: 1,840 sq. ft.
Second Floor: 840 sq. ft.
Total: 2,680 sq. ft.
Bonus Space: 295 sq. ft.
Width: 66'-0"  Depth: 65'-10"

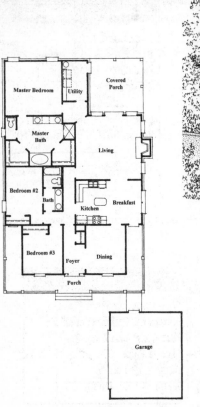

## Plan HPT840225

**Price Code:** A4
**Bedrooms:** 3 **Bathrooms:** 2
**Square Footage:** 2,155
**Width:** 50'-4" **Depth:** 101'-9"

The hipped roof with its eyebrow dormers settles beautifully above the columns and shuttered windows of this three-bedroom home. A courtyard separates the house from the street. Inside, three bedrooms line the left of the plan, while shared living area sits to the right. The master suite features a large bath with two walk-in closets. A hearth-warmed living room accesses the rear porch. The island kitchen easily serves the formal dining room.

## Plan HPT840226

**Price Code:** A4
**Bedrooms:** 3 **Bathrooms:** 2
**Square Footage:** 2,033
**Width:** 51'-0" **Depth:** 94'-0"

A beautiful wraparound porch with columns and two dormers set above welcomes guests inside from the courtyard entry. The foyer introduces the formal dining area to the right, nearby the island kitchen and breakfast nook. A fireplace warms the living room, while plenty of windows draw in natural light. The master suite sits at the rear of the plan and features a plush bath with two walk-in closets. Two family bedrooms share a dual-vanity bath.

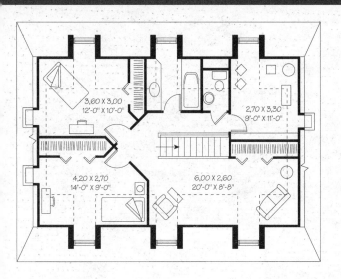

3,60 X 3,00
12'-0" X 10'-0"

2,70 X 3,30
9'-0" X 11'-0"

4,20 X 2,70
14'-0" X 9'-0"

6,00 X 2,60
20'-0" X 8'-8"

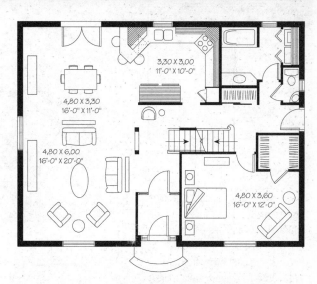

3,30 X 3,00
11'-0" X 10'-0"

4,80 X 3,30
16'-0" X 11'-0"

4,80 X 6,00
16'-0" X 20'-0"

4,80 X 3,60
16'-0" X 12'-0"

Quaint French cottage style creates a sumptuous floor plan perfect for any family. Stucco, corner quoins, French shutters and a shingled roof are of notable European influence, while the front dormers possess a countryside simplicity. To the left, the family room is open to the formal dining room. Double doors from the dining room open to the rear property. The adjoining island countertop kitchen features a breakfast bar. Down the hall, the first-floor master suite—secluded for extra privacy—features a walk-in closet. Upstairs, a huge loft area makes a perfect media room and is illuminated by two front-facing dormers. This home is designed with a basement foundation.

## Plan HPT840227

**Price Code:** A4
**Bedrooms:** 3 **Bathrooms:** 2½
**First Floor:** 1,196 sq. ft.
**Second Floor:** 934 sq. ft.
**Total:** 2,130 sq. ft.
**Width:** 40'-0" **Depth:** 30'-0"

## Plan HPT840229

**Price Code:** A4
**Bedrooms:** 3  **Bathrooms:** 2½
**First Floor:** 1,278 sq. ft.
**Second Floor:** 1,027 sq. ft.
**Total:** 2,305 sq. ft.
**Width:** 42'-6"  **Depth:** 61'-2"

This quaint French Country house is perfect for narrow lots. The timber framed porch invites you into an entry that moves you conveniently from an office/study on the left, to the great room with a vaulted ceiling straight ahead. To the right, a well-appointed kitchen opens to a family-style keeping room. Upstairs, the second floor features a master bedroom suite that provides a huge walk-in closet.

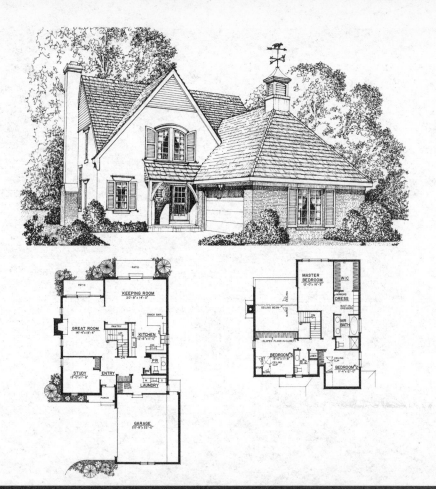

## Plan HPT840228

**Price Code:** C2
**Bedrooms:** 5  **Bathrooms:** 3
**First Floor:** 1,724 sq. ft.
**Second Floor:** 701 sq. ft.
**Total:** 2,425 sq. ft.
**Width:** 50'-0"  **Depth:** 51'-8"

Stucco siding and intricate windows decorate the facade of this home. Front and rear porches offer plenty of outdoor opportunities. Two family bedrooms are located away from the master suite for privacy. Two more family bedrooms are located on the second level. Please specify basement, crawlspace or slab foundation when ordering.

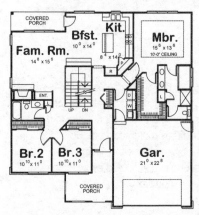

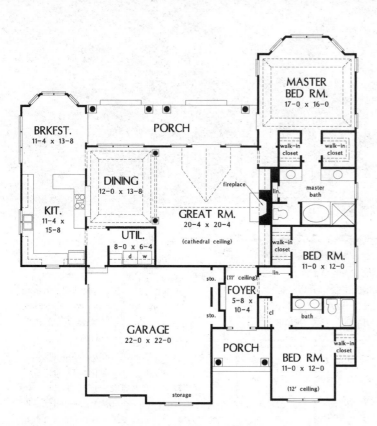

## Plan HPT840230

**Price Code:** C1
**Bedrooms:** 3 **Bathrooms:** 2
**Square Footage:** 2,098
**Width:** 60'-0" **Depth:** 63'-8"

This three-bedroom home fits nicely into any neighborhood with its complex hipped roof and stucco facade offering a European/Mediterranean flair. The vaulted great room, with fireplace, built-ins and a window wall that opens to the covered porch, adjoins the elegant dining room where decorative columns and a tray ceiling set a formal tone. The rear porch can also be accessed by the master bedroom and the breakfast nook, which enjoys a sunny location adjoining the kitchen. ©2000 Donald A. Gardner, Inc.

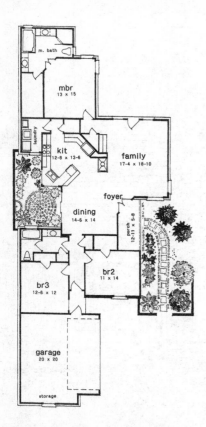

## Plan HPT840232

**Price Code:** A3
**Bedrooms:** 3 **Bathrooms:** 2
**Square Footage:** 1,823
**Width:** 38'-10" **Depth:** 94'-10"

This splendid European cottage boasts the romantic influence of the French countryside. French shutters, stucco and brick detailing highlight the eye-catching exterior. A covered front porch welcomes you inside to a foyer flanked on either side by a dining area and family room. The master suite is secluded for privacy and includes a private bath with a walk-in closet. Two additional bedrooms and a hall bath are located at the front of the plan.

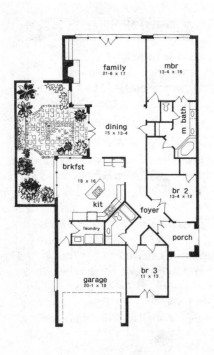

## Plan HPT840231

**Price Code:** A4
**Bedrooms:** 3 **Bathrooms:** 2
**Square Footage:** 2,048
**Width:** 38'-10" **Depth:** 75'-0"

Presenting a narrow frontage, this plan provides spacious rooms for a family. Enter through a front corner porch or through a side courtyard that opens to the dining room. A fireplace warms the family room, which accesses the rear yard through French doors. A bright corner breakfast nook highlights the kitchen, which provides a cooktop island and laundry-room access. The master suite features a walk-in closet and separate vanities in the compartmented bath.

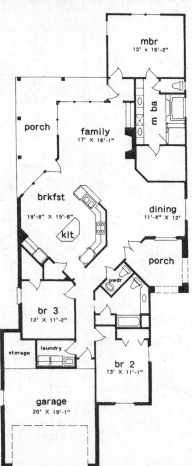

## Plan HPT840233

**Price Code:** A4
**Bedrooms:** 3 **Bathrooms:** 2½
**Square Footage:** 2,007
**Width:** 40'-0" **Depth:** 94'-10"

An ornate stucco facade with brick highlights refines this charming French cottage. The double-door entrance sits to the side—perfect for a courtyard welcome. A dining and family room utilize an open layout for easy traffic flow. The circular kitchen space features an island and complementary breakfast bay. Bedrooms 2 and 3 share a hall bath. The master suite, apart from the main living areas, enjoys privacy and a full bath with a spacious walk-in closet. The rear porch encourages outdoor relaxation.

### Plan HPT840234

**Price Code:** A4
**Bedrooms:** 3 **Bathrooms:** 2
**Square Footage:** 2,000
**Width:** 68'-0" **Depth:** 64'-0"

Steep rooflines and columns make this home one to remember. Starburst windows align the exterior and offer a nice touch of sophistication. Extra amenities run rampant through this one-story home. The sun room can be enjoyed during every season. An eating nook is right off the kitchen and brightens the rear of the home well. A utility and storage area are also found at the rear of the home. A cozy study privately accesses the side porch. The master bedroom is complete with dual vanities and His and Hers closets. Two family bedrooms are to the left of the plan. Please specify crawlspace or slab foundation when ordering.

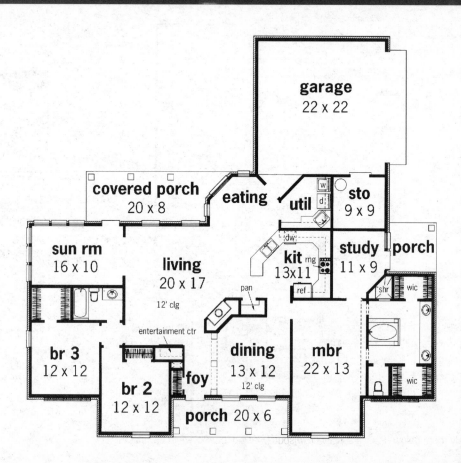

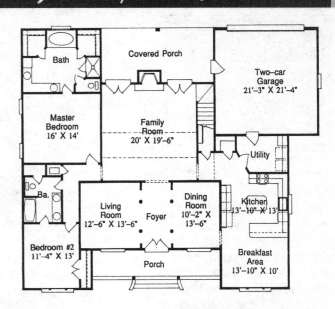

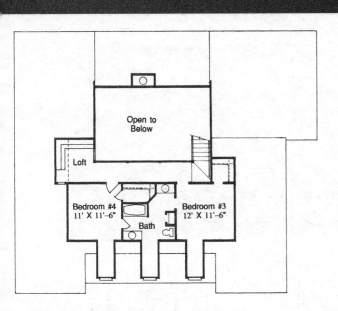

Open to Below

Loft

Bedroom #4
11' X 11'-6"

Bedroom #3
12' X 11'-6"

Bath

Bath

Covered Porch

Two-car Garage
21'-3" X 21'-4"

Master Bedroom
16' X 14'

Family Room
20' X 19'-6"

Utility

Ba.

Living Room
12'-6" X 13'-6"

Foyer

Dining Room
10'-2" X 13'-6"

Kitchen
13'-10" X 13'

Bedroom #2
11'-4" X 13'

Porch

Breakfast Area
13'-10" X 10'

Wonderful windows, sunburst transoms, French doors, dormers and Palladian windows flood the interior of this home with light. The formal areas of the home and the rear covered porch are wonderful for grand entertainment events. Relax in the two-story family room watching a crackling fire in the fireplace. The master suite and one family bedroom occupy the left side of the plan. Preparing meals will be a breeze in the U-shaped kitchen with its island work space and serving bar to the breakfast room. Upstairs, dormer windows adorn Bedrooms 3 and 4. Note the private loft, with views of the family room below. Please specify crawlspace or slab foundation when ordering.

## Plan HPT840235

**Price Code:** C1
**Bedrooms:** 4  **Bathrooms:** 3
**First Floor:** 2,152 sq. ft.
**Second Floor:** 717 sq. ft.
**Total:** 2,869 sq. ft.
**Width:** 62'-4"  **Depth:** 53'-0"

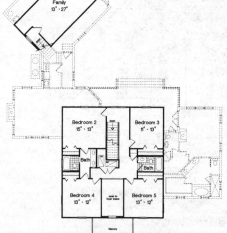

## Plan HPT840237

**Price Code:** C2

**Bedrooms:** 5  **Bathrooms:** 3½

**First Floor:** 2,250 sq. ft.

**Second Floor:** 1,180 sq. ft.

**Total:** 3,430 sq. ft.

**Bonus Space:** 438 sq. ft.

**Width:** 76'-3"  **Depth:** 95'-7"

A real French country classic—two-story for that large family that likes a formal setting. The formal living room, den and master suite are to the right. To the left is the formal dining room and family areas. The master suite enjoys a private bath with dual vanities and large walk-in closet. The kitchen, overlooking the breakfast nook and family room, is a dream with its cooktop island and large pantry.

## Plan HPT840236

**Price Code:** C3

**Bedrooms:** 4  **Bathrooms:** 3½

**First Floor:** 1,234 sq. ft.

**Second Floor:** 1,316 sq. ft.

**Total:** 2,550 sq. ft.

**Width:** 48'-0"  **Depth:** 48'-0"

Symmetry fares well on this French Country home. A living room or study greets guests and leads into the family room. A bayed morning room has access to the backyard. A columned dining room is well situated close to the kitchen. The sleeping quarters are located on the second level. Please specify basement, crawlspace or slab foundation when ordering.

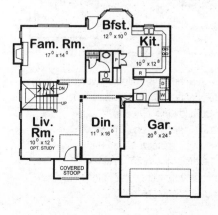

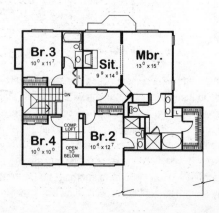

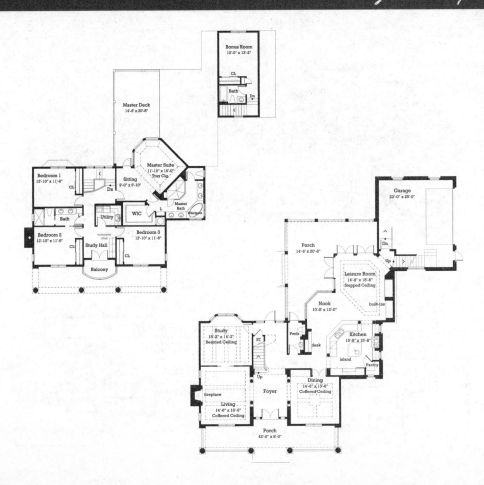

Bonus Room
12'-0" x 13'-2"
CL
Bath
Dn

Master Deck
14'-6" x 20'-8"

Master Suite
11'-10" x 15'-0"
Tray Clg.

Bedroom 1
12'-10" x 11'-6"
CL

Sitting
9'-0" x 9'-10"
Dn

Master Bath
Whirlpool

Bath
Utility
WIC
L

Bedroom 2
12'-10" x 11'-6"
CL

Study Hall
CL
Balcony

Bedroom 3
12'-10" x 11'-6"

Garage
22'-0" x 25'-0"

Porch
14'-6" x 20'-8"
Dn
Up

Leisure Room
14'-8" x 18'-8"
Stepped Ceiling
built-ins

Nook
10'-8" x 12'-0"

Study
15'-2" x 14'-2"
Beamed Ceiling
ST

Pwdr.
desk

Kitchen
15'-8" x 15'-8"
island
Pantry

fireplace
Up
Foyer

Dining
14'-6" x 13'-6"
Coffered Ceiling

Living
14'-6" x 16'-8"
Coffered Ceiling

Porch
42'-0" x 8'-0"

## Plan HPT840238

**Price Code:** C4
**Bedrooms:** 4  **Bathrooms:** 2½
**First Floor:** 1,865 sq. ft.
**Second Floor:** 1,477 sq. ft.
**Total:** 3,342 sq. ft.
**Bonus Space:** 584 sq. ft.
**Width:** 79'-0"  **Depth:** 79'-2"

This eloquent French cottage design features an enchanting country layout. Double doors open inside to a formal welcoming foyer. To the left, a living room is warmed by a fireplace, which connects to a bay-windowed study. A formal dining room is found to the right. The island kitchen opens to a nook and leisure room with built-ins. Three sets of double doors open onto the rear porch. Upstairs, the study hall opens to a romantic front balcony. Three family bedrooms share a hall bath. The master suite is an impressive retreat with a large sitting area accessing the master deck, a private whirlpool bath and a huge walk-in closet. Please specify basement or crawlspace foundation when ordering.

## Plan HPT840240

**Price Code:** C2
**Bedrooms:** 5 **Bathrooms:** 3½
**First Floor:** 2,542 sq. ft.
**Second Floor:** 909 sq. ft.
**Total:** 3,451 sq. ft.
**Width:** 74'-0" **Depth:** 84'-11"

European charm is written all over the facade of this lovely home. A paneled entry, a delicate balustrade and a hipped roof announce a thoughtful plan with an open interior and room to grow. A center island in the kitchen features a cooktop and space for food preparation. Privately located on the first floor, the master suite enjoys a luxurious bath. Three family bedrooms share a full bath on the second level.

## Plan HPT840239

**Price Code:** C1
**Bedrooms:** 3 **Bathrooms:** 2½
**First Floor:** 1,407 sq. ft.
**Second Floor:** 1,157 sq. ft.
**Total:** 2,564 sq. ft.
**Width:** 62'-3" **Depth:** 51'-2"

Although one of the massive chimneys on this French stucco home is decorative, fireplaces in the family, living and dining rooms will ensure that you have no trouble keeping warm. The front of the house appears symmetrical, but the front door is off-center, adding a bit of eccentricity. The entrance opens into the formal rooms, then leads back to the kitchen, which opens into a breakfast area with French doors to the patio.

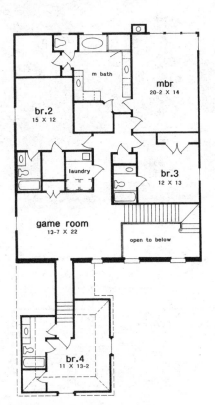

br.2
15 X 12

m bath

mbr
20-2 X 14

laundry

br.3
12 X 13

game room
13-7 X 22

open to below

br.4
11 X 13-2

brkfst
12-6 X 13-9

family
20 X 22-4

kit
15 X 16

storage

dining
14 X 17

study
17-6 X 11-8

foyer

garage
20 X 20

## Plan HPT840241

**Price Code:** C4
**Bedrooms:** 4 **Bathrooms:** 4½
**First Floor:** 1,909 sq. ft.
**Second Floor:** 1,992 sq. ft.
**Total:** 3,901 sq. ft.
**Width:** 39'-9" **Depth:** 76'-10"

A garage-top bedroom may be the perfect place for your teenager, offering privacy, a separate bathroom, a large walk-in closet and a view out of two arched dormer windows. There are plenty of great spaces for children and adults in this elegant home. A downstairs study and an upstairs game room are two extras that set this home apart. Four bedrooms each have a private bathroom, with an additional powder room located downstairs. Notice that there is plenty of extra storage space in this home and that the laundry room is conveniently located near the cluster of bedrooms.

## Plan HPT840242

**Price Code:** C3
**Bedrooms:** 4 **Bathrooms:** 3
**First Floor:** 1,904 sq. ft.
**Second Floor:** 792 sq. ft.
**Total:** 2,696 sq. ft.
**Width:** 67'-8" **Depth:** 64'-10"

This charming cottage has all the accoutrements of an English manor. Inside, the angled foyer directs the eye to the arched entrances of the formal dining room and the great room with its fireplace and patio access. The master bedroom and a guest bedroom are located on the opposite side of the house for privacy. Please specify basement, crawlspace or slab foundation when ordering.

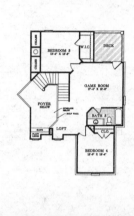

## Plan HPT840243

**Price Code:** C1
**Bedrooms:** 3 **Bathrooms:** 2
**First Floor:** 2,188 sq. ft.
**Second Floor:** 396 sq. ft.
**Total:** 2,584 sq. ft.
**Future Space:** 836 sq. ft.
**Width:** 72'-0" **Depth:** 45'-8"

This two-story stucco home fits a corner lot perfectly with a side-loading two-car garage. The heart of this design is the great room where beautiful views frame the elegant fireplace. The formal dining room and breakfast area are placed near the island kitchen for convenience. Two bedrooms share a full bath on the left near the master suite. Please specify basement, crawlspace or slab foundation when ordering.

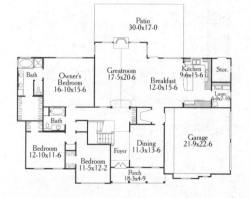

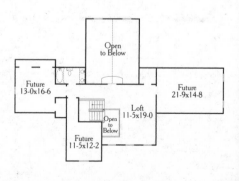

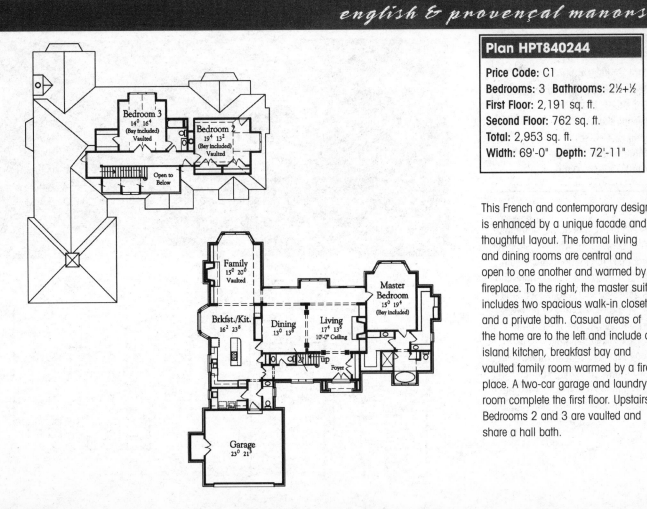

**Plan HPT840244**

**Price Code:** C1
**Bedrooms:** 3 **Bathrooms:** 2½+½
**First Floor:** 2,191 sq. ft.
**Second Floor:** 762 sq. ft.
**Total:** 2,953 sq. ft.
**Width:** 69'-0" **Depth:** 72'-11"

This French and contemporary design is enhanced by a unique facade and a thoughtful layout. The formal living and dining rooms are central and open to one another and warmed by a fireplace. To the right, the master suite includes two spacious walk-in closets and a private bath. Casual areas of the home are to the left and include an island kitchen, breakfast bay and vaulted family room warmed by a fire-place. A two-car garage and laundry room complete the first floor. Upstairs, Bedrooms 2 and 3 are vaulted and share a hall bath.

## Plan HPT840246

**Price Code:** C1
**Bedrooms:** 3  **Bathrooms:** 2½
**First Floor:** 1,781 sq. ft.
**Second Floor:** 730 sq. ft.
**Total:** 2,511 sq. ft.
**Width:** 54'-0"  **Depth:** 63'-8"

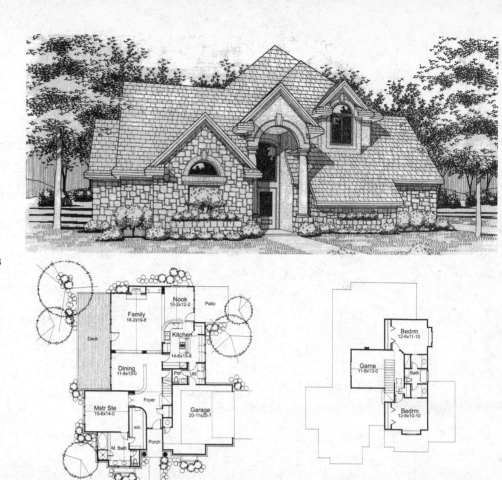

This romantic cottage is structured in contemporary and European designs. Inside, the deluxe master suite features a pampering bath and huge walk-in closet. The foyer leads to the formal dining room and family room warmed by a fireplace. The cooktop-island kitchen connects to a casual morning nook. Upstairs, two family bedrooms share a Jack-and-Jill bath and a second-floor game room. Please specify basement, crawlspace or slab foundation when ordering.

## Plan HPT840245

**Price Code:** A4
**Bedrooms:** 4  **Bathrooms:** 2½
**First Floor:** 1,658 sq. ft.
**Second Floor:** 538 sq. ft.
**Total:** 2,196 sq. ft.
**Bonus Room:** 496 sq. ft.
**Width:** 50'-0"  **Depth:** 56'-0"

The stone accents of this home give it a European flavor. The vaulted foyer introduces the formal dining room plus a built-in shelf to the right and the den/Bedroom 4 to the left. The massive great room also enjoys a vaulted ceiling. The vaulted master bedroom includes a large walk-in closet and a private entrance to the utility room. The private bath is entered through French doors and boasts an oversized soaking tub.

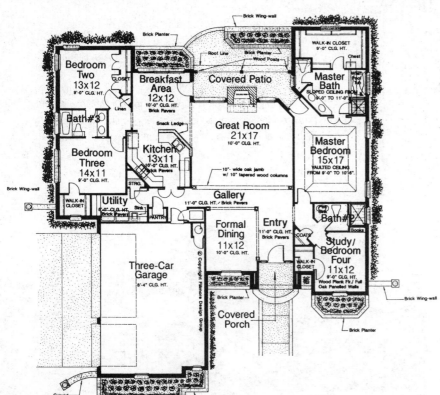

## Plan HPT840247

**Price Code:** C1
**Bedrooms:** 4  **Bathrooms:** 3
**Square Footage:** 2,391
**Width:** 64'-0"  **Depth:** 68'-5"

This exquisite one-story European cottage offers an amenity-filled layout favorable for the whole family. Inside, the entry is flanked by the formal dining room and study. A gallery hall separates these rooms from the great room, warmed by a country hearth. The kitchen serves the breakfast room with ease. Two family bedrooms share a Jack-and-Jill bath. The master bedroom is vaulted and features a pampering bath with a walk-in closet and private access to the rear covered patio. A three-car garage and utility room complete the floor plan.

## Plan HPT840249

**Price Code:** C1
**Bedrooms:** 4 **Bathrooms:** 2½
**Square Footage:** 2,757
**Width:** 69'-6" **Depth:** 68'-3"

Country French appointments give this home an elegant Old World look. The foyer opens to the well-proportioned dining room, with a twelve-foot ceiling. A stairway is conveniently located in the home to provide access to the optional basement below and the attic above. Double French doors with transoms open to the rear porch. Three additional bedrooms include a flex room that easily converts to a home office or study. Please specify basement, crawlspace or slab foundation when ordering.

A gentle European charm flavors the facade of this ultra-modern home. The foyer opens to a formal dining room, which leads to the kitchen through privacy doors. Here, a center cooktop island complements wrapping counter space, a walk-in pantry and a snack counter. Casual living space shares a through-fireplace with the formal living room and provides its own access to the rear porch. Please specify basement, crawlspace or slab foundation when ordering.

## Plan HPT840248

**Price Code:** C2
**Bedrooms:** 4 **Bathrooms:** 2½
**Square Footage:** 2,745
**Width:** 69'-6" **Depth:** 76'-8"

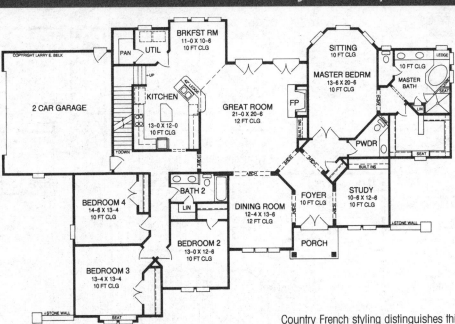

**Plan HPT840250**

Price Code: C1

Bedrooms: 4  Bathrooms: 2½

Square Footage: 2,960

Width: 90'-2"  Depth: 58'-6"

Country French styling distinguishes this split-bedroom, one-story home. Inside, twelve-foot ceilings are used in the dining room and great room. A study is located to the right of the foyer for quiet seclusion. The master suite features a bay-window seating area and an amenity-filled bath that extends into a double walk-in closet. Family bedrooms on the opposite side of the home share a full hall bath. A rear staircase is included in the plan, which can go up to the expandable attic space or down to the basement. Please specify basement, crawlspace or slab foundation when ordering.

## Plan HPT840251

**Price Code:** A4
**Bedrooms:** 4  **Bathrooms:** 2½
**First Floor:** 1,482 sq. ft.
**Second Floor:** 971 sq. ft.
**Total:** 2,453 sq. ft.
**Width:** 47'-0"  **Depth:** 58'-0"

A dual-pitched roof, brick and half-timbering combine to create a wonderful Tudor facade. A vaulted foyer with a skylight leads to the curved staircase, which climbs to the cluster of bedrooms. The master bedroom has a private bath, while three other bedrooms share a roomy central bath. Downstairs, a formal dining room, a sunken living room with bay window, a den, laundry room, sunken family room and kitchen with a breakfast nook complete this plan.

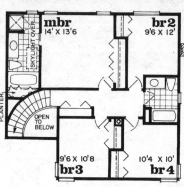

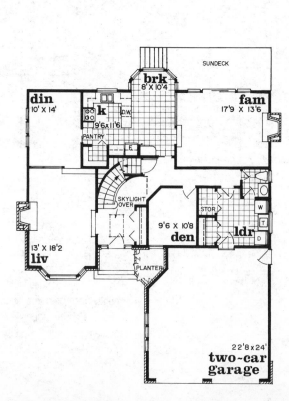

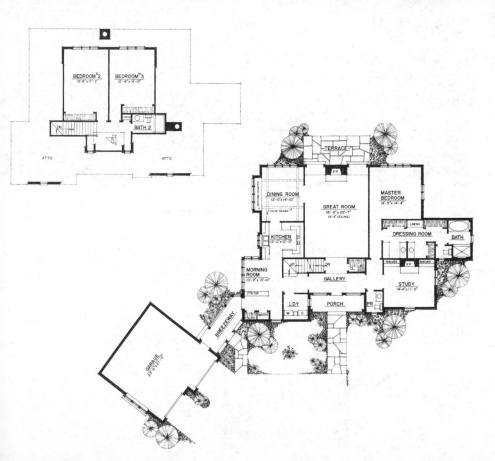

## Plan HPT840252

**Price Code:** C2
**Bedrooms:** 3  **Bathrooms:** 2½
**First Floor:** 2,122 sq. ft.
**Second Floor:** 719 sq. ft.
**Total:** 2,841 sq. ft.
**Width:** 107'-0"  **Depth:** 71'-0"

This breathtaking European design is enhanced with French stucco and Tudor detailing. The front porch enters inside to the welcoming gallery. To the right, a quiet study is enhanced by a fireplace and flanking built-ins. The master suite features a large dressing room and a private bath. The great room is central to the plan and is warmed by a second fireplace. The kitchen serves the formal dining room and morning room with ease. Upstairs, two additional family bedrooms share a hall bath. A breezeway connects the main house to the garage.

This country cottage offers a fine picture of comfort and luxury within 2,500 square feet. A formal dining room is accented by columns and sits across a gallery from the great room. A large fireplace provides a warm visual display for this area and the dining room. To the right, the master suite is provided with privacy and the convenient comforts of a full bath and oversized walk-in closet.

## Plan HPT840254

**Price Code:** C1
**Bedrooms:** 4  **Bathrooms:** 3
**Square Footage:** 2,483
**Width:** 64'-5"  **Depth:** 67'-5"

## Plan HPT840253

**Price Code:** A4
**Bedrooms:** 3  **Bathrooms:** 2½
**Square Footage:** 1,807
**Width:** 74'-0"  **Depth:** 44'-0"

The striking European-style facade of this home includes a beautiful stone exterior, complete with stone quoins, a shingled rooftop and French-style shutters on the front windows. An element of privacy has been observed, with the master bedroom separated from the other two bedrooms, which share a full bath.

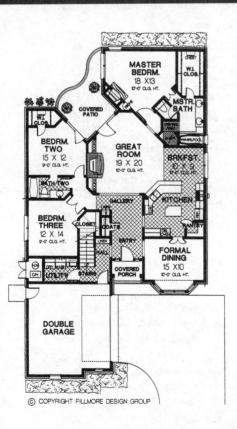

© COPYRIGHT FILLMORE DESIGN GROUP

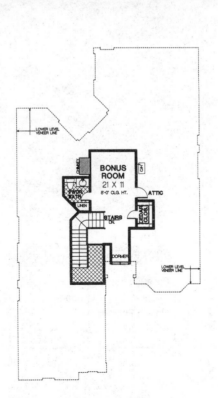

## Plan HPT840255

**Price Code:** C1
**Bedrooms:** 3 **Bathrooms:** 2½
**First Floor:** 2,168 sq. ft.
**Second Floor:** 308 sq. ft.
**Total:** 2,476 sq. ft.
**Bonus Room:** 308 sq. ft.
**Width:** 44'-10" **Depth:** 79'-10"

A touch of Tudor and a touch of the English cottage—this home is designed for comfort. A tiled entry, gallery, kitchen and breakfast nook give a sense of casual space. The formal dining area is set to the right and enjoys a bumped-out bay window. Two bedrooms share a hall bath on the right of the plan. The master suite looks out to the rear covered patio and is pampered by a full bath and walk-in closet. The great room is the hub of this plan, featuring a warm fireplace and patio access. A bonus room is perfect for a guest bedroom or recreation room.

## Plan HPT840256

**Price Code:** C2
**Bedrooms:** 4 **Bathrooms:** 3½
**First Floor:** 2,144 sq. ft.
**Second Floor:** 920 sq. ft.
**Total:** 3,064 sq. ft.
**Width:** 59'-0" **Depth:** 79'-3"

Fieldstone, stucco and brick give this cottage harmony in variety. The foyer opens to a private study with bay windows and a fireplace. The formal dining room is just down the hall and opens through column accents to the living room. The kitchen serves both the formal and casual spaces. The family room is cozy with a fireplace and rear-window display.

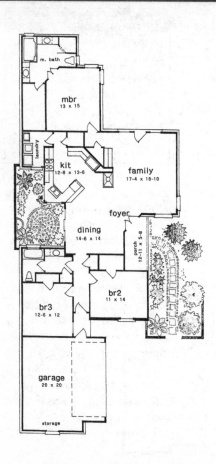

## Plan HPT840257

**Price Code:** A3
**Bedrooms:** 3 **Bathrooms:** 2
**Square Footage:** 1,823
**Width:** 38'-10" **Depth:** 94'-10"

This home's long, narrow footprint is ideal for a slim lot. A beautiful facade using stucco, brick, shuttered windows and steepled rooftops is as inviting as the floor plan. A courtyard entrance is flanked by the open dining and family spaces. Two family bedrooms are split from the master suite, which fosters privacy. The master bedroom, at the rear of the home, enjoys simple luxuries in the dual-vanity bath.

## Plan HPT840258

**Price Code:** L1
**Bedrooms:** 4   **Bathrooms:** 4
**First Floor:** 1,840 sq. ft.
**Second Floor:** 1,888 sq. ft.
**Total:** 3,728 sq. ft.
**Width:** 61'-6"   **Depth:** 64'-4"

With an informal European Country flavor, this home speaks volumes about great design. Romantic rooflines sweep over the entry, which leads through double doors to a fabulous foyer. The formal dining room connects with the kitchen via a spacious butler's pantry. Double-hung floor-length windows provide plenty of natural light in the study. A curved wall of windows enhances the two-story great room, which features a fireplace. The island kitchen overlooks the breakfast room, also warmed by a fireplace. A screened porch resides to the rear of the plan and is accessed by the breakfast room. Upstairs, the spacious master suite boasts a bay window and features a romantic fireplace. This home is designed with a walkout basement foundation.

## Plan HPT840260

**Price Code:** A3
**Bedrooms:** 3  **Bathrooms:** 2½
**First Floor:** 1,487 sq. ft.
**Second Floor:** 497 sq. ft.
**Total:** 1,984 sq. ft.
**Width:** 62'-0"  **Depth:** 42'-6"

European styling comes into play on this stone-and-stucco elevation, which showcases an elegant stair tower. A wall of windows adds interest to the secluded master bedroom. Two bedrooms on the second floor share a full hall bath that includes dual vanities. Please specify basement or slab foundation when ordering.

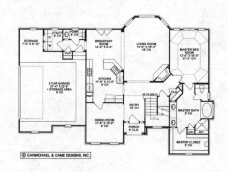

## Plan HPT840259

**Price Code:** C2
**Bedrooms:** 4  **Bathrooms:** 3½
**First Floor:** 1,678 sq. ft.
**Second Floor:** 1,766 sq. ft.
**Total:** 3,444 sq. ft.
**Width:** 72'-6"  **Depth:** 55'-8"

This enchanting European-style home is enhanced by mixed exterior detailing. Inside, the foyer is flanked on either side by the library and formal dining room. The great room is sunken and is warmed by a fireplace. The kitchen offers an island counter and casual breakfast room. Upstairs, the master suite includes a luxurious bath, dressing area and walk-in closet. The second floor is completed by three additional bedrooms and two baths.

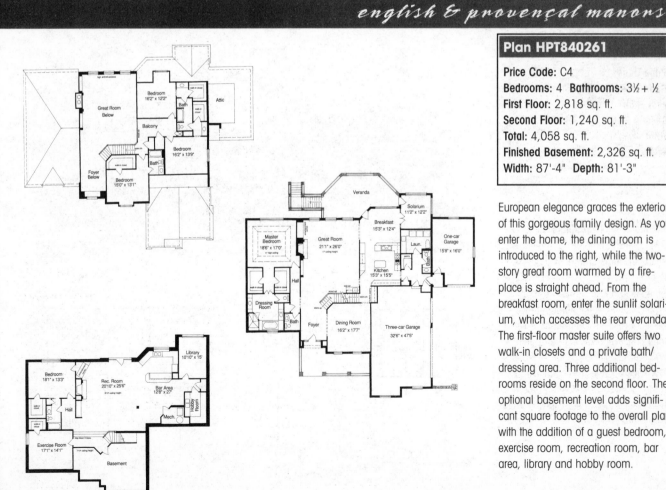

## Plan HPT840261

**Price Code:** C4
**Bedrooms:** 4  **Bathrooms:** 3½ + ½
**First Floor:** 2,818 sq. ft.
**Second Floor:** 1,240 sq. ft.
**Total:** 4,058 sq. ft.
**Finished Basement:** 2,326 sq. ft.
**Width:** 87'-4"  **Depth:** 81'-3"

European elegance graces the exterior of this gorgeous family design. As you enter the home, the dining room is introduced to the right, while the two-story great room warmed by a fireplace is straight ahead. From the breakfast room, enter the sunlit solarium, which accesses the rear veranda. The first-floor master suite offers two walk-in closets and a private bath/dressing area. Three additional bedrooms reside on the second floor. The optional basement level adds significant square footage to the overall plan with the addition of a guest bedroom, exercise room, recreation room, bar area, library and hobby room.

## Plan HPT840262

**Price Code:** C3
**Bedrooms:** 4 **Bathrooms:** 3½
**First Floor:** 2,654 sq. ft.
**Second Floor:** 1,013 sq. ft.
**Total:** 3,667 sq. ft.
**Width:** 75'-4" **Depth:** 74'-2"

European accents shape the exterior of this striking family home. Inside, the foyer is open to the dining room on the right and the living room straight ahead. Here, two sets of double doors open onto the rear covered porch. Casual areas of the home include a family room warmed by a fireplace and an island kitchen opening to a bayed breakfast room. Please specify basement, crawlspace or slab foundation when ordering.

## Plan HPT840263

**Price Code:** L2
**Bedrooms:** 5 **Bathrooms:** 4
**First Floor:** 2,042 sq. ft.
**Second Floor:** 2,137 sq. ft.
**Total:** 4,179 sq. ft.
**Width:** 63'-0" **Depth:** 66'-0"

© Stephen Fuller, Inc.

Quaint and traditional, this home features natural and informal materials, which add to its charm. The height of the elevation lends a stately presence to the entire home. Inside, formal living and dining areas flank the foyer. The great room is warmed by a fireplace and overlooks the rear porch. The gourmet island kitchen is thoughtfully placed between the dining room and the vaulted breakfast/sun room. This home is designed with a walkout basement foundation.

## Plan HPT840264

**Price Code:** L1
**Bedrooms:** 5  **Bathrooms:** 4½
**First Floor:** 2,095 sq. ft.
**Second Floor:** 1,954 sq. ft.
**Total:** 4,049 sq. ft.
**Width:** 56'-0"  **Depth:** 63'-0"

The French Country facade of this lovely design hints to the enchanting amenities found within. A two-story foyer welcomes you inside. To the right, a bayed living room is separated from the formal dining room by graceful columns. A butler's pantry leads to the gourmet island kitchen. The breakfast room accesses a rear covered porch and shares a casual area with the two-story family room. Here, a fireplace flanked by built-ins adds to the relaxing atmosphere. Bedroom 5 with a private bath converts to an optional study. Upstairs, the master suite offers palatial elegance. Please specify basement or crawlspace foundation when ordering.

## Plan HPT840266

**Price Code:** C2
**Bedrooms:** 4 **Bathrooms:** 3
**First Floor:** 2,067 sq. ft.
**Second Floor:** 1,129 sq. ft.
**Total:** 3,196 sq. ft.
**Width:** 69'-0" **Depth:** 63'-0"

This French chateau boasts all the charm of Europe and features all the modern conveniences for today's busy lifestyles. Inside, the foyer is flanked by the formal dining room and an optional room perfect for a guest suite, connecting to a hall bath. The great room is truly magnificent with an enormous hearth and two sets of double doors opening onto the rear porch. The kitchen connects to a breakfast/sun room for casual family dining. This home is designed with a walkout basement foundation.

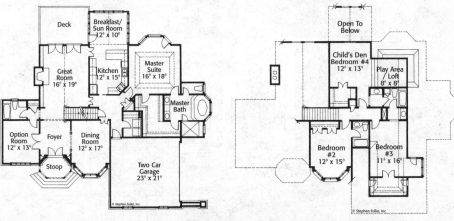

## Plan HPT840265

**Price Code:** C4
**Bedrooms:** 3 **Bathrooms:** 3½
**First Floor:** 2,200 sq. ft.
**Second Floor:** 835 sq. ft.
**Total:** 3,035 sq. ft.
**Width:** 95'-6" **Depth:** 64'-0"

This enchanting design features a unique facade and interior layout. The foyer introduces a beautiful staircase and is flanked on either side by a library and dining room. The master suite features a plush bath and double walk-in closet. Casual areas include the island kitchen, morning nook and family room warmed by a fireplace. Two additional bedrooms and a bonus room reside upstairs.

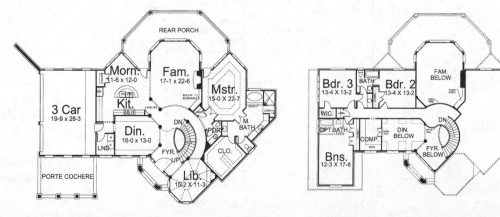

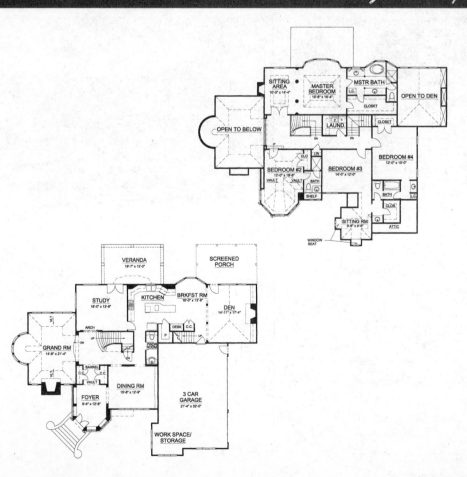

## Plan HPT840267

**Price Code:** C3
**Bedrooms:** 4  **Bathrooms:** 3½
**First Floor:** 2,007 sq. ft.
**Second Floor:** 1,959 sq. ft.
**Total:** 3,966 sq. ft.
**Width:** 77'-0"  **Depth:** 52'-0"

Interesting windows and rooflines give a unique character to this stucco facade. The European influences are unmistakable. To the right of the foyer, the study is highlighted by a beam ceiling, built-ins and floor-to-ceiling windows. The grand room is by itself to the left of the plan and includes a bayed sitting area and a fireplace. Another bay window brightens the breakfast room, which is found between the island kitchen and a den with a second fireplace. The living room and a grand stair hall complete the first floor. The elegant stairway leads up to three family bedrooms and a sumptuous master suite.

## Plan HPT840269

**Price Code:** L1
**Bedrooms:** 3 **Bathrooms:** 4½
**First Floor:** 2,480 sq. ft.
**Second Floor:** 1,315 sq. ft.
**Total:** 3,795 sq. ft.
**Finished Basement:** 1,136 sq. ft.
**Width:** 91'-9" **Depth:** 79'-2"

This incredible French Country design offers all the elegance of a chateau and all the amenities of the modern era. The first floor includes a sumptuous master suite, formal rooms and a gourmet kitchen. Two additional suites and a home office reside upstairs. The basement is reserved for future developments. The main and lower levels feature hillside terraces for outdoor enjoyment.

## Plan HPT840268

**Price Code:** C3
**Bedrooms:** 4 **Bathrooms:** 4
**Square Footage:** 3,064
**Bonus Room:** 366 sq. ft.
**Width:** 79'-6" **Depth:** 91'-0"

From a more graceful era, this estate evokes a sense of quiet refinement. Exquisite exterior detailing makes it a one-of-a-kind. Inside are distinctive treatments that make the floor plan unique and functional. The central foyer is enhanced with columns that define the dining room and formal living room. A beamed ceiling complements the den. The master suite includes a private garden with a fountain, pool access, a walk-in closet and a fireplace to the outdoor spa.

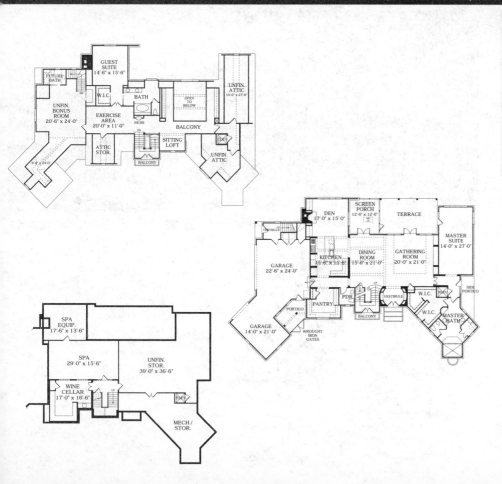

## Plan HPT840270

**Price Code:** L2
**Bedrooms:** 2  **Bathrooms:** 2½
**First Floor:** 2,911 sq. ft.
**Second Floor:** 1,345 sq. ft.
**Total:** 4,256 sq. ft.
**Finished Basement:** 857 sq. ft.
**Bonus Space:** 721 sq. ft.
**Width:** 107'-1"  **Depth:** 67'-7"

This captivating European manor speaks all the romance of the Old World. The right wing of the home is devoted to the master suite, which provides a deluxe master bath and double walk-in closet. The dining and gathering rooms combine for easy entertaining and open to the rear terrace and screened porch. The kitchen is opposite of a large pantry and faces the hearth-warmed den. The second floor includes a guest suite, an exercise room and unfinished space to be used as the family grows. The basement level adds luxury to exquisite planning with room for a spa and wine cellar.

## Plan HPT840272

**Price Code:** C4
**Bedrooms:** 4  **Bathrooms:** 3½
**First Floor:** 2,995 sq. ft.
**Second Floor:** 1,102 sq. ft.
**Total:** 4,097 sq. ft.
**Width:** 120'-6"  **Depth:** 58'-8"

This enchanted chateau sings of refined European luxury. A formal dining room and study flank the entry. The master bedroom is a sumptuous retreat with a bayed sitting area, pampering bath and two walk-in closets. A massive stone fireplace warms the great room. Casual areas include the kitchen, breakfast and recreation rooms. Three additional bedrooms are located upstairs.

## Plan HPT840271

**Price Code:** C3
**Bedrooms:** 4  **Bathrooms:** 3½
**Square Footage:** 3,549
**Bonus Room:** 426 sq. ft.
**Width:** 85'-0"  **Depth:** 85'-4"

With brick and stone and multiple rooflines, this luxurious European cottage is sure to be the envy of the neighborhood. A formal dining room and study flank the entry. The great room is warmed by a massive hearth flanked by built-ins. The master suite is located to the left of the plan and includes a sitting bay, private bath and huge walk-in closet. Three additional bedrooms are located on the right side of the plan.

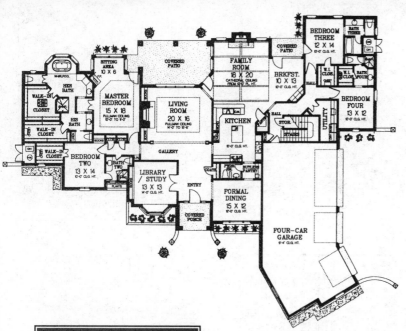

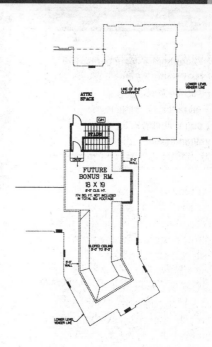

## Plan HPT840273

**Price Code:** C4

**Bedrooms:** 4  **Bathrooms:** 5½

**Square Footage:** 4,270

**Bonus Room:** 774 sq. ft.

**Width:** 112'-4"  **Depth:** 91'-3"

Both formal and informal spaces grace the floor plan of this Tudor one-story home. Inside, a formal dining room and library/study flank the entry. Fireplaces warm the living and family rooms. The master suite and one family bedroom sit on the left side of the plan, while two additional bedrooms reside on the right. The family room has a beam ceiling and cozy fireplace. Bonus space over the four-car garage adds 774 square feet—perfect for a guest suite or home office.

## Plan HPT840275

**Price Code:** C2
**Bedrooms:** 3  **Bathrooms:** 2½+½
**First Floor:** 2,532 sq. ft.
**Second Floor:** 650 sq. ft.
**Total:** 3,182 sq. ft.
**Bonus Room:** 383 sq. ft.
**Width:** 80'-0"  **Depth:** 77'-6"

A garage with barn doors gives this French country home a true country look. A recessed entry opens to the foyer, where columns and arches define the dining and living rooms. A butler's pantry leads to the island kitchen, which occupies part of a large open area that includes a sizable nook and a vaulted family room. To the right of the foyer are a den and the master suite.

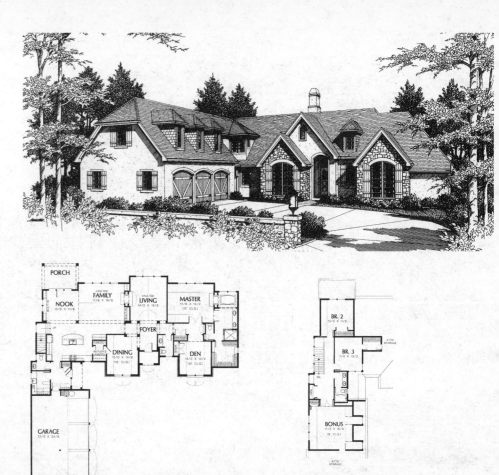

## Plan HPT840274

**Price Code:** C3
**Bedrooms:** 3  **Bathrooms:** 3½
**First Floor:** 2,698 sq. ft.
**Second Floor:** 819 sq. ft.
**Total:** 3,517 sq. ft.
**Bonus Room:** 370 sq. ft.
**Width:** 90'-6"  **Depth:** 84'-0"

If you've ever traveled the European countryside, you may have come upon a home much like this one. Stone accents combined with stucco add a touch of charm that introduces the marvelous floor plan found inside. The foyer opens onto a great room. To the left, you'll find a formal dining room; to the right, a quiet den. Just steps away resides the sitting room that introduces the grand master suite.

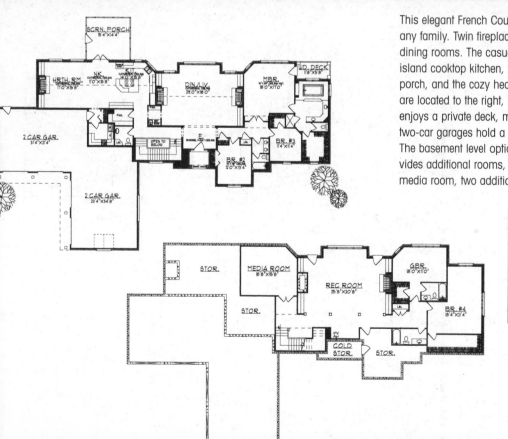

This elegant French Country estate is the perfect retreat for any family. Twin fireplaces warm the combined living and dining rooms. The casual area of the home includes the island cooktop kitchen, the nook accessing the screened porch, and the cozy hearth room. Three family bedrooms are located to the right, including the master suite, which enjoys a private deck, master bath and walk-in closet. Two two-car garages hold a sizable collection of family cars. The basement level option—perfect for a hillside site—provides additional rooms, which include a recreation room, media room, two additional bedrooms and a storage area.

## Plan HPT840276

**Price Code:** C1
**Bedrooms:** 4  **Bathrooms:** 4½
**Square Footage:** 2,941
**Finished Basement:** 2,127 sq. ft.
**Width:** 118'-4"  **Depth:** 64'-4"

## Plan HPT840277

**Price Code:** C1
**Bedrooms:** 3 **Bathrooms:** 2½
**First Floor:** 1,802 sq. ft.
**Second Floor:** 670 sq. ft.
**Total:** 2,472 sq. ft.
**Width:** 49'-0" **Depth:** 79'-0"

With all the charm and romance of the French countryside, this European design features great amenities for today's modern family. French shutters and a stucco facade dazzle the exterior. Inside, the foyer is flanked by the efficient kitchen and formal dining room. The kitchen serves the petite eating nook with ease. The living room is enhanced by a corner fireplace, wet bar and a built-in entertainment center complete with library shelves. The first-floor master suite features a bay-windowed wall, a private bath and two walk-in closets. Two additional bedrooms are located upstairs, sharing a bath.

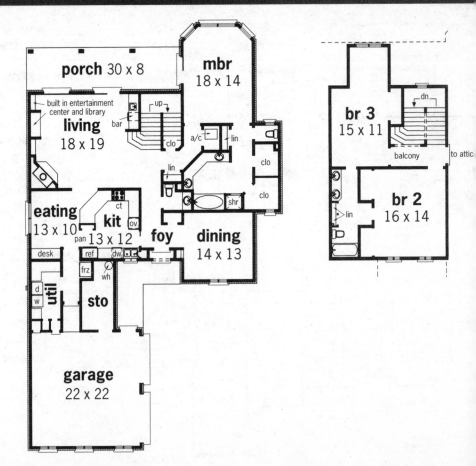

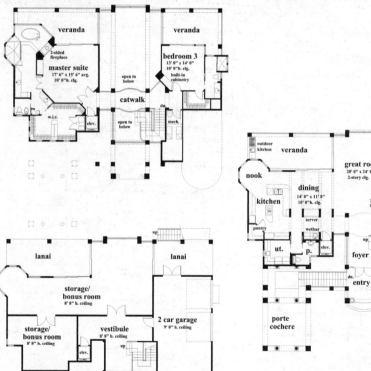

**Plan HPT840278**

**Price Code:** L2
**Bedrooms:** 3   **Bathrooms:** 3½
**First Floor:** 2,391 sq. ft.
**Second Floor:** 1,539 sq. ft.
**Total:** 3,930 sq. ft.
**Lower-Level Entry:** 429 sq. ft.
**Width:** 71'-0"   **Depth:** 69'-0"

Impressive pillars, keystone lintel arches, a covered carport, an abundance of windows and an alluring fountain are just a few of the decorative touches of this elegant design. The two-story foyer leads to a two-story great room, which enjoys built-in cabinetry, a two-sided fireplace and spectacular views to the rear property. To the left of the great room is the dining area, with a wet bar, island kitchen and nearby bayed breakfast nook. Bedroom 2 boasts a semi-circular wall of windows, a full bath and a walk-in closet. The second-floor master suite is filled with amenities, including a two-sided fireplace.

## Plan HPT840279

**Price Code:** C3
**Bedrooms:** 4  **Bathrooms:** 4½
**First Floor:** 2,035 sq. ft.
**Second Floor:** 1,543 sq. ft.
**Total:** 3,578 sq. ft.
**Bonus Room:** 366 sq. ft.
**Width:** 62'-0"  **Depth:** 76'-0"

Twin columns give entry into the two-story foyer of this fine home. A quiet study to the left would make a good home office. Entertaining will be pleasant, with a formal living room—complete with a fireplace—a formal dining room and a spacious family room. All of these entertainment areas open to a large covered porch, which is perfect for catching the ocean breezes. Note the fireplace in the family room as well as the one on the porch. The kitchen will please the gourmet of the family, with its abundance of amenities. The lavish master suite is designed to pamper with a private deck, a huge walk-in closet and a deluxe bath.

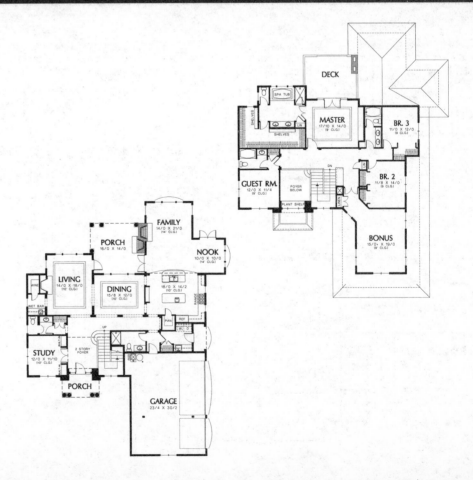

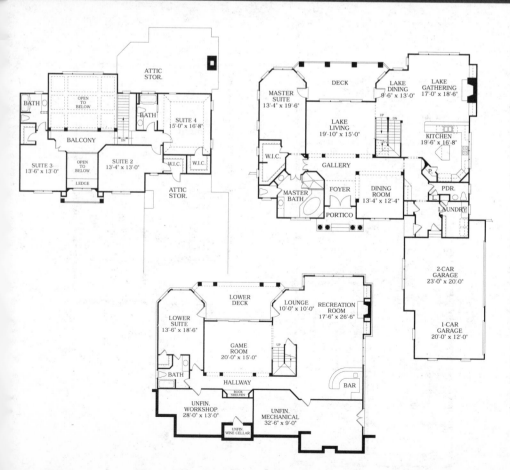

ATTIC STOR.

BATH

OPEN TO BELOW

BATH

SUITE 4
15'-0" x 16'-8"

BALCONY

SUITE 3
13'-6" x 13'-0"

OPEN TO BELOW

LEDGE

SUITE 2
13'-4" x 13'-0"

W.I.C.

W.I.C.

ATTIC STOR.

MASTER SUITE
13'-4" x 19'-6"

DECK

LAKE DINING
9'-6" x 13'-0"

LAKE GATHERING
17'-0" x 18'-6"

LAKE LIVING
19'-10" x 15'-0"

KITCHEN
19'-6" x 16'-8"

W.I.C.

GALLERY

MASTER BATH

FOYER

DINING ROOM
13'-4" x 12'-4"

PDR.

PORTICO

LAUNDRY

2-CAR GARAGE
23'-0" x 20'-0"

1-CAR GARAGE
20'-0" x 12'-0"

LOWER DECK

LOUNGE
10'-0" x 10'-0"

RECREATION ROOM
17'-6" x 26'-6"

LOWER SUITE
13'-6" x 18'-6"

GAME ROOM
20'-0" x 15'-0"

BATH

HALLWAY

BOOK SHELVES

BAR

UNFIN. WORKSHOP
28'-0" x 13'-0"

UNFIN. MECHANICAL
32'-6" x 9'-0"

UNFIN. WINE CELLAR

## Plan HPT840280

**Price Code:** L1
**Bedrooms:** 4  **Bathrooms:** 3½
**First Floor:** 2,538 sq. ft.
**Second Floor:** 1,171 sq. ft.
**Total:** 3,709 sq. ft.
**Finished Basement:** 1,784 sq. ft.
**Width:** 67'-7"  **Depth:** 85'-1"

This impressive Mediterranean design is dazzled in Italianate style. A front portico offers a warm welcome into the main level. The master suite is located to the left and includes rear-deck access, a double walk-in closet and pampering master bath. The island kitchen serves the formal and casual dining areas with ease. The casual gathering area is warmed by a fireplace. Three additional family suites reside upstairs, along with two baths and a balcony overlooking the two-story living room.

## Plan HPT840281

**Price Code:** A3
**Bedrooms:** 3 **Bathrooms:** 2½
**First Floor:** 1,270 sq. ft.
**Second Floor:** 630 sq. ft.
**Total:** 1,900 sq. ft.
**Width:** 28'-0" **Depth:** 76'-0"

Possessing an irresistible charm, this electric French design will elicit accolades from all who pass by. The double front porch provides a shady spot for a cool drink and a moment of relaxation. A spacious foyer, ample enough for a cherished antique, greets those who enter. Just beyond, the great room with its soaring ceiling gives additional flair to this open and inviting plan. An open-railed stairwell leads to a dramatic landing that overlooks the great room below. Access the second-floor porch easily from this landing. Two spacious bedrooms share a compartmented bath; each has a separate vanity and a walk-in closet.

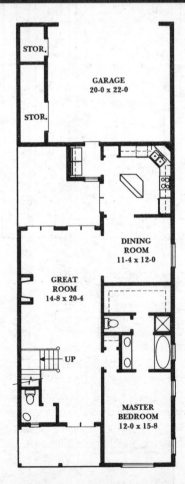

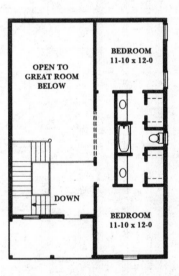

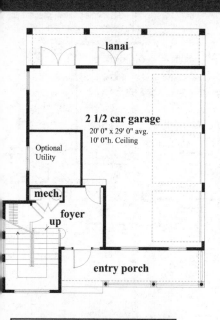

lanai

2 1/2 car garage
20' 0" x 29' 0" avg.
10' 0"h. Ceiling

Optional
Utility

mech.

foyer
up

entry porch

veranda

window
seat

built-in
cabinetry

great room
18' 0" x 20' 0"
10' 0"h. clg.

fireplace

built-in
cabinetry

window
seat

dn.

up

ut.

p.

dining
10' 0" x 13' 0"
10' 0"h. clg.

kitchen
15' 0" x 15' 0"
10' 0"h. clg.

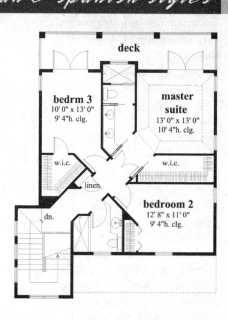

deck

bedrm 3
10' 0" x 13' 0"
9' 4"h. clg.

master
suite
13' 0" x 13' 0"
10' 4"h. clg.

w.i.c.

w.i.c.

linen

dn.

bedroom 2
12' 8" x 11' 0"
9' 4"h. clg.

## Plan HPT840282

**Price Code:** A3
**Bedrooms:** 3 **Bathrooms:** 2½
**First Floor:** 874 sq. ft.
**Second Floor:** 880 sq. ft.
**Total:** 1,754 sq. ft.
**Lower-Level Entry:** 242 sq. ft.
**Width:** 34'-0" **Depth:** 43'-0"

A stately tower adds a sense of grandeur to contemporary high-pitched rooflines on this dreamy Mediterranean-style villa. Surrounded by outdoor views, the living space extends to a veranda through three sets of French doors. Decorative columns announce the dining area, which boasts a ten-foot ceiling and views of its own. Tall arch-top windows bathe a winding staircase with sunlight or moonlight. The upper-level sleeping quarters include a master retreat that offers a bedroom with views and access to the observation deck. Secondary bedrooms share a full bath and linen storage. Bedroom 3 features a walk-in closet and French doors to the deck.

## Plan HPT840283

**Price Code:** A3
**Bedrooms:** 3 **Bathrooms:** 2
**First Floor:** 1,342 sq. ft.
**Second Floor:** 511 sq. ft.
**Total:** 1,853 sq. ft.
**Width:** 44'-0" **Depth:** 40'-0"

Historic architectural details and time-less materials come together in this outrageously beautiful home. With a perfect Mediterranean spirit, arch-top windows create curb appeal and allow the beauty and warmth of nature with-in. To the rear of the plan, an elegant dining room easily flexes to serve tra-ditional events as well as impromptu gatherings. An angled island counter accents the gourmet kitchen and per-mits wide interior vistas. The master bedroom features a spacious bedroom that leads outside to a private porch. On the upper level, an open deck extends the square footage of one of the secondary bedrooms.

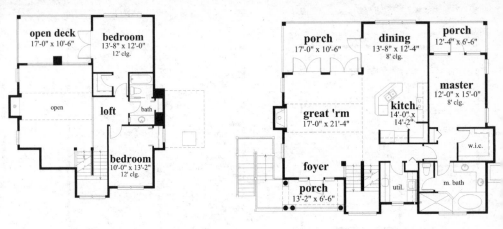

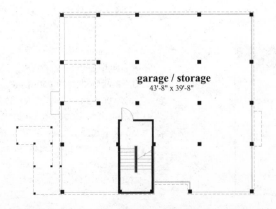

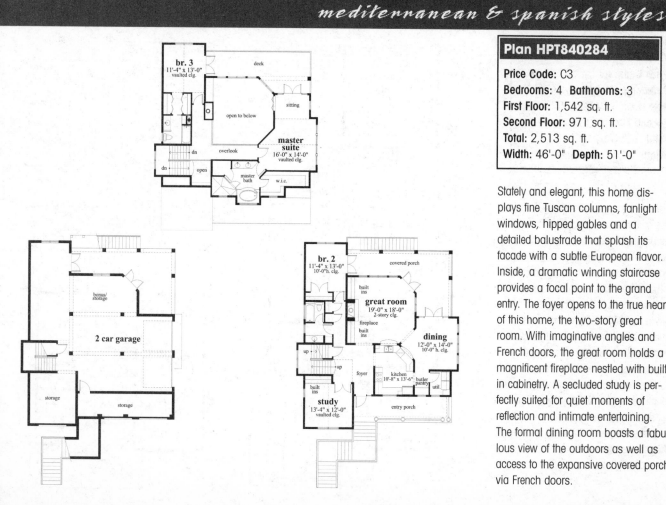

**br. 3**
11'-4" x 13'-0"
vaulted clg.

deck

open to below

sitting

open to below

**master suite**
16'-0" x 14'-0"
vaulted clg.

overlook

dn

dn

open

master bath

w.i.c.

bonus/ storage

**2 car garage**

storage

storage

**br. 2**
11'-4" x 13'-0"
10'-0" h. clg.

covered porch

built ins

**great room**
19'-0" x 18'-0"
2-story clg.

fireplace

built ins

**dining**
12'-0" x 14'-0"
10'-0" h. clg.

up

up

foyer

kitchen
10'-8" x 13'-6"

butler pantry

util.

built ins

**study**
13'-4" x 12'-0"
vaulted clg.

entry porch

## Plan HPT840284

**Price Code:** C3
**Bedrooms:** 4 **Bathrooms:** 3
**First Floor:** 1,542 sq. ft.
**Second Floor:** 971 sq. ft.
**Total:** 2,513 sq. ft.
**Width:** 46'-0" **Depth:** 51'-0"

Stately and elegant, this home displays fine Tuscan columns, fanlight windows, hipped gables and a detailed balustrade that splash its facade with a subtle European flavor. Inside, a dramatic winding staircase provides a focal point to the grand entry. The foyer opens to the true heart of this home, the two-story great room. With imaginative angles and French doors, the great room holds a magnificent fireplace nestled with built-in cabinetry. A secluded study is perfectly suited for quiet moments of reflection and intimate entertaining. The formal dining room boasts a fabulous view of the outdoors as well as access to the expansive covered porch via French doors.

Photo caption: ©Jeffrey Jacobs/Architectural Photography courtesy of Looney Ricks Kiss Architects

This home, as shown in the photograph, may differ from the actual blueprints. For more detailed information, please check the floor plans carefully.

## Plan HPT840285

**Price Code:** C4
**Bedrooms:** 5 **Bathrooms:** 3½
**First Floor:** 1,915 sq. ft.
**Second Floor:** 1,360 sq. ft.
**Total:** 3,275 sq. ft.
**Width:** 39'-2" **Depth:** 97'-2"

This exquisite facade weds a distinctly modern look with traditional details such as a bay window, gabled roofline and Doric-style columns. Inside, the formal rooms flank a foyer that leads to a gallery hall. The living room's fireplace is positioned to allow dinner guests to enjoy its glow. A U-shaped kitchen also serves a casual eating area, which opens to the family room. Tall windows and a single door allow plenty of natural light to brighten the master suite. Upstairs, four family bedrooms share two full baths, a sitting area and gallery hall.

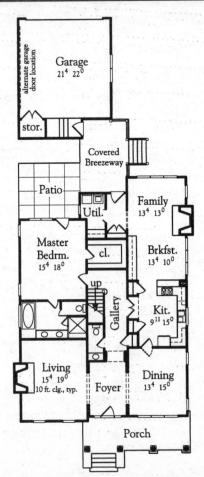

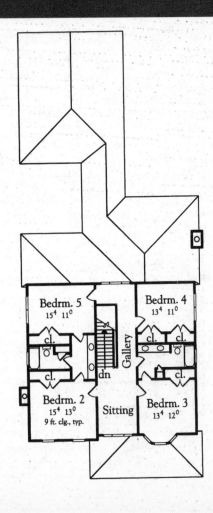

This Mediterranean dream home is much more than just a pretty face. Form follows function throughout a well-arranged interior—with rooms that flex and dynamic space that suits changing lifestyles. The dining room converts from a private place for planned occasions to an extension of the living area, which offers a fireplace. The master bedroom features a magnificent bay window and a corner garden tub. Three bedrooms reside upstairs—two of these secondary bedrooms are enhanced by soaring cathedral ceilings. ©2000 Donald A. Gardner, Inc.

## Plan HPT840286

**Price Code:** C2
**Bedrooms:** 4 **Bathrooms:** 2½
**First Floor:** 1,679 sq. ft.
**Second Floor:** 921 sq. ft.
**Total:** 2,600 sq. ft.
**Width:** 58'-0" **Depth:** 58'-10"

## Plan HPT840287

Price Code: C3
Bedrooms: 4   Bathrooms: 2½
First Floor: 1,650 sq. ft.
Second Floor: 1,557 sq. ft.
Total: 3,207 sq. ft.
Width: 45'-6"   Depth: 75'-6"

This large and roomy contemporary home offers plenty of space for the family on the grow. The open-plan living/dining room features glass-block accents, an archway entry from the two-level foyer, and a gas fireplace for added warmth. The spacious kitchen, featuring a pantry, telephone desk and breakfast bar, opens to an informal eating area with double-door access to the rear deck. The den can function as a home office or as a guest room. The master bedroom, featuring a gas fireplace as a room divider, has its own walk-in closet and private bath with a soaking tub. The upstairs bedrooms share a three-piece bathroom, brightened by a skylight.

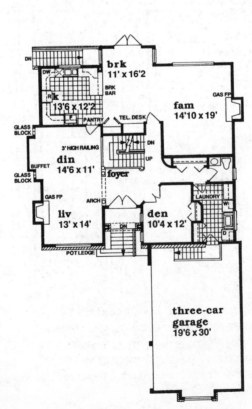

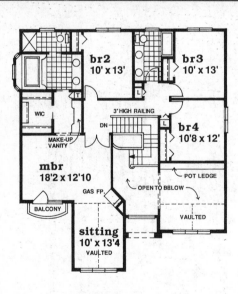

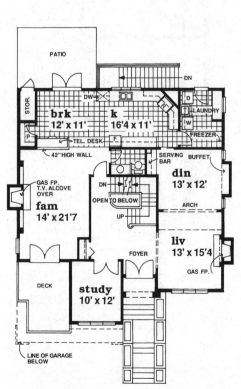

## Plan HPT840288

**Price Code:** C3
**Bedrooms:** 4  **Bathrooms:** 2½
**First Floor:** 1,664 sq. ft.
**Second Floor:** 1,404 sq. ft.
**Total:** 3,068 sq. ft.
**Width:** 42'-4"  **Depth:** 50'-4"

This spacious four-bedroom design offers plenty of extras. Open living and dining areas boast distinctive styling, including the lovely archways from the foyer. Among the extras in the dining area are a serving bar and built-in space for a buffet. The large kitchen offers ample counter space and opens to the breakfast area with a telephone desk, pantry and double French doors to the patio. The family room features a TV alcove over the gas fireplace. The study, accessed from the front foyer, overlooks the front yard. The luxurious master bedroom boasts its own separate sitting room with a vaulted ceiling.

## Plan HPT840289

**Price Code:** A4
**Bedrooms:** 4 **Bathrooms:** 3
**Square Footage:** 2,391
**Width:** 61'-10" **Depth:** 64'-11"

Quoins, keystone lintels and two picture windows adorn the stucco exterior of this charming four-bedroom home. Inside, the foyer introduces a dining room adorned with graceful columns. The nearby kitchen features a sunny breakfast nook, walk-in pantry and an angled serving bar to the living room. A hearth with built-in shelves enhances the living room, which also includes rear-porch access. Two family bedrooms to the right share a two-sink bath, while on the left a third family bedroom comes with a walk-in closet and a private bath. A tray ceiling accents the master suite, which also enjoys two walk-in closets, two vanities and a separate shower and tub.

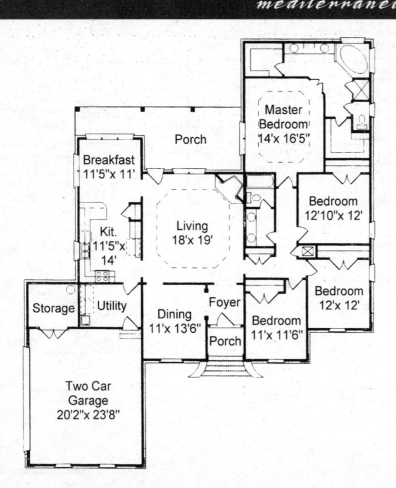

## Plan HPT840290

**Price Code:** A4
**Bedrooms:** 4  **Bathrooms:** 2
**Square Footage:** 2,243
**Width:** 62'-10"  **Depth:** 75'-3"

This stunning Contemporary design, spiced with Mediterranean influences, will be the envy of the neighborhood. Stucco, corner quoins and varied rooflines enhance the exterior, while interior spaces are packed with modern amenities. Inside, the foyer is flanked by family bedrooms and a formal dining room. The formal living room is warmed by a corner fireplace and features rear-porch access. The compact kitchen serves the casual breakfast room with ease. The master bedroom suite includes two walk-in closets and a pampering bath. Three additional bedrooms share a hall bath. The plan is completed by a utility room that connects to the two-car garage with storage.

## Plan HPT840291

**Price Code:** A4
**Bedrooms:** 4 **Bathrooms:** 3½
**First Floor:** 2,112 sq. ft.
**Second Floor:** 361 sq. ft.
**Total:** 2,473 sq. ft.
**Width:** 59'-10" **Depth:** 69'-5"

This exciting Contemporary design is enhanced by distinctively European details. Just inside, the foyer is flanked by family bedrooms and a formal dining room. Straight ahead, the formal two-story living room is warmed by a cozy fireplace. The kitchen is open to the casual breakfast room. The master suite is located to the left and includes a roomy walk-in closet, private bath and rear-porch/patio access. On the opposite side of the home, two additional family bedrooms share a hall bath. A utility room, powder room and two-car garage complete the first floor. Upstairs, an additional bedroom features a private bath and walk-in closet—perfect for a guest suite. Please specify crawlspace or slab foundation when ordering.

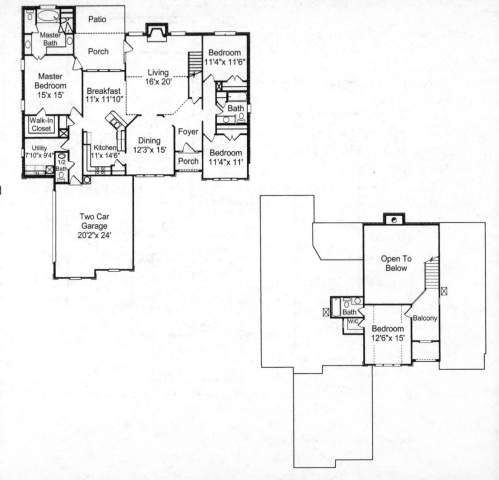

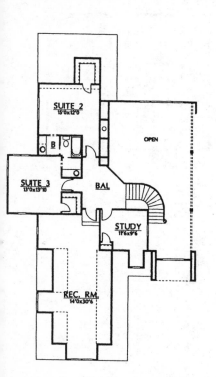

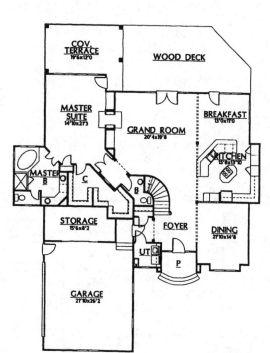

### Plan HPT840292

**Price Code:** C3
**Bedrooms:** 3 **Bathrooms:** 2½
**First Floor:** 2,062 sq. ft.
**Second Floor:** 905 sq. ft.
**Total:** 2,967 sq. ft.
**Bonus Space:** 550 sq. ft.
**Width:** 61'-6" **Depth:** 79'-0"

This dramatic Transitional-style home is a pampering delight for the whole family. A portico and grand arching entrance announce your entry. The island kitchen easily serves the formal dining room and casual breakfast room. The two-story grand room shares a see-through fireplace with the master suite. The lavish first-floor suite also includes a double walk-in closet and sumptuous private bath. The rear covered terrace and wood deck are ideal for outdoor entertaining year round. Two additional suites—each with a walk-in closet and sharing a full bath—reside upstairs. A second-floor study and recreation room add to this enriching family design.

## Plan HPT840293

**Price Code:** C3
**Bedrooms:** 4  **Bathrooms:** 2½
**First Floor:** 1,884 sq. ft.
**Second Floor:** 1,335 sq. ft.
**Total:** 3,219 sq. ft.
**Width:** 68'-3"  **Depth:** 50'-8"

This distinctively European and Mediterranean design offers two levels of exquisite luxury. Inside, the entry is flanked on either side by the study brightened by a bay window and the formal living room warmed by a fireplace. The kitchen features an island workstation and serves the dining room and breakfast bay with ease. The casual family room is vaulted and is warmed by the glow of a country fireplace flanked by built-ins. The rear stone terrace encourages outdoor relaxation. A vaulted master suite resides upstairs, with its pampering bath, dressing room and two walk-in closets. Three other family bedrooms share a hall bath.

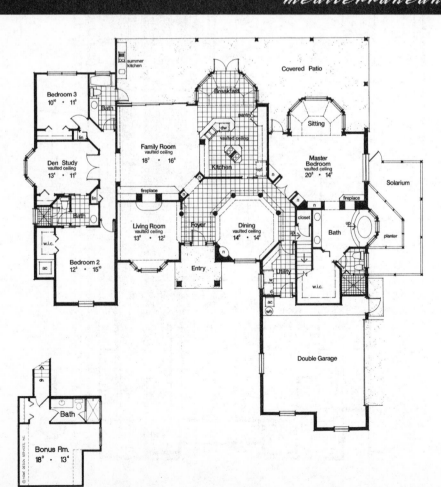

## Plan HPT840294

**Price Code:** C3
**Bedrooms:** 3  **Bathrooms:** 3
**Square Footage:** 2,908
**Bonus Room:** 379 sq. ft.
**Width:** 77'-0"  **Depth:** 82'-8"

This exquisite design features a contemporary layout for the modern family. Inside, formal rooms flank the entry—the living room is warmed by a fireplace, while columns frame the octagon shape of the dining room. The island kitchen is central and connects to a bayed nook that opens to the rear covered patio. The master wing features a brilliant bayed sitting area, a private whirlpool bath and huge walk-in closet. The side solarium is a serene touch. Two additional bedrooms, an optional study and two baths are located on the opposite side of the home.

## Plan HPT840295

**Price Code:** L2
**Bedrooms:** 4  **Bathrooms:** 3½
**Square Footage:** 2,262
**Finished Basement:** 1,822 sq. ft.
**Width:** 109'-11"  **Depth:** 46'-0"

This exquisite home is definitely Mediterranean, with its corner quoins, lintels and tall entry. This home features a dining room, a massive family room with a fireplace, a gourmet kitchen with a breakfast area, and a laundry room. Finishing the first floor is a lavish master suite which enjoys a vast walk-in closet, a sitting area and a pampering private bath. The lower level features three suites, two full baths, a pool room and a recreation room/theater along with two storage rooms.

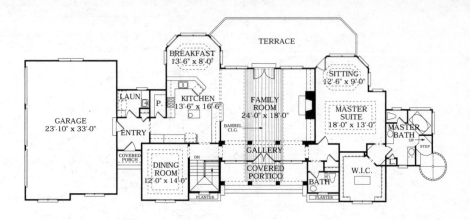

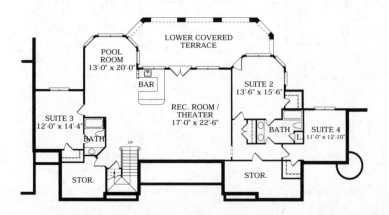

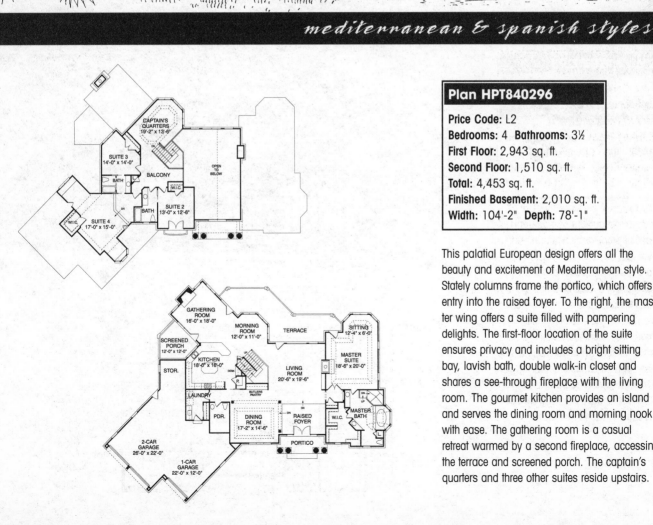

### Plan HPT840296

**Price Code:** L2
**Bedrooms:** 4  **Bathrooms:** 3½
**First Floor:** 2,943 sq. ft.
**Second Floor:** 1,510 sq. ft.
**Total:** 4,453 sq. ft.
**Finished Basement:** 2,010 sq. ft.
**Width:** 104'-2"  **Depth:** 78'-1"

This palatial European design offers all the beauty and excitement of Mediterranean style. Stately columns frame the portico, which offers entry into the raised foyer. To the right, the master wing offers a suite filled with pampering delights. The first-floor location of the suite ensures privacy and includes a bright sitting bay, lavish bath, double walk-in closet and shares a see-through fireplace with the living room. The gourmet kitchen provides an island and serves the dining room and morning nook with ease. The gathering room is a casual retreat warmed by a second fireplace, accessing the terrace and screened porch. The captain's quarters and three other suites reside upstairs.

## Plan HPT840297

Price Code: A4
Bedrooms: 3  Bathrooms: 2
Square Footage: 2,000
Width: 65'-10"  Depth: 51'-11"

An arched entrance, a sunburst and sidelights around the four-paneled door provide a touch of class to this European-style home. An angled bar opens the kitchen and breakfast room to the living room with bookcases and a fireplace. The master suite boasts a sloped ceiling and private bath with a five-foot turning radius. Two family bedrooms provide ample closet space and share a hall bath.

*mediterranean & spanish styles*

## Plan HPT840298

Price Code: A4
Bedrooms: 3  Bathrooms: 2
Square Footage: 1,932
Width: 53'-5"  Depth: 65'-10"

Enter this beautiful home through graceful archways and columns. The foyer, dining room and living room are one open space, defined by a creative room arrangement. The living room opens to the breakfast room and porch. The bedrooms are off a small hall reached through an archway. Two family bedrooms share a bath, while the master suite enjoys a private bath with a double-bowl vanity. Please specify slab or crawlspace foundation when ordering.

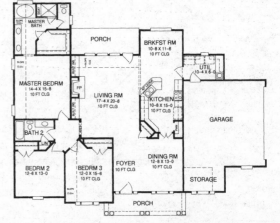

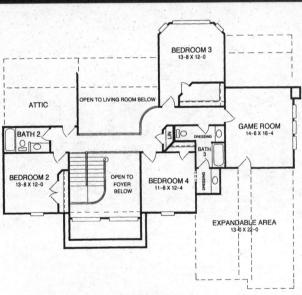

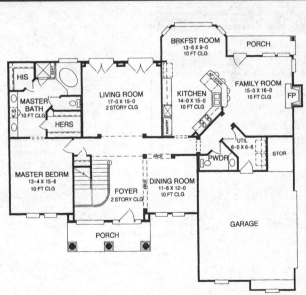

### Plan HPT840299

**Price Code:** C3
**Bedrooms:** 4  **Bathrooms:** 3½
**First Floor:** 1,919 sq. ft.
**Second Floor:** 1,190 sq. ft.
**Total:** 3,109 sq. ft.
**Bonus Space:** 286 sq. ft.
**Width:** 64'-6"  **Depth:** 55'-10"

Flower boxes, arches and multi-pane windows all combine to create the elegant facade of this four-bedroom home. Inside, the two-story foyer has a formal dining room to its right and leads to a two-story living room that is filled with light. An efficient kitchen has a bayed breakfast room and shares a snack bar with a cozy family room. Located on the first floor for privacy, the master suite is graced with a luxurious bath. Upstairs, three secondary bedrooms share two full baths and have access to a large game room. Please specify basement, crawlspace or slab foundation when ordering.

## Plan HPT840300

**Price Code:** C4
**Bedrooms:** 3  **Bathrooms:** 3½
**Square Footage:** 3,398
**Width:** 121'-5"  **Depth:** 96'-2"

Bringing the outdoors in through a multitude of bay windows is what this design is all about. The grand foyer opens to the living room with a magnificent view of the covered lanai. The study and dining room flank the foyer. The master suite is found on the left with an opulent bath and views of the private garden. The kitchen adjoins the nook that boasts a mitered glass bay window overlooking the lanai.

## Plan HPT840301

**Price Code:** C1
**Bedrooms:** 3  **Bathrooms:** 2½
**First Floor:** 1,336 sq. ft.
**Second Floor:** 1,186 sq. ft.
**Total:** 2,522 sq. ft.
**Width:** 58'-9"  **Depth:** 54'-10"

L

A covered porch leads inside this extravagant two-story home to a wide tiled foyer. A curving staircase makes an elegant statement in the open space between the formal living and dining rooms. A through-fireplace warms the nook and the family room, which accesses the rear terrace. Look for a wet bar and glass shelves here. Upstairs, the exclusive master bedroom includes a sitting area, walk-in closet, pampering whirlpool tub and private deck.

**QUOTE ONE®**

Cost to build? See page 246
to order complete cost estimate
to build this house in your area!

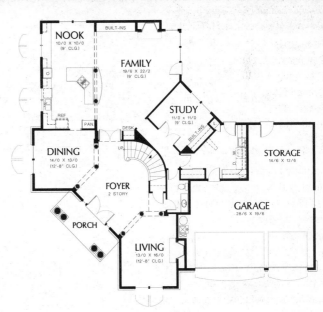

### Plan HPT840302

**Price Code:** C3
**Bedrooms:** 4  **Bathrooms:** 2½
**First Floor:** 1,923 sq. ft.
**Second Floor:** 1,710 sq. ft.
**Total:** 3,633 sq. ft.
**Width:** 66'-0"  **Depth:** 60'-0"

This uniquely designed home is dazzled in Mediterranean influences and eye-catching luxury. A grand arching entrance welcomes you inside to a spacious foyer that introduces a curved staircase and flanking living and dining rooms on either side. Casual areas of the home are clustered to the rear left of the plan and include a kitchen, nook and family room warmed by a fireplace. The professional study is a quiet retreat. The three-car garage offers spacious storage. Upstairs, the master bedroom enjoys a private bath and roomy walk-in closet. Three additional bedrooms share a hall bath and open playroom.

## Plan HPT840303

**Price Code:** A4
**Bedrooms:** 4 **Bathrooms:** 3
**Square Footage:** 2,409
**Width:** 65'-0" **Depth:** 85'-0"

This classic design is impressive at every turn. The entry is adorned with square and round columns and a keystone lintel above a transom and double doors. The tiled foyer faces the living room with its wall of glass. To the right is the dining room, featuring a clerestory window. The master wing enjoys a sitting area and a luxurious bath. Two family bedrooms share a full bath.

Mediterranean splendor abounds as you enter under the tiered portico. The foyer opens to the living room on the left and the dining room on the right where attention to details creates elegance and excitement. The living and gathering rooms share a see-through fireplace. The magnificent master suite offers a wet bar in the bayed sitting area.

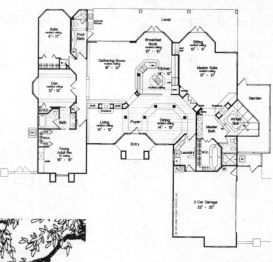

## Plan HPT840304

**Price Code:** C2
**Bedrooms:** 4 **Bathrooms:** 3
**Square Footage:** 3,280
**Width:** 72'-4" **Depth:** 82'-0"

**Plan HPT840305**

**Price Code:** A4
**Bedrooms:** 4  **Bathrooms:** 3
**Square Footage:** 2,348
**Width:** 61'-4"  **Depth:** 65'-0"

This home boasts great curb appeal with its Mediterranean influences—glass-block and muntin windows, a decorative oval window, impressive pillars and a stucco facade. The family side of this home abounds with thoughtful design features, like the island in the kitchen, the media/fireplace wall in the family room and the mitered glass breakfast nook. A dramatic arched entry into the master suite leads to a gently curving wall of glass block, a double vanity, oversized shower, compartmented toilet and large walk-in closet. Another special feature is the design of the three secondary bedrooms, which share private bath facilities.

## Plan HPT840306

**Price Code:** A4
**Bedrooms:** 3 **Bathrooms:** 2
**Square Footage:** 2,367
**Width:** 76'-0" **Depth:** 71'-4"

The impressive entry into this Mediterranean-style home leads directly into a spacious gathering room, with unique angles and a mitered glass window. This is the perfect home for the family that entertains! The large gathering room and covered porch with a summer kitchen are ready for a pool party! Elegance and style grace this split floor plan, with large bedrooms and a very spacious kitchen/breakfast nook area. The kitchen includes a center island and a walk-in pantry. The master suite showcases a fireplace next to French doors, which lead onto the covered porch at the rear.

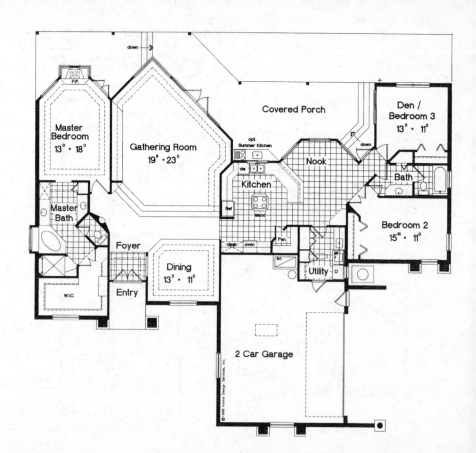

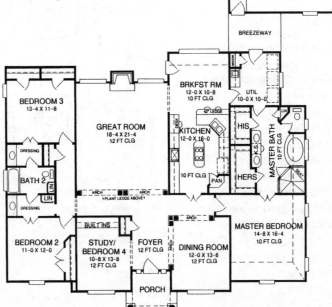

Offering unique design features, this cozy bungalow is charming with stucco, corner quoins and brick accents. The foyer leads to a spacious great room with a warming fireplace. The dining room resides across from the kitchen for easy entertaining. The kitchen is well-appointed with an angled sink and pantry storage. A two-car garage is located at the rear of the plan. The master bedroom includes His and Hers walk-in closets and a private bath. Two additional bedrooms share a Jack-and-Jill bath, but have their own dressing room with vanity sink. Please specify crawlspace or slab foundation when ordering.

## Plan HPT840307

**Price Code:** C1
**Bedrooms:** 3 **Bathrooms:** 2
**Square Footage:** 2,583
**Width:** 67'-1" **Depth:** 79'-4"

## Plan HPT840308

**Price Code:** C1
**Bedrooms:** 3  **Bathrooms:** 2½
**Square Footage:** 2,257
**Width:** 64'-0"  **Depth:** 67'-6"

A covered and skylit rear patio, graced by an array of columns and a built-in barbe-cue, is the highlight of this casual design. The interior is open and lives easily. The breakfast room and efficient kitchen over-look the sunken family room, which is warmed by a hearth. The master bedroom boasts a walk-in closet, private patio and luxurious bath with a sunken whirlpool tub. A den, with a walk-in closet, can be used as a fourth bedroom. Additional bedrooms share a full bath that has patio access.

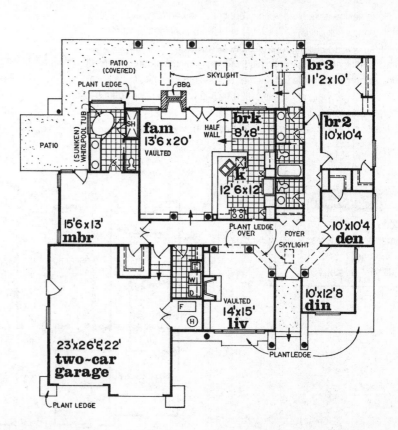

J.N.HANSEN S.D.C.

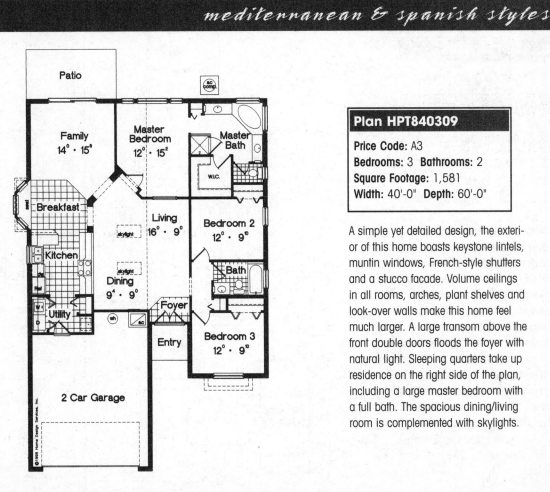

### Plan HPT840309

**Price Code:** A3
**Bedrooms:** 3 **Bathrooms:** 2
**Square Footage:** 1,581
**Width:** 40'-0" **Depth:** 60'-0"

A simple yet detailed design, the exterior of this home boasts keystone lintels, muntin windows, French-style shutters and a stucco facade. Volume ceilings in all rooms, arches, plant shelves and look-over walls make this home feel much larger. A large transom above the front double doors floods the foyer with natural light. Sleeping quarters take up residence on the right side of the plan, including a large master bedroom with a full bath. The spacious dining/living room is complemented with skylights.

## Plan HPT840310

**Price Code:** C1
**Bedrooms:** 4 **Bathrooms:** 3
**Square Footage:** 2,781
**Bonus Room:** 319 sq. ft.
**Width:** 64'-10" **Depth:** 76'-9"

A multi-faceted facade and classic arches blend with an intricate hipped-roof design, dressing this home with a sheer sense of elegance. The dining and living rooms meld with the breakfast nook, creating an expansive common area that spills out onto the rear covered porch. The four bedrooms are split with two on each side of the plan—the master suite on the left boasts a lavish master bath and twin walk-in closets. The unfinished game room easily converts to a home office or attic storage. Please specify crawlspace or slab foundation when ordering.

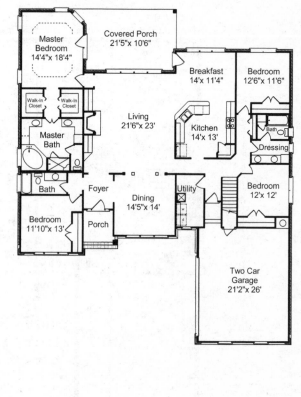

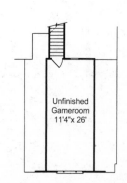

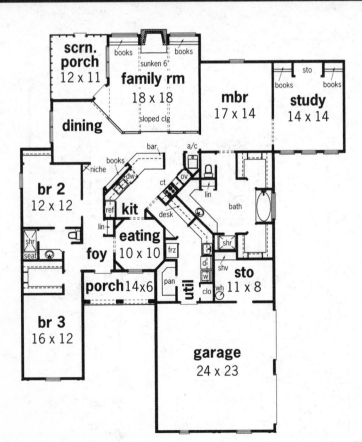

**scrn. porch** 12 x 11

books | books
sunken 6"

**family rm** 18 x 18

sloped clg

**mbr** 17 x 14

sto
books | books

**study** 14 x 14

**dining**

bar | a/c

books

niche

**br 2** 12 x 12

dw
ref | ct | ov
**kit** | desk | lin

**bath**

shr | seat

lin

**eating** 10 x 10

**foy**

frz

shr

**br 3** 16 x 12

**porch** 14 x 6

pan

util

d/w | shv | **sto** 11 x 8
wh | clo

**garage** 24 x 23

### Plan HPT840311

**Price Code:** A4
**Bedrooms:** 3  **Bathrooms:** 2
**Square Footage:** 2,349
**Width:** 63'-0"  **Depth:** 74'-0"

This stunning Sun Country design offers a convenient arrangement of rooms all on one level. Inside, the kitchen with a serving bar offers easy access to the casual eating room and the dining room. Two family bedrooms are located to the left and share a hall bath. The master bedroom enjoys a spacious bath with twin walk-in closets and a private study with built-in bookshelves. A sloped ceiling shapes the cozy family room warmed by a fireplace with flanking bookshelves. The rear screened porch is a brisk retreat. The utility room leads to the two-car garage with storage. Please specify crawlspace or slab foundation when ordering.

## Plan HPT840312

**Price Code:** C1
**Bedrooms:** 4 **Bathrooms:** 3
**Square Footage:** 2,743
**Width:** 67'-0" **Depth:** 75'-0"

Monumental arches grace this classic facade, allowing light to spill into the spacious interior of this four-bedroom home. The dining room sits to the right of the foyer, open to the living room and conveniently near the kitchen. Two family bedrooms share a full bath and convenient access to the garage at the right of the design. The kitchen, breakfast nook and family room feature an open layout. The U-shaped kitchen enjoys a serving bar, walk-in pantry, built-in desk and rectangular island work area. Enjoy plenty of evenings at home in this beautiful family room with its corner fireplace, built-in shelves and lovely views of the backyard.

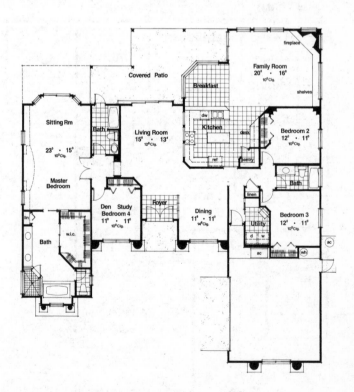

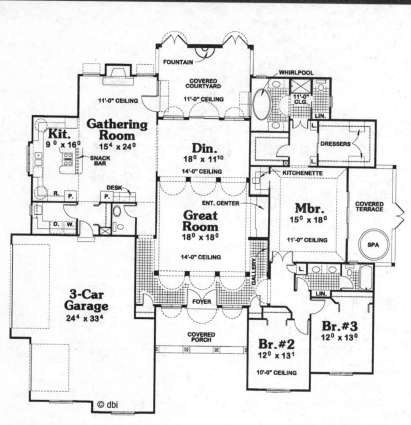

## Plan HPT840313

**Price Code:** C3
**Bedrooms:** 3 **Bathrooms:** 2½
**Square Footage:** 2,715
**Width:** 72'-0" **Depth:** 64'-8"

This exquisite Sun Country features stunning Mediterranean accents that combine Old World style with modern convenience. Three arches welcome you to a covered front porch, which opens into a spacious tiled foyer. Enchanting arches frame the great room and formal dining room. The computer alcove is a modern touch. The island snack-bar kitchen opens to a casual gathering room warmed by a fireplace. At the rear, a covered courtyard is a relaxing retreat, featuring a serene built-in fountain. The luxurious master wing offers a private covered terrace with a spa, a kitchenette, a whirlpool bath and two huge walk-in closets—one with built-in dressers. Please specify basement, crawlspace or slab foundation when ordering.

© desian basics inc.

## Plan HPT840315

**Price Code:** C3
**Bedrooms:** 3  **Bathrooms:** 2½
**Square Footage:** 2,647
**Width:** 66'-8"  **Depth:** 79'-8"

A convenient one-story floor plan is provided for this attractive Sun country home. A covered front porch welcomes you inside to a foyer flanked on either side by a den and a formal dining room. A fireplace in the great room warms family and friends. The kitchen opens to a breakfast nook. The rear screened porch is enhanced by a cathedral ceiling. Please specify basement, crawlspace or slab foundation when ordering.

## Plan HPT840314

**Price Code:** L1
**Bedrooms:** 5  **Bathrooms:** 3½
**Main Level:** 2,812 sq. ft.
**Lower Level:** 2,827 sq. ft.
**Total:** 5,639 sq. ft.
**Width:** 95'-0"  **Depth:** 62'-0"

Mediterranean elegance shapes the facade of this tempting design. A formal dining room and den flank the entry inside. The snack-bar kitchen, breakfast bay and hearth room are open to one another for casual family gatherings. The main-level master suite boasts a private wood deck, master bath and walk-in closet. The basement level offers four additional bedrooms, a family room, toy room and exercise room.

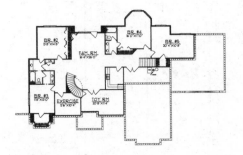

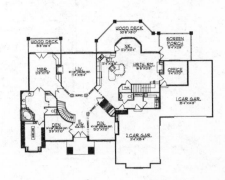

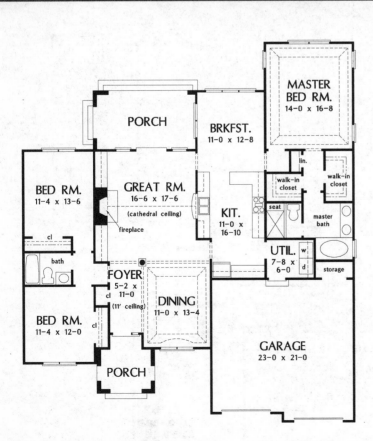

PORCH

BRKFST.
11-0 x 12-8

MASTER
BED RM.
14-0 x 16-8

BED RM.
11-4 x 13-6

GREAT RM.
16-6 x 17-6

(cathedral ceiling)

fireplace

KIT.
11-0 x
16-10

lin.

walk-in
closet

walk-in
closet

seat

master
bath

UTIL.
7-8 x
6-0

w
d

storage

cl

bath

FOYER
5-2 x
11-0
cl  11' ceiling)

DINING
11-0 x 13-4

cl

BED RM.
11-4 x 12-0

cl

PORCH

GARAGE
23-0 x 21-0

## Plan HPT840316

**Price Code:** A4
**Bedrooms:** 3 **Bathrooms:** 2
**Square Footage:** 1,831
**Width:** 54'-6" **Depth:** 60'-6"

This one-story, three-bedroom design takes its inspiration from the French and Neo-French Eclectic periods with the steeply pitched hipped roof and the entry's elevated arch. Very modern in design, the interior boasts an efficient arrangement of private and social areas. The hub of social activities is definitely the great room which adjoins the dining room and opens to the rear porch while enjoying a pass-through to the kitchen. Tray ceilings grace the formal dining room and the master suite that includes two walk-in closets, double-sink vanity, tub and compartmented shower and toilet. ©2000 Donald A. Gardner, Inc.

## Plan HPT840317

**Price Code:** C1
**Bedrooms:** 3 **Bathrooms:** 2½
**First Floor:** 1,378 sq. ft.
**Second Floor:** 977 sq. ft.
**Total:** 2,355 sq. ft.
**Width:** 56'-6" **Depth:** 50'-0"

Here's a versatile contemporary plan with an attractive, low-maintenance stucco finish, bold portico entry and distinctive windows. An alternate brick-and-siding exterior has an air of state-ly elegance. The vaulted foyer is brightly lit by a second-floor window and a skylight. Decorative columns and a plant ledge visually separate the sunken living room from the foyer and dining room. Double doors open from the dining room onto an expansive, partially covered deck. The kitchen has a walk-in pantry, a built-in planning desk and a breakfast room.

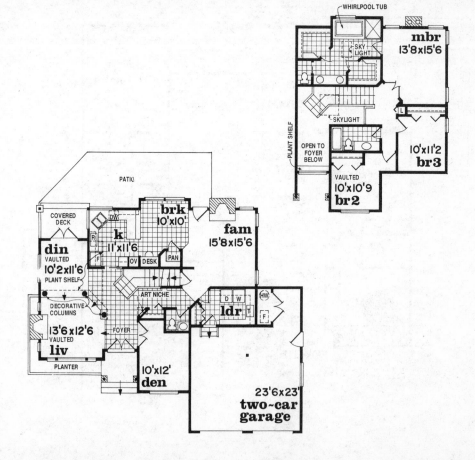

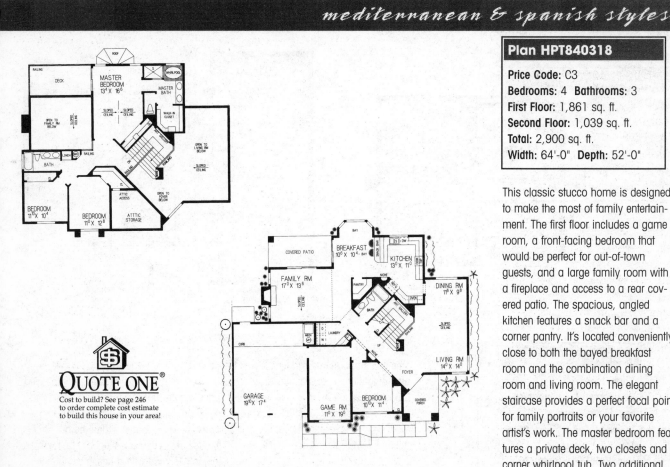

## Quote One®

Cost to build? See page 246
to order complete cost estimate
to build this house in your area!

### Plan HPT840318

**Price Code:** C3
**Bedrooms:** 4 **Bathrooms:** 3
**First Floor:** 1,861 sq. ft.
**Second Floor:** 1,039 sq. ft.
**Total:** 2,900 sq. ft.
**Width:** 64'-0" **Depth:** 52'-0"

This classic stucco home is designed to make the most of family entertainment. The first floor includes a game room, a front-facing bedroom that would be perfect for out-of-town guests, and a large family room with a fireplace and access to a rear covered patio. The spacious, angled kitchen features a snack bar and a corner pantry. It's located conveniently close to both the bayed breakfast room and the combination dining room and living room. The elegant staircase provides a perfect focal point for family portraits or your favorite artist's work. The master bedroom features a private deck, two closets and a corner whirlpool tub. Two additional bedrooms share a galley-style bath.

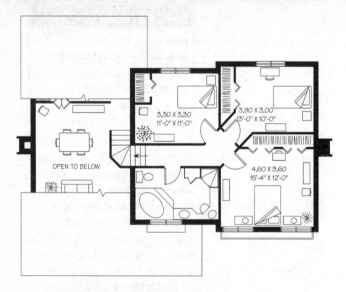

OPEN TO BELOW

3,30 X 3,30
11'-0" X 11'-0"

3,90 X 3,00
13'-0" X 10'-0"

4,60 X 3,60
15'-4" X 12'-0"

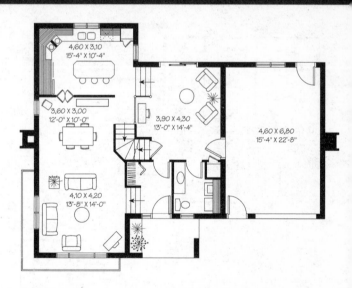

4,60 X 3,10
15'-4" X 10'-4"

3,60 X 3,00
12'-0" X 10'-0"

3,90 X 4,30
13'-0" X 14'-4"

4,60 X 6,80
15'-4" X 22'-8"

4,10 X 4,20
13'-8" X 14'-0"

## Plan HPT840319

**Price Code:** A4
**Bedrooms:** 3 **Bathrooms:** 1½
**First Floor:** 1,394 sq. ft.
**Second Floor:** 753 sq. ft.
**Total:** 2,147 sq. ft.
**Width:** 46'-0" **Depth:** 36'-0"

This contemporary design features all the livability of the Mediterranean lifestyle. A gleaming stucco facade, intricately detailed railing and a Castilian-style, red-shingled roof enhance the exterior. Inside, the living and dining rooms are open to one another for easy entertaining. The island kitchen will be an Italian cook's delight! The casual family room accesses the garage and utility room. Three family bedrooms are arranged upstairs for family privacy. The full hall bath includes a corner whirlpool tub, two-sink vanity, separate shower and toilet. This home is designed with a basement foundation.

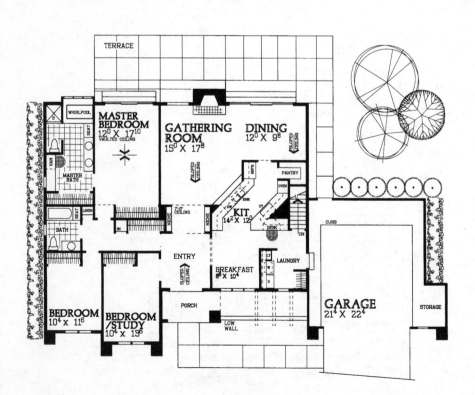

## Plan HPT840320

**Price Code:** C1
**Bedrooms:** 3  **Bathrooms:** 2
**Square Footage:** 1,845
**Width:** 75'-0"  **Depth:** 47'-5"

Beyond the grand entry, a comfortable gathering room with a central fireplace shares sweeping, open spaces with the dining room. An efficiently patterned kitchen makes use of a large walk-in pantry and a breakfast area. A snack bar offers a third mealtime eating option. Away from the hustle and bustle of the day, the sleeping wing offers a study with a wide opening off the foyer. If desired as a bedroom, the size and location of the doorway could be moved to the bedroom hallway to afford the proper amount of privacy. In the master bedroom, look for double closets and a pampering bath with a double-vanity sink and a whirlpool bath.

## Plan HPT840321

**Price Code:** C2
**Bedrooms:** 4  **Bathrooms:** 2½ + ½
**First Floor:** 3,058 sq. ft.
**Second Floor:** 279 sq. ft.
**Total:** 3,337 sq. ft.
**Width:** 104'-6"  **Depth:** 58'-4"

**L**

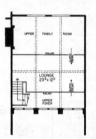

QUOTE ONE®

Cost to build? See page 246
to order complete cost estimate
to build this house in your area!

A centrally located interior atrium is just one of the interesting features of this Spanish design. The atrium has a built-in seat and will bring light to the adjacent living room, dining room and breakfast room. Beyond the foyer and down one step, a tiled reception hall includes a powder room. This area leads to the sleeping wing and up one step to the family room with its raised-hearth fireplace and sliding glass doors to the rear terrace. Overlooking the family room is a railed lounge that can be used for various activities. Sleeping areas include a deluxe master suite and three family bedrooms.

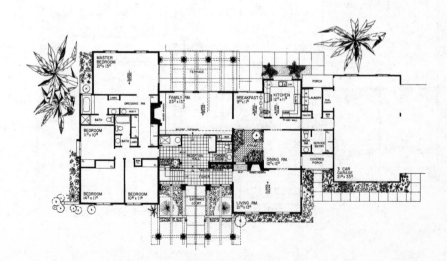

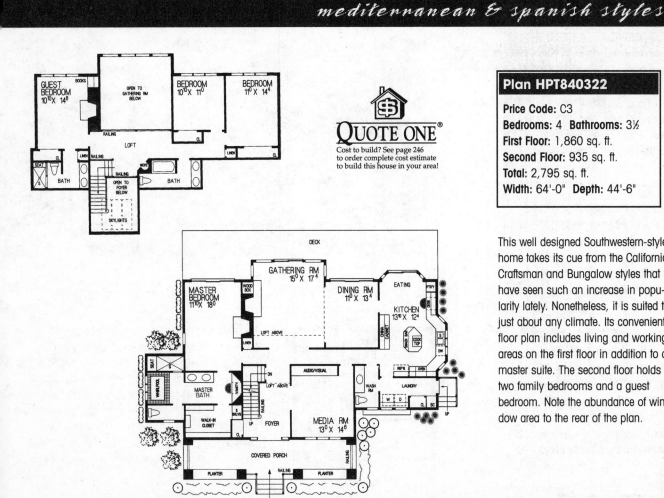

**Quote One**®

Cost to build? See page 246
to order complete cost estimate
to build this house in your area!

**Plan HPT840322**

**Price Code:** C3
**Bedrooms:** 4 **Bathrooms:** 3½
**First Floor:** 1,860 sq. ft.
**Second Floor:** 935 sq. ft.
**Total:** 2,795 sq. ft.
**Width:** 64'-0" **Depth:** 44'-6"

This well designed Southwestern-style home takes its cue from the California Craftsman and Bungalow styles that have seen such an increase in popularity lately. Nonetheless, it is suited to just about any climate. Its convenient floor plan includes living and working areas on the first floor in addition to a master suite. The second floor holds two family bedrooms and a guest bedroom. Note the abundance of window area to the rear of the plan.

## Plan HPT840323

**Price Code:** A4
**Bedrooms:** 4 **Bathrooms:** 2½
**First Floor:** 1,172 sq. ft.
**Second Floor:** 884 sq. ft.
**Total:** 2,056 sq. ft.
**Width:** 54'-4" **Depth:** 47'-8"

**L D**

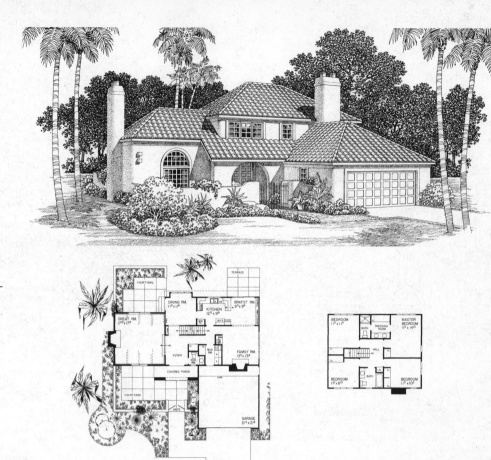

An arched entry welcomes you to a sunny courtyard that leads to a charming stucco home. The sunken great room will be the place for wonderful gatherings with its beamed ceiling, central fireplace and access to a rear terrace. Dining areas reign at the rear of the plan; a formal dining room, a kitchen and a breakfast nook. Upstairs, three family bedrooms share a full hall bath while a master bedroom revels in its own private bath.

## Plan HPT840324

**Price Code:** A3
**Bedrooms:** 3 **Bathrooms:** 2½
**First Floor:** 1,000 sq. ft.
**Second Floor:** 780 sq. ft.
**Total:** 1,780 sq. ft.
**Width:** 40'-0" **Depth:** 66'-6"

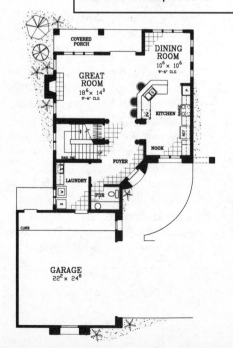

Heavily influenced by the Spanish Eclectic style, the tower and second-floor balcony on this two-story home will clearly draw attention. The dramatic two-story foyer is breathtaking with the grand staircase, tiled floor and decorative columns that lead to the great room. The kitchen is situated neatly between the sunlit dining room and the breakfast nook. The master suite boasts an efficient private bath while two additional bedrooms share a bath on the second floor.

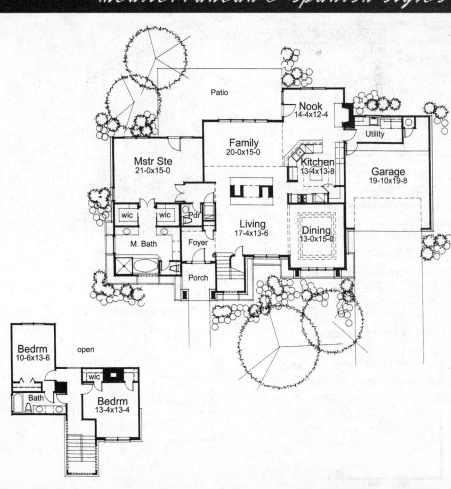

This unique contemporary design is highlighted by an unusual exterior that encloses an amenity-filled layout. A two-sided fireplace warms the formal living room and family room. The gourmet island kitchen connects to a nook warmed by a second fireplace. The master suite is enhanced by twin walk-in closets and a private bath. The rear outdoor patio encourages entertaining alfresco. A useful utility room is placed just outside of the two-car garage. Two additional bedrooms share a full bath upstairs. Please specify basement, crawlspace or slab foundation when ordering.

## Plan HPT840325

**Price Code:** A4
**Bedrooms:** 3 **Bathrooms:** 1½
**First Floor:** 1,893 sq. ft.
**Second Floor:** 501 sq. ft.
**Total:** 2,394 sq. ft.
**Width:** 76'-0" **Depth:** 49'-4"

Patio

Nook
14-4x12-4

Utility

Family
20-0x15-0

Mstr Ste
21-0x15-0

Kitchen
13-4x13-8

Garage
19-10x19-8

wic · wic · Pdr

Living
17-4x13-6

Dining
13-0x15-0

M. Bath

Foyer

Porch

Bedrm
10-6x13-6

open

wic

Bath

Bedrm
13-4x13-4

*mediterranean & spanish styles*

## Plan HPT840331

**Price Code:** C1
**Bedrooms:** 4  **Bathrooms:** 3½
**First Floor:** 2,083 sq. ft.
**Second Floor:** 1,013 sq. ft.
**Total:** 3,096 sq. ft.
**Width:** 74'-0"  **Depth:** 88'-0"

This country villa design is accented by a gazebo-style front porch and an abundance of arched windows. Many rooms in this house are graced with tray, stepped or vaulted ceilings, enhancing the entire plan. The first-floor master suite boasts multiple amenities, including a private lanai, His and Hers walk-in closets and a bayed whirlpool tub. Other highlights on this floor include a study with a window seat and built-in cabinetry, a bayed breakfast nook, a butler's pantry in the island kitchen, a utility room and an outdoor kitchen on the lanai. Three secondary bedrooms reside upstairs, along with two full baths.

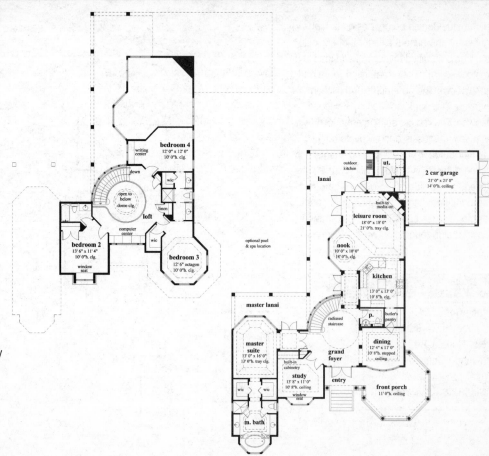

Villa enchantment is romantically enhanced by the facade of this Italianate design—Mediterranean allure creates the soft European appeal dressed in stucco attire. The wraparound entry porch is majestically inviting. Enter through double doors into the two-story foyer—notice the study with built-in cabinetry to the right and the formal dining room to the left. Straight ahead, an octagonal great room with a multi-faceted vaulted ceiling, illuminates the entire plan. The island kitchen is brightened by a bayed window and a pass-through to the lanai. Two spacious walk-in closets and a whirlpool bath await to pamper the homeowner in the master suite.

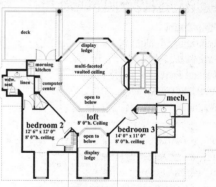

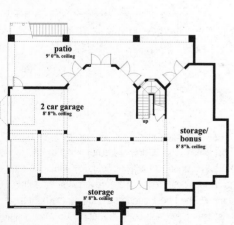

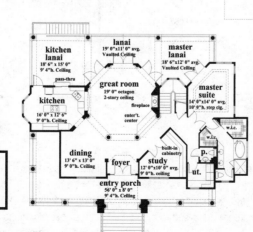

## Plan HPT840332

**Price Code:** C1
**Bedrooms:** 3  **Bathrooms:** 3½
**First Floor:** 1,855 sq. ft.
**Second Floor:** 901 sq. ft.
**Total:** 2,756 sq. ft.
**Bonus Space:** 1,010 sq. ft.
**Width:** 66'-0"  **Depth:** 50'-0"

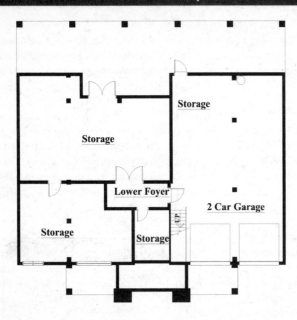

Storage

Storage

Lower Foyer

2 Car Garage

Storage

Storage

UP

DN DN

Deck

Deck

Deck

Master Suite
16'-8" x 13'-6"
10'-0" Ceiling

Nook
11'-3" x 11'-4"
Vaulted

Guest Suite #1
12'-0" x 12'-0"
10'-0" Ceiling

A/C

A/C

Great Room
18'-6" x 18'-10"
Vaulted

Kitchen
12'-4" x 13'-3"
Vaulted

W.I.C.

W.I.C.

M. Bath

Study
11'-0" x 13'-2"
Vaulted Ceiling

UP

Foyer

DN

Utility

Guest Suite #2
11'-0" x 13'-2"
Vaulted

Balcony

Entry

Balcony

UP

## Plan HPT840333

**Price Code:** A4
**Bedrooms:** 3  **Bathrooms:** 3
**Square Footage:** 2,385
**Lower-level Entry:** 109 sq. ft.
**Width:** 60'-0"  **Depth:** 52'-0"

This enticing European Villa boasts an Italian charm and a distinct Mediterranean feel. Stucco and columns dramatically enhance the exterior facade. Once inside, the foyer steps lead up to the formal living areas. To the left, a study is expanded by a vaulted ceiling and double doors that open to the front balcony. Vaulted ceilings create a spacious feel throughout the home, especially in the central great room, which overlooks the rear deck. The island kitchen is conveniently open to a breakfast nook. The guest quarters reside on the right side of the plan—one boasts a private bath, while the second suite uses a full hall bath. The secluded master suite features two walk-in closets and a pampering whirlpool tub.

# LET US SHOW YOU OUR HOME BLUEPRINT PACKAGE.

## BUILDING A HOME?  PLANNING A HOME?

### OUR BLUEPRINT PACKAGE HAS NEARLY EVERYTHING YOU NEED TO GET THE JOB DONE RIGHT,

whether you're working on your own or with help from an architect, designer, builder or subcontractors. Each Blueprint Package is the result of many hours of work by licensed architects or professional designers.

## QUALITY

Hundreds of hours of painstaking effort have gone into the development of your blueprint plan. Each home has been quality-checked by professionals to insure accuracy and buildability.

## VALUE

Because we sell in volume, you can buy professional quality blueprints at a fraction of their development cost. With our plans, your dream home design costs substantially less than the fees charged by architects.

## SERVICE

Once you've chosen your favorite home plan, you'll receive fast, efficient service whether you choose to mail or fax your order to us or call us toll free at 1-800-521-6797. After you have received your order, call for customer service toll free 1-888-690-1116.

## SATISFACTION

Over 50 years of service to satisfied home plan buyers provide us unparalleled experience and knowledge in producing quality blueprints.

## ORDER TOLL FREE 1-800-521-6797

After you've looked over our Blueprint Package and Important Extras, call toll free on our Blueprint Hotline: 1-800-521-6797, for current pricing and availability prior to mailing the order form on page 253. We're ready and eager to serve you. After you have received your order, call for customer service toll free 1-888-690-1116.

Each set of blueprints is an interrelated collection of detail sheets which includes components such as floor plans, interior and exterior elevations, dimensions, cross-sections, diagrams and notations. These sheets show exactly how your house is to be built.

## SETS MAY INCLUDE:

### FRONTAL SHEET
This artist's sketch of the exterior of the house gives you an idea of how the house will look when built and landscaped. Large floor plans show all levels of the house and provide an overview of your new home's livability, as well as a handy reference for deciding on furniture placement.

### FOUNDATION PLANS
This sheet shows the foundation layout including support walls, excavated and unexcavated areas, if any, and foundation notes. If slab construction rather than basement, the plan shows footings and details for a monolithic slab. This page, or another in the set, may include a sample plot plan for locating your house on a building site.

### DETAILED FLOOR PLANS
These plans show the layout of each floor of the house. Rooms and interior spaces are carefully dimensioned and keys are given for cross-section details provided later in the plans. The positions of electrical outlets and switches are shown.

### HOUSE CROSS-SECTIONS
Large-scale views show sections or cut-aways of the foundation, interior walls, exterior walls, floors, stairways and roof details. Additional cross-sections may show important changes in floor, ceiling or roof heights or the relationship of one level to another. Extremely valuable for construction, these sections show exactly how the various parts of the house fit together.

### INTERIOR ELEVATIONS
Many of our drawings show the design and placement of kitchen and bathroom cabinets, laundry areas, fireplaces, bookcases and other built-ins. Little "extras," such as mantelpiece and wainscoting drawings, plus molding sections, provide details that give your home that custom touch.

### EXTERIOR ELEVATIONS
These drawings show the front, rear and sides of your house and give necessary notes on exterior materials and finishes. Particular attention is given to cornice detail, brick and stone accents or other finish items that make your home unique.

## MATERIALS LIST

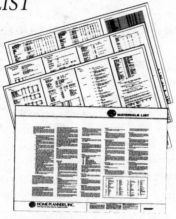

*(Note: Because of the diversity of local building codes, our Materials List does not include mechanical materials.)*

For many of the designs in our portfolio, we offer a customized materials take-off that is invaluable in planning and estimating the cost of your new home. This Materials List outlines the quantity, type and size of materials needed to build your house (with the exception of mechanical system items). Included are framing lumber, windows and doors, kitchen and bath cabinetry, rough and finish hardware, and much more. This handy list helps you or your builder cost out materials and serves as a reference sheet when you're compiling bids. Some Materials Lists may be ordered before blueprints are ordered, call for information.

## SPECIFICATION OUTLINE

This valuable 16-page document is critical to building your house correctly. Designed to be filled in by you or your builder, this book lists 166 stages or items crucial to the building process. It provides a comprehensive review of the construction process and helps in choosing materials. When combined with the blueprints, a signed contract, and a schedule, it becomes a legal document and record for the building of your home.

## QUOTE ONE®

**SUMMARY COST REPORT**     **MATERIAL COST REPORT**

A product for estimating the cost of building select designs, the Quote One® system is available in two separate stages: The Summary Cost Report and the Material Cost Report.

The **Summary Cost Report** is the first stage in the package and shows the total cost per square foot for your chosen home in your zip-code area and then breaks that cost down into various categories showing the costs for building materials, labor and installation. The report includes three grades: Budget, Standard and Custom. These reports allow you to evaluate your building budget and compare the costs of building a variety of homes in your area.

Make even more informed decisions about your home-building project with the second phase of our package, our **Material Cost Report.** This tool is invaluable in planning and estimating the cost of your new home. The material and installation (labor and equipment) cost is shown for each of over 1,000 line items provided in the Materials List (Standard grade), which is included when you purchase this estimating tool. It allows you to determine building costs for your specific zip-code area and for your chosen home design. Space is allowed for additional estimates from contractors and subcontractors, such as for mechanical materials, which are not included in our packages. This invaluable tool includes a Materials List. A Material Cost Report cannot be ordered before blueprints are ordered. Call for details. In addition, ask about our Home Planners Estimating Package.

If you are interested in a plan that is not indicated as Quote One®, please call and ask our sales reps. They will be happy to verify the status for you. To order these invaluable reports, use the order form.

# CONSTRUCTION INFORMATION

*IF YOU WANT TO KNOW MORE ABOUT TECHNIQUES—*
*and deal more confidently with subcontractors —*
*we offer these useful sheets. Each set is an excellent*
*tool that will add to your understanding of these*
*technical subjects. These helpful details provide*
*general construction information and*
*are not specific to any single plan.*

## PLUMBING

The Blueprint Package includes locations for all the plumbing fixtures, including sinks, lavatories, tubs, showers, toilets, laundry trays and water heaters. However, if you want to know more about the complete plumbing system, these Plumbing Details will prove very useful. Prepared to meet requirements of the National Plumbing Code, these fact-filled sheets give general information on pipe schedules, fittings, sump-pump details, water-softener hookups, septic system details and much more. Sheets also include a glossary of terms.

## ELECTRICAL

The locations for every electrical switch, plug and outlet are shown in your Blueprint Package. However, these Electrical Details go further to take the mystery out of household electrical systems. Prepared to meet requirements of the National Electrical Code, these comprehensive drawings come packed with helpful information, including wire sizing, switch-installation schematics, cable-routing details, appliance wattage, doorbell hook-ups, typical service panel circuitry and much more. A glossary of terms is also included.

## CONSTRUCTION

The Blueprint Package contains information an experienced builder needs to construct a particular house. However, it doesn't show all the ways that houses can be built, nor does it explain alternate construction methods. To help you understand how your house will be built—and offer additional techniques—this set of Construction Details depicts the materials and methods used to build foundations, fireplaces, walls, floors and roofs. Where appropriate, the drawings show acceptable alternatives.

## MECHANICAL

These Mechanical Details contain fundamental principles and useful data that will help you make informed decisions and communicate with subcontractors about heating and cooling systems. Drawings contain instructions and samples that allow you to make simple load calculations, and preliminary sizing and costing analysis. Covered are the most commonly used systems from heat pumps to solar fuel systems. The package is filled with illustrations and diagrams to help you visualize components and how they relate to one another.

# THE HANDS-ON HOME FURNITURE PLANNER

Effectively plan the space in your home using The **Hands-On Home Furniture Planner**. It's fun and easy—no more moving heavy pieces of furniture to see how the room will go together. And you can try different layouts, moving furniture at a whim.

The kit includes reusable peel and stick furniture templates that fit onto a 12" x 18" laminated layout board—space enough to layout every room in your home.

Also included in the package are a number of helpful planning tools. You'll receive:

- ✓ Helpful hints and solutions for difficult situations.
- ✓ Furniture planning basics to get you started.
- ✓ Furniture planning secrets that let you in on some of the tricks of professional designers.

The **Hands-On Home Furniture Planner** is the one tool that no new homeowner or home remodeler should be without. It's also a perfect housewarming gift!

# To Order, Call Toll Free
# 1-800-521-6797

After you've looked over our Blueprint Package and Important Extras on these pages, call for current pricing and availability prior to mailing the order form. We're ready and eager to serve you. After you have received your order, call for customer service toll free 1-888-690-1116.

## THE DECK BLUEPRINT PACKAGE

Many of the homes in this book can be enhanced with a professionally designed Home Planners Deck Plan. Those homes marked with a **D** have a complementary Deck Plan, sold separately, which includes a Deck Plan Frontal Sheet, Deck Framing and Floor Plans, Deck Elevations and a Deck Materials List. A Standard Deck Details Package, also available, provides all the how-to information necessary for building *any* deck. Our Complete Deck Building Package contains one set of Custom Deck Plans of your choice, plus one set of Standard Deck Building Details, all for one low price. Our plans and details are carefully prepared in an easy-to-understand format that will guide you through every stage of your deck-building project. This page shows a sample Deck layout to match your favorite house. See Blueprint Price Schedule for ordering information.

## THE LANDSCAPE BLUEPRINT PACKAGE

For the homes marked with an **L** in this book, Home Planners has created a front-yard Landscape Plan that is complementary in design to the house plan. These comprehensive blueprint packages include a Frontal Sheet, Plan View, Regionalized Plant & Materials List, a sheet on Planting and Maintaining Your Landscape, Zone Maps and Plant Size and Description Guide. These plans will help you achieve professional results, adding value and enjoyment to your property for years to come. Each set of blueprints is a full 18" x 24" in size with clear, complete instructions and easy-to-read type. A sample Landscape Plan is shown below. See Blueprint Price Schedule for ordering information.

**CONTEMPORARY LEISURE DECK**
Deck ODA021

**CAPE COD COTTAGE**
Landscape OLA003

## REGIONAL ORDER MAP

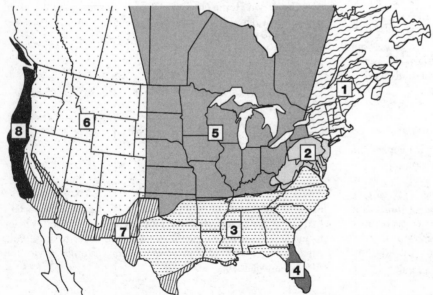

Most Landscape Plans are available with a Plant & Materials List adapted by horticultural experts to 8 different regions of the country. Please specify the Geographic Region when ordering your plan. See Blueprint Price Schedule for ordering information and regional availability.

| | | |
|---|---|---|
| **Region** | 1 | Northeast |
| **Region** | 2 | Mid-Atlantic |
| **Region** | 3 | Deep South |
| **Region** | 4 | Florida & Gulf Coast |
| **Region** | 5 | Midwest |
| **Region** | 6 | Rocky Mountains |
| **Region** | 7 | Southern California & Desert Southwest |
| **Region** | 8 | Northern California & Pacific Northwest |

# BLUEPRINT PRICE SCHEDULE

*Prices guaranteed through December 31, 2002*

| TIERS | 1-SET STUDY PACKAGE | 4-SET BUILDING PACKAGE | 8-SET BUILDING PACKAGE | 1-SET REPRODUCIBLE* |
|-------|------|------|------|------|
| P1 | $20 | $50 | $90 | $140 |
| P2 | $40 | $70 | $110 | $160 |
| P3 | $70 | $100 | $140 | $190 |
| P4 | $100 | $130 | $170 | $220 |
| P5 | $140 | $170 | $210 | $270 |
| P6 | $180 | $210 | $250 | $310 |
| A1 | $440 | $480 | $520 | $660 |
| A2 | $480 | $520 | $560 | $720 |
| A3 | $520 | $560 | $600 | $780 |
| A4 | $565 | $605 | $645 | $850 |
| C1 | $610 | $655 | $700 | $915 |
| C2 | $655 | $700 | $745 | $980 |
| C3 | $700 | $745 | $790 | $1050 |
| C4 | $750 | $795 | $840 | $1125 |
| L1 | $825 | $875 | $925 | $1240 |
| L2 | $900 | $950 | $1000 | $1350 |
| L3 | $1000 | $1050 | $1100 | $1500 |
| L4 | $1100 | $1150 | $1200 | $1650 |

\* Requires a fax number

## OPTIONS FOR PLANS IN TIERS A1–L4

Additional Identical Blueprints
in same order for "A1–L4" price plans ............................................$50 per set
Reverse Blueprints (mirror image)
with 4- or 8-set order for "A1–L4" plans.............................................$50 fee per order
Specification Outlines...............................................................$10 each
Materials Lists for "A1–C3" plans ...................................................$60 each
Materials Lists for "C4–L4" plans....................................................$70 each

## OPTIONS FOR PLANS IN TIERS P1–P6

Additional Identical Blueprints
in same order for "P1–P6" price plans...............................................$10 per set
Reverse Blueprints (mirror image) for "P1–P6" price plans .............$10 fee per order
Set of Deck Construction Details ..............................................$14.95 each
Deck Construction Package ....................................**add $10 to Building Package price**
*(includes 1 set of "P1–P6" plans, plus 1 set Standard Deck Construction Details)*

## IMPORTANT NOTES

The 1-set study package is marked "not for construction."
Prices for 4- or 8-set Building Packages honored only at time of original order.
Some foundations carry a $225 surcharge.
Right-reading reverse blueprints, if available, will incur a $165 surcharge.
Additional identical blueprints may be purchased within 60 days of original order.

*TO USE THE INDEX,* refer to the design number listed in numerical order (a helpful page reference is also given). Note the price tier and refer to the Blueprint Price Schedule above for the cost of one, four or eight sets of blueprints or the cost of a reproducible drawing. Additional prices are shown for identical and reverse blueprint sets, as well as a very useful Materials List for some of the plans. Also note in the Plan Index those plans that have Deck Plans or Landscape Plans. Refer to the schedules above for prices of these plans. The letter "Y" identifies plans that are part of our Quote One® estimating service and those that offer Materials Lists.

*TO ORDER,* Call toll free 1-800-521-6797 for current pricing and availability prior to mailing the order form. FAX: 1-800-224-6699 or 520-544-3086.

# PLAN INDEX

| DESIGN | PRICE | PAGE | MATERIALS LIST | QUOTE ONE® | DECK | DECK PRICE | LANDSCAPE | LANDSCAPE PRICE | REGIONS |
|--------|-------|------|----------------|-----------|------|-----------|-----------|-----------------|---------|
| HPT840001 | C4 | 5 | | | | | | | |
| HPT840002 | C4 | 6 | | | | | | | |
| HPT840003 | C4 | 6 | | | | | | | |
| HPT840004 | C4 | 7 | | | | | | | |
| HPT840005 | A4 | 8 | | | | | | | |
| HPT840006 | C1 | 8 | | Y | | | | | |
| HPT840007 | C1 | 9 | | Y | | | | | |
| HPT840008 | A3 | 10 | | | | | | | |
| HPT840009 | C1 | 10 | | | | | | | |
| HPT840010 | C1 | 11 | | | | | | | |
| HPT840011 | A2 | 12 | | | | | | | |
| HPT840012 | A1 | 12 | | Y | | | | | |
| HPT840013 | A3 | 13 | | Y | | | | | |
| HPT840014 | A4 | 14 | | | | | | | |
| HPT840015 | A4 | 14 | | | | | | | |
| HPT840016 | C2 | 15 | | | | | | | |
| HPT840017 | C1 | 16 | | | | | | | |
| HPT840018 | A4 | 17 | | Y | | | | | |
| HPT840019 | C4 | 18 | | | | | | | |
| HPT840020 | A4 | 18 | | Y | | | | | |
| HPT840021 | A3 | 19 | | | | | | | |
| HPT840022 | A2 | 20 | | | | | | | |
| HPT840023 | A2 | 20 | | | | | | | |
| HPT840024 | A2 | 21 | | | | | | | |
| HPT840025 | A4 | 22 | | | | | | | |
| HPT840026 | A2 | 22 | | | | | | | |
| HPT840027 | A2 | 23 | | Y | | | | | |
| HPT840028 | A2 | 24 | | | | | | | |
| HPT840029 | A3 | 24 | | | | | | | |
| HPT840030 | C1 | 25 | | Y | | | | | |
| HPT840031 | C2 | 26 | | Y | | | | | |
| HPT840032 | C1 | 26 | | | | | | | |
| HPT840033 | A4 | 27 | | | | | | | |
| HPT840034 | C4 | 28 | | | | | | | |
| HPT840035 | C1 | 28 | | Y | | | | | |
| HPT840036 | C1 | 29 | | Y | | | | | |
| HPT840037 | A4 | 30 | | | | | | | |
| HPT840038 | A4 | 30 | | | | | | | |
| HPT840039 | C2 | 31 | | Y | | | | | |
| HPT840040 | C3 | 32 | | Y | | | | | |
| HPT840041 | C2 | 32 | | Y | | | | | |
| HPT840042 | L2 | 33 | | Y | | | | | |
| HPT840043 | L2 | 34 | | | | | | | |
| HPT840044 | C3 | 34 | | | | | | | |
| HPT840045 | C4 | 35 | | Y | | | | | |
| HPT840046 | C2 | 36 | | | | | | | |
| HPT840047 | C2 | 36 | | | | | | | |
| HPT840048 | C2 | 37 | | Y | | | | | |
| HPT840049 | C3 | 38 | | | | | | | |
| HPT840050 | C2 | 38 | | | | | | | |
| HPT840051 | C3 | 39 | | | | | | | |
| HPT840052 | C4 | 40 | | | | | | | |
| HPT840053 | C3 | 40 | | | | | | | |
| HPT840054 | C4 | 41 | | | | | | | |
| HPT840055 | A3 | 42 | | | | | | | |
| HPT840056 | A4 | 42 | | Y | | | | | |
| HPT840057 | C4 | 43 | | | | | | | |
| HPT840058 | C3 | 44 | | | | | | | |
| HPT840059 | A3 | 44 | | | | | | | |
| HPT840060 | C1 | 45 | | | | | | | |
| HPT840061 | C2 | 46 | | | | | | | |
| HPT840062 | C1 | 46 | | | | | | | |
| HPT840063 | C1 | 47 | | | | | | | |
| HPT840064 | C3 | 48 | | | | | | | |
| HPT840065 | C3 | 48 | | | | | | | |
| HPT840066 | C4 | 49 | | | | | | | |
| HPT840067 | C3 | 50 | | | | | | | |

250

*BEFORE FILLING OUT THE ORDER FORM, PLEASE CALL US ON OUR TOLL-FREE BLUEPRINT HOTLINE 1-800-521-6797. YOU MAY WANT TO LEARN MORE ABOUT OUR SERVICES AND PRODUCTS. HERE'S SOME INFORMATION YOU WILL FIND HELPFUL.*

## OUR EXCHANGE POLICY

With the exception of reproducible plan orders, we will exchange your entire first order for an equal or greater number of blueprints within our plan collection within 90 days of the original order. The entire content of your original order must be returned before an exchange will be processed. Please call our customer service department for your return authorization number and shipping instructions. If the returned blueprints look used, redlined or copied, we will not honor your exchange. Fees for exchanging your blueprints are as follows: 20% of the amount of the original order...plus the difference in cost if exchanging for a design in a higher price bracket or less the difference in cost if exchanging for a design in a lower price bracket. **(Reproducible blueprints are not exchangeable or refundable.)** Please call for current postage and handling prices. Shipping and handling charges are not refundable.

## ABOUT REPRODUCIBLES

When purchasing a reproducible you may be required to furnish a fax number. The designer will fax documents that you must sign and return to them before shipping will take place.

## ABOUT REVERSE BLUEPRINTS

Although lettering and dimensions will appear backward, reverses will be a useful aid if you decide to flop the plan. See Price Schedule and Plans Index for pricing.

## REVISING, MODIFYING AND CUSTOMIZING PLANS

Like many homeowners who buy these plans, you and your builder, architect or engineer may want to make changes to them. We recommend purchase of a reproducible plan for any changes made by your builder, licensed architect or engineer. As set forth below, we cannot assume any responsibility for blueprints which have been changed, whether by you, your builder or by professionals selected by you or referred to you by us, because such individuals are outside our supervision and control.

## ARCHITECTURAL AND ENGINEERING SEALS

Some cities and states are now requiring that a licensed architect or engineer review and "seal" a blueprint, or officially approve it, prior to construction due to concerns over energy costs, safety and other factors. Prior to application for a building permit or the start of actual construction, we strongly advise that you consult your local building official who can tell you if such a review is required.

## ABOUT THE DESIGNS

The architects and designers whose work appears in this publication are among America's leading residential designers. Each plan was designed to meet the requirements of a nationally recognized model building code in effect at the time and place the plan was drawn. Because national building codes change from time to time, plans may not comply with any such code at the time they are sold to a customer. In addition, building officials may not accept these plans as final construction documents of record as the plans may need to be modified and additional drawings and details added to suit local conditions and requirements. We strongly advise that purchasers consult a licensed architect or engineer, and their local building official, before starting any construction related to these plans.

## LOCAL BUILDING CODES AND ZONING REQUIREMENTS

At the time of creation, our plans are drawn to specifications published by the Building Officials and Code Administrators (BOCA) International, Inc.; the Southern Building Code Congress (SBCCI) International, Inc.; the International Conference of Building Officials (ICBO); or the Council of American Building Officials (CABO). Our plans are designed to meet or exceed national building standards. Because of the great differences in geography and climate throughout the United States and Canada, each state, county and municipality has its own building codes, zone requirements, ordinances and building regulations. Your plan may need to be modified to comply with local requirements regarding snow loads, energy codes, soil and seismic conditions and a wide range of other matters. In addition, you may need to obtain permits or inspections from local governments before and in the course of construction. Prior to using blueprints ordered from us, we strongly advise that you consult a licensed architect or engineer—and speak with your local building official—before applying for any permit or beginning construction. We authorize the use of our blueprints on the express condition that you strictly comply with all local building codes, zoning requirements and other applicable laws, regulations, ordinances and requirements. Notice: Plans for homes to be built in Nevada must be re-drawn by a Nevada-registered professional. Consult your building official for more information on this subject.

**TOLL FREE**
**1-800-521-6797**

**REGULAR OFFICE HOURS:**
8:00 a.m.-9:00 p.m. EST, Monday-Friday

If we receive your order by 3:00 p.m. EST, Monday-Friday, we'll process it and ship within **two business days**. When ordering by phone, please have your credit card or check information ready. We'll also ask you for the Order Form Key Number at the bottom of the order form.

By FAX: Copy the Order Form on the next page and send it on our FAX line: 1-800-224-6699 or 520-544-3086.

**Canadian Customers**
**Order Toll Free 1-877-223-6389**

## HOW MANY BLUEPRINTS DO YOU NEED?

Although a standard building package may satisfy many states, cities and counties, some plans may require certain changes. For your convenience, we have developed a Reproducible plan which allows a local professional to modify and make up to 10 copies of your revised plan. As our plans are all copyright protected, with your purchase of the Reproducible, we will supply you with a Copyright release letter. The number of copies you may need: 1 for owner; 3 for builder; 2 for local building department and 1-3 sets for your mortgage lender.

# ORDER TOLL FREE!

**For information about any of our services or to order call**
**1-800-521-6797**

**Browse our website:**
**www.eplans.com**

**BLUEPRINTS ARE NOT REFUNDABLE EXCHANGES ONLY**

**For Customer Service, call toll free**
**1-888-690-1116.**

---

 **HOME PLANNERS, LLC wholly owned by Hanley-Wood, LLC**
3275 WEST INA ROAD, SUITE 110 • TUCSON, ARIZONA • 85741

### THE BASIC BLUEPRINT PACKAGE

Rush me the following (please refer to the Plans Index and Price Schedule in this section):

____Set(s) of reproducibles*, plan number(s) _____  $_____
indicate foundation type _____  surcharge (if applicable): $_____
____Set(s) of blueprints, plan number(s) _____  $_____
indicate foundation type _____  surcharge (if applicable): $_____
____Additional identical blueprints (standard or reverse) in same order @ $50 per set  $_____
____Reverse blueprints @ $50 fee per order. Right-reading reverse @ $165 surcharge  $_____

### IMPORTANT EXTRAS

Rush me the following:

____Materials List: $60 (Must be purchased with Blueprint.) Add $10 for Schedule C4–L4 plans  $_____
____**Quote One**® Summary Cost Report @ $29.95 for one, $14.95 for each additional, for plans _____.
Building location: City _____ Zip Code _____  $_____
____**Quote One**® Material Cost Report @ $120 Schedules P1–C3; $130 Schedules C4–L4, for plan _____ (Must be purchased with Blueprints set.)
Building location: City _____ Zip Code _____  $_____
____Specification Outlines @ $10 each  $_____
____Detail Sets @ $14.95 each; any two $22.95; any three $29.95; all four for $39.95 (save $19.85)  $_____
❑ Plumbing ❑ Electrical ❑ Construction ❑ Mechanical
____Home Furniture Planner @ $15.95 each  $_____

### DECK BLUEPRINTS

(Please refer to the Plans Index and Price Schedule in this section)

____Set(s) of Deck Plan _____
____Additional identical blueprints in same order @ $10 per set.  $_____
____Reverse blueprints @ $10 fee per order.  $_____
____Set of Standard Deck Details @ $14.95 per set.  $_____
____Set of Complete Deck Construction Package (Best Buy!) Add $10 to Building Package.  $_____
Includes Custom Deck Plan _____ Plus Standard Deck Details

### LANDSCAPE BLUEPRINTS

(Please refer to the Plans Index and Price Schedule in this section.)

____Set(s) of Landscape Plan _____
____Additional identical blueprints in same order @ $10 per set  $_____
____Reverse blueprints @ $10 fee per order  $_____
**Please indicate appropriate region of the country for Plant & Material List. Region _____**

| POSTAGE AND HANDLING *SIGNATURE IS REQUIRED FOR ALL DELIVERIES.* | 1–3 sets | 4+ sets |
|---|---|---|
| **DELIVERY** No COD's (Requires street address—No P.O. Boxes) •Regular Service (Allow 7–10 business days delivery) | ❑ $20.00 | ❑ $25.00 |
| •Priority (Allow 4–5 business days delivery) | ❑ $25.00 | ❑ $35.00 |
| •Express (Allow 3 business days delivery) | ❑ $35.00 | ❑ $45.00 |
| **OVERSEAS DELIVERY** | fax, phone or mail for quote | |

Note: All delivery times are from date Blueprint Package is shipped.

**POSTAGE (From box above)**  $_____
**SUBTOTAL**  $_____
**SALES TAX** (AZ & MI residents, please add appropriate state and local sales tax.)  $_____
**TOTAL (Subtotal and tax)**  $_____

### YOUR ADDRESS (please print legibly)

Name _____

Street _____

City _____ State _____ Zip _____

Daytime telephone number (required) (_____) _____

* Fax number (required for reproducible orders) _____
TeleCheck® Checks By Phone℠ available

### FOR CREDIT CARD ORDERS ONLY

Credit card number _____ Exp. Date: (M/Y) _____

Check one ❑ Visa ❑ MasterCard ❑ Discover Card ❑ American Express

Order Form Key

Signature (required) _____  HPT84

Please check appropriate box: ❑ Licensed Builder-Contractor ❑ Homeowner

 **ORDER TOLL FREE!**
**1-800-521-6797**

BY FAX: Copy the order form above and send it on our FAXLINE: 1-800-224-6699 OR 520-544-3086

# HELPFUL BOOKS FROM HOME PLANNERS

TO ORDER BY PHONE
**1-800-322-6797**

**254**

**1  BIGGEST & BEST**

1001 of our best-selling plans in one volume. 1,074 to 7,275 square feet. 704 pgs $12.95 1K1

**2  ONE-STORY**

450 designs for all lifestyles. 800 to 4,900 square feet. 384 pgs $9.95 OS

**3  MORE ONE-STORY**

475 superb one-level plans from 800 to 5,000 square feet. 448 pgs $9.95 MO2

**4  TWO-STORY**

443 designs for one-and-a-half and two stories. 1,500 to 6,000 square feet. 448 pgs $9.95 TS

**5  VACATION**

430 designs for recreation, retirement and leisure. 448 pgs $9.95 VS3

**6  HILLSIDE**
208 designs for split-levels, bi-levels, multi-levels and walkouts. 224 pgs $9.95 HH

**7  FARMHOUSE**

300 Fresh Designs from Classic to Modern. 320 pgs. $10.95 FCP

**8  COUNTRY HOUSES**

208 unique home plans that combine traditional style and modern livability. 224 pgs $9.95 CN

**9  BUDGET-SMART**
200 efficient plans from 7 top designers, that you can really afford to build! 224 pgs $8.95 BS

**10  BARRIER-FREE**
Over 1,700 products and 51 plans for accessible living. 128 pgs $15.95 UH

**11  ENCYCLOPEDIA**
500 exceptional plans for all styles and budgets—the best book of its kind! 528 pgs $9.95 ENC

**12  ENCYCLOPEDIA II**
500 completely new plans. Spacious and stylish designs for every budget and taste. 352 pgs $9.95 E2

**13  AFFORDABLE**

300 Modest plans for savvy homebuyers.256 pgs. $9.95 AH2

**14  VICTORIAN**

210 striking Victorian and Farmhouse designs from today's top designers. 224 pgs $15.95 VDH2

**15  ESTATE**

Dream big! Eighteen designers showcase their biggest and best plans. 224 pgs $16.95 EDH3

**16  LUXURY**
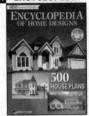
170 lavish designs, over 50% brand-new plans added to a most elegant collection. 192 pgs $12.95 LD3

**17  EUROPEAN STYLES**
200 homes with a unique flair of the Old World. 224 pgs $15.95 EURO

**18  COUNTRY CLASSICS**

Donald Gardner's 101 best Country and Traditional home plans. 192 pgs $17.95 DAG

**19  COUNTRY**

85 Charming Designs from American Home Gallery. 160 pgs. $17.95 CTY

**20  TRADITIONAL**

85 timeless designs from the Design Traditions Library. 160 pgs $17.95 TRA

**21  COTTAGES**

245 Delightful retreats from 825 to 3,500 square feet. 256 pgs. $10.95 COOL

**22  CABINS TO VILLAS**

Enchanting Homes for Mountain Sea or Sun, from the Sater collection. 144 pgs $19.95 CCV

**23  CONTEMPORARY**

The most complete and imaginative collection of contemporary designs available anywhere. 256 pgs $10.95 CM2

**24  FRENCH COUNTRY**
Live every day in the French countryside using these plans, landscapes and interiors. 192 pgs. $14.95 PN

**25  SOUTHERN**

207 homes rich in Southern styling and comfort. 240 pgs $8.95 SH

**26  SOUTHWESTERN**

138 designs that capture the spirit of the Southwest. 144 pgs $10.95 SW

**27  SHINGLE-STYLE**

155 Home plans from Classic Colonials to Breezy Bungalows. 192 pgs. $12.95 SNG

**28  NEIGHBORHOOD**

170 designs with the feel of main street America. 192 pgs $12.95 TND

**29  CRAFTSMAN**

170 Home plans in the Craftsman and Bungalow style. 192 pgs $12.95 CC

**30  GRAND VISTAS**

200 Homes with a View. 224 pgs. $10.95 GV

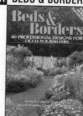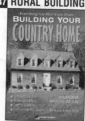